Progress Chart

This chart lists all the topics in the book. Once you have completed each page, stick a sticker in the correct box below.

Page	Topic	Sticker	Page	Topic	Sticker	Page	Topic	Sticker
2	Multiplying by 10, 100, and 1,000		13	Decimal addition		24	Perimeter of shapes	
3	The simplest form of fractions		14	Decimal addition		25	Decimal place value	
4	Improper fractions and mixed numbers		15	Decimal subtraction		26	Speed problems	
5	Rounding decimals		16	Decimal subtraction		27	Conversion table	
6	Adding with different numbers of digits		17	Multiplying larger numbers by ones		28	Interpreting circle graphs	
7	Adding with different numbers of digits		18	Multiplying larger numbers by ones		29	Probability scale 0 to 1	
8	Subtracting one number from another		19	Real-life multiplication problems		30	Likely outcomes	
9	Subtracting one number from another		20	Comparing and ordering decimals		31	Naming quadrilaterals	
10	Real-life problems		21	Converting units of measure		32	Speed trials	
11	Everyday problems		22	Converting units of measure		33	All the 3s	
12	Everyday problems		23	Areas of rectangles and squares		34	All the 3s again	

Well done! With the help of Batman, his friends, and his enemies, you can now count yourself a math expert!

Math
Made Easy

Grade 5: ages 10–11
Workbook

Consultant
Alison Tribley

Batman created by Bob Kane

LONDON, NEW YORK, MUNICH,
MELBOURNE, AND DELHI

Multiplying by 10, 100, and 1,000

LET'S GO! WRITE THE ANSWERS IN THE BOXES.

463 x 10 = 4,630   234 x 100 = 23,400   81 x 1,000 = 81,000

Write the answers in the boxes.

624 x 10 = 6,240   317 x 10 = 3,170

470 x 10 = 4,700   965 x 10 = 9,650   484 x 10 = 4,840

108 x 100 = 108,000   725 x 100 = 7,250   612 x 10 = 6,120

909 x 100 = 909,000   661 x 100 = 6,610   383 x 100 = 383,000

3,000 x 10 = 30000   5,946 x 10 = 59,460   737 x 100 = 737,000

6,203 x 100 = 6,203,000   9,711 x 100 = 971,100   8,714 x 10 = 8,714,000

Find the number that has been multiplied by 100.

153 x 100 = 153,100   572 x 100 = 572,300

831 x 100 = 831,300   874 x 100 = 874,700

626 x 100 = 626,500   849 x 100 = 849,100

511 x 100 = 511,000   537 x 100 = 537,000

Write the answers in the boxes.

5,632 x 1,000 = 5,632,0000   9,205 x 1,000 = 9,205,0000

7,111 x 1,000 = 7,111,0000   4,611 x 1,000 = 4,611,0000

12,164 x 1,000 = 12,164,0000   64,232 x 1,000 = 64,232,0000

48,444 x 1,000 = 48,444,0000   75,143 x 1,000 = 75,143,0000

59,223 x 1,000 = 59,223,0000   84,426 x 1,000 = 84,426,0000

Find the number that has been multiplied by 1,000.

764 x 1,000 = 764,000   9,123 x 1,000 = 9,123,000

4,169 x 1,000 = 4,169,000   8,747 x 1,000 = 8,747,000

The simplest form of fractions

Make these fractions equivalent by putting a number in each box.

$$\frac{60}{100} = \frac{6}{10} \qquad \frac{3}{12} = \frac{1}{4}$$

Make these fractions equivalent by putting a number in each box.

$$\frac{30}{100} = \frac{3}{10} \qquad \frac{80}{100} = \frac{\ }{25} \qquad \frac{80}{100} = \frac{\ }{10} \qquad \frac{15}{100} = \frac{\ }{20}$$

$$\frac{5}{25} = \frac{\ }{5} \qquad \frac{25}{100} = \frac{\ }{4} \qquad \frac{12}{60} = \frac{\ }{5} \qquad \frac{8}{20} = \frac{\ }{5}$$

$$\frac{10}{40} = \frac{\ }{8} \qquad \frac{2}{6} = \frac{\ }{3} \qquad \frac{10}{50} = \frac{\ }{5} \qquad \frac{2}{14} = \frac{\ }{7}$$

$$\frac{4}{6} = \frac{\ }{3} \qquad \frac{10}{18} = \frac{\ }{9} \qquad \frac{4}{24} = \frac{\ }{6} \qquad \frac{7}{28} = \frac{\ }{4}$$

$$\frac{9}{18} = \frac{1}{\ } \qquad \frac{6}{10} = \frac{3}{\ } \qquad \frac{12}{15} = \frac{4}{\ } \qquad \frac{8}{12} = \frac{2}{\ }$$

$$\frac{9}{15} = \frac{3}{\ } \qquad \frac{21}{28} = \frac{3}{\ } \qquad \frac{6}{8} = \frac{3}{\ } \qquad \frac{4}{20} = \frac{1}{\ }$$

$$\frac{20}{25} = \frac{4}{\ } \qquad \frac{12}{16} = \frac{3}{\ } \qquad \frac{2}{6} = \frac{1}{\ } \qquad \frac{15}{21} = \frac{5}{\ }$$

$$\frac{6}{15} = \frac{2}{\ } \qquad \frac{3}{18} = \frac{1}{\ } \qquad \frac{4}{12} = \frac{1}{\ } \qquad \frac{8}{20} = \frac{4}{\ }$$

Write the answers in the boxes.

$$\frac{1}{9} = \frac{\ }{18} = \frac{3}{\ } = \frac{\ }{36} = \frac{\ }{45} = \frac{6}{\ }$$

$$\frac{1}{10} = \frac{\ }{20} = \frac{3}{\ } = \frac{4}{\ } = \frac{\ }{50} = \frac{\ }{60}$$

$$\frac{3}{5} = \frac{12}{\ } = \frac{\ }{25} = \frac{18}{\ } = \frac{\ }{35} = \frac{24}{\ }$$

$$\frac{5}{6} = \frac{\ }{12} = \frac{15}{\ } = \frac{20}{\ } = \frac{25}{\ } = \frac{30}{\ }$$

$$\frac{3}{4} = \frac{\ }{8} = \frac{\ }{16} = \frac{\ }{20} = \frac{18}{\ } = \frac{\ }{28}$$

$$\frac{1}{7} = \frac{\ }{14} = \frac{\ }{21} = \frac{4}{\ } = \frac{\ }{35} = \frac{6}{\ }$$

EQUALIZE THIS!

3

Improper fractions and mixed numbers

THERE'S SOMETHING IMPROPER HERE!

Change this improper fraction to a mixed number. Don't forget you may need to reduce.

$$\frac{27}{12} = 27 \div 12 = 2\ r\ 3 = 2\frac{3}{12} = 2\frac{3 \div 3 = 1}{12 \div 3 = 4} = 2\frac{1}{4}$$

Change these mixed numbers to improper fractions.

$$1\frac{3}{4} = \frac{(1 \times 4) + 3 = 7}{4} \qquad 6\frac{1}{2} = \frac{(6 \times 2) + 1 = 13}{2}$$

Change these improper fractions to mixed numbers.

$$\frac{8}{3} = \qquad\qquad \frac{29}{12} = \qquad\qquad \frac{36}{7} =$$

$$\frac{19}{6} = \qquad\qquad \frac{13}{9} = \qquad\qquad \frac{14}{5} =$$

$$\frac{22}{5} = \qquad\qquad \frac{23}{3} = \qquad\qquad \frac{8}{5} =$$

$$\frac{7}{2} = \qquad\qquad \frac{21}{2} = \qquad\qquad \frac{15}{4} =$$

$$\frac{22}{4} = \qquad\qquad \frac{18}{8} = \qquad\qquad \frac{42}{9} =$$

Change these mixed numbers to improper fractions.

$$3\frac{1}{4} = \qquad\qquad 5\frac{1}{2} = \qquad\qquad 2\frac{1}{4} =$$

$$2\frac{1}{3} = \qquad\qquad 6\frac{3}{4} = \qquad\qquad 3\frac{3}{10} =$$

$$5\frac{3}{8} = \qquad\qquad 2\frac{2}{5} = \qquad\qquad 3\frac{5}{6} =$$

$$2\frac{3}{4} = \qquad\qquad 2\frac{3}{8} = \qquad\qquad 2\frac{7}{12} =$$

$$2\frac{7}{10} = \qquad\qquad 3\frac{9}{10} = \qquad\qquad 4\frac{1}{8} =$$

$$4\frac{1}{4} = \qquad\qquad 8\frac{1}{2} = \qquad\qquad 1\frac{5}{12} =$$

Rounding decimals

Round these decimals to the nearest tenth.

7.34 is	1.54 is	3.24 is
4.87 is	2.73 is	9.42 is
6.38 is	8.82 is	7.83 is
2.79 is	3.46 is	6.46 is

Round these decimals to the nearest tenth.

8.75 is	4.65 is	2.75 is
2.66 is	1.87 is	3.52 is
1.35 is	8.47 is	9.45 is
2.87 is	9.36 is	1.54 is

Round these decimals to the nearest tenth.

22.73 is	16.84 is	46.21 is
35.61 is	33.56 is	26.75 is
18.87 is	72.72 is	83.64 is
12.65 is	88.88 is	39.55 is
45.26 is	34.76 is	65.43 is

Adding with different numbers of digits

Work out the sum of each problem.

$$\begin{array}{r} 256 \\ + \ 31 \\ \hline \rule{1cm}{0.4pt} \end{array} \qquad \begin{array}{r} 283 \\ + \ 15 \\ \hline \rule{1cm}{0.4pt} \end{array} \qquad \begin{array}{r} 207 \\ + \ 83 \\ \hline \end{array} \qquad \begin{array}{r} 576 \\ + \ 12 \\ \hline \end{array}$$

$$\begin{array}{r} 317 \\ + \ 72 \\ \hline \rule{1cm}{0.4pt} \end{array} \qquad \begin{array}{r} 542 \\ + \ 29 \\ \hline \rule{1cm}{0.4pt} \end{array} \qquad \begin{array}{r} 271 \\ + \ 18 \\ \hline \end{array} \qquad \begin{array}{r} 324 \\ + \ 45 \\ \hline \end{array}$$

HURRY UP! GET ON THE CASE...

Write the answer in the box.

48 + 311 =

382 + 214 =

32 + 563 =

275 + 386 =

Write the missing numbers in the boxes.

$$\begin{array}{r} 242 \\ + \ 27 \\ \hline 2 \ \ 9 \end{array} \qquad \begin{array}{r} 93 \\ + \ 37 \\ \hline 976 \end{array} \qquad \begin{array}{r} 8 \ \ 5 \\ + \ 32 \\ \hline 837 \end{array} \qquad \begin{array}{r} 6 \ \ 3 \\ + \ 72 \\ \hline 695 \end{array}$$

Write the answer in the colored box. Use the space for working them out.

Robin has saved $276. For his birthday he is given another $32. How much does he have now?

The Joker sells 207 adult tickets for his show and 87 children's tickets. How many tickets are sold altogether?

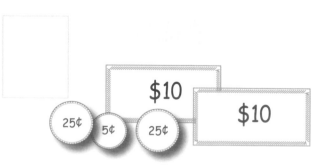

Adding with different numbers of digits

Work out the sum of each problem.

```
    1 11                    1 11
     987                   2,767
+ 423,123               + 12,844
  424,110                 15,611
```

Remember to regroup if you need to.

Work out the sum of each problem.

```
    3,756          6,855,967              56
+  27,594       +   153,462        +   2,738
_____      _____        _____
```

```
    5,783            205,836           5,776
+  32,368       +      2,791     + 878,142
_____      _____        _____
```

Write the answer in the box.

6,783,201 + 914,875 =

415,739 + 24,683 =

YOU CAN'T
BEAT ME...

Write in the missing numbers in these sums.

```
  5, 8              21          6,75
+   848        +  8,189     +    909
_____         _____       _____
 6,235          8,51         7,661
```

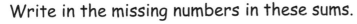

Work out the answer to the problem.
Use the space for working it out.

Harley Quinn has 1,253 playing cards in
her collection. The Joker has 831. How
many do they have altogether?

Subtracting one number from another

Find the difference for each problem.

$$\begin{array}{r} \overset{7\ 13}{8\cancel{3}4} \\ -\ 44 \\ \hline 790 \end{array} \qquad \begin{array}{r} \overset{3\ 12\ 11}{\cancel{4}\cancel{3}\cancel{1}} \\ -\ 84 \\ \hline 347 \end{array}$$

Find the difference for each problem.

$$\begin{array}{r} 834 \\ -\ 12 \\ \hline \end{array} \qquad \begin{array}{r} 580 \\ -\ 60 \\ \hline \end{array} \qquad \begin{array}{r} 437 \\ -\ 56 \\ \hline \end{array} \qquad \begin{array}{r} 175 \\ -\ 54 \\ \hline \end{array}$$

$$\begin{array}{r} 579 \\ -\ 42 \\ \hline \end{array} \qquad \begin{array}{r} 364 \\ -\ 62 \\ \hline \end{array} \qquad \begin{array}{r} 289 \\ -\ 68 \\ \hline \end{array} \qquad \begin{array}{r} 280 \\ -\ 30 \\ \hline \end{array}$$

$$\begin{array}{r} 483 \\ -\ 26 \\ \hline \end{array} \qquad \begin{array}{r} 756 \\ -\ 17 \\ \hline \end{array} \qquad \begin{array}{r} 253 \\ -\ 16 \\ \hline \end{array} \qquad \begin{array}{r} 841 \\ -\ 28 \\ \hline \end{array}$$

Write the answer in the box.

431 - 21 = ⬜   636 - 22 = ⬜

785 - 63 = ⬜   866 - 34 = ⬜

Find the difference for each problem.

There are 585 children in Gotham high school. If 38 children are on a field trip, how many children are still at school?

There are 256 bats in the Batcave. If 37 fly away, how many are left?

Subtracting one number from another

SUBLIMINAL SUBTRACTION!

Work out the answer to each problem.

```
  1 16 16 7 15
  27,685
-  8,726
  18,959
```

```
  1 10 14   3 12
  2,147,423
-   165,351
  1,982,072
```

Work out the answer to each problem.

```
  568,232
-   3,846
```

```
  6,262,422
-   347,566
```

```
  10,684
-  2,845
```

```
  337,481
-  19,802
```

```
  7,157,864
- 3,633,976
```

```
  892,223
- 746,489
```

```
  82,818
-  7,465
```

```
  67,444
- 28,647
```

```
  3,732,522
-     3,176
```

```
  872,813
-  52,284
```

```
  4,794,872
-   355,257
```

```
  116,387
-   2,799
```

Write the answer in the box.

4,635,652 - 1,754,871 =

975,830 - 7,642 =

Work out the answer to the problem. Use the space for working it out.

Batman was traveling in his Whirly-Bat at 2,635 feet above ground. He suddenly descended 142 feet. How high above ground was he now?

I HOPE ALFRED FIXED THE ENGINE...

9

Real-life problems

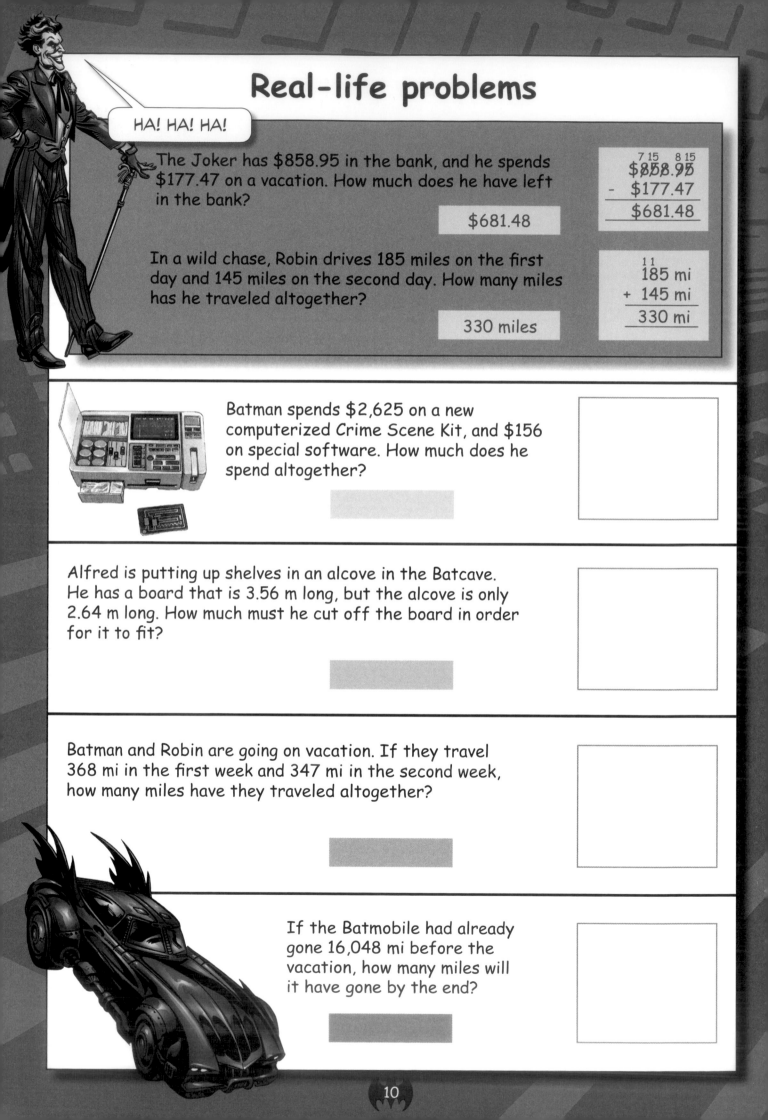

HA! HA! HA!

The Joker has $858.95 in the bank, and he spends $177.47 on a vacation. How much does he have left in the bank?

$681.48

$$\begin{array}{r} {}^{7\,15}\;\;{}^{8\,15} \\ \$8\cancel{58}.\cancel{95} \\ -\quad \$177.47 \\ \hline \$681.48 \end{array}$$

In a wild chase, Robin drives 185 miles on the first day and 145 miles on the second day. How many miles has he traveled altogether?

330 miles

$$\begin{array}{r} {}^{1\,1} \\ 185 \text{ mi} \\ +\; 145 \text{ mi} \\ \hline 330 \text{ mi} \end{array}$$

Batman spends $2,625 on a new computerized Crime Scene Kit, and $156 on special software. How much does he spend altogether?

Alfred is putting up shelves in an alcove in the Batcave. He has a board that is 3.56 m long, but the alcove is only 2.64 m long. How much must he cut off the board in order for it to fit?

Batman and Robin are going on vacation. If they travel 368 mi in the first week and 347 mi in the second week, how many miles have they traveled altogether?

If the Batmobile had already gone 16,048 mi before the vacation, how many miles will it have gone by the end?

Everyday problems

Alfred buys 415 ft of cable. If he uses 234 ft, how much does he have left?

181 ft

$$\begin{array}{r} \overset{3\ 11}{\cancel{4}\cancel{1}5}\ \text{ft} \\ -\ \ 234\ \text{ft} \\ \hline 181\ \text{ft} \end{array}$$

Bruce Wayne travels by train for 120 mi, by bus for 48 mi, and then walks the final 3 mi to Wayne Manor. How far does he travel?

171 mi

$$\begin{array}{r} \overset{1}{1}20\ \text{mi} \\ 48\ \text{mi} \\ +\ \ \ 3\ \text{mi} \\ \hline 171\ \text{mi} \end{array}$$

Commissioner Gordon works 185 hours a month. His wife works 72 hours a month. How many hours do they work altogether in a month?

Gotham high school collects money for the local children's home. If the pupils collect $275 in the first month, $210 in the second month, and $136 in the third month, how much do they collect altogether?

Batman and Robin are racing to a crime scene. Batman gets there in 12.75 seconds. Robin gets there in 14.83 seconds. Who got there first?

How much faster was the crime buster who got there first?

Arkham Asylum orders 8,755 lb of potatoes. 6,916 lb are eaten. How many pounds of potatoes are left?

Everyday problems

The Riddler, Query, and Echo want to put their money together to buy a some new equipment. If the Riddler has $25.25, Query has $24.75, and Echo has $12.50, how much will they have to spend on the equipment?

```
0 1 1 1
  $25.25
  $24.75
+ $12.50
  $62.50
```

They will have $62.50 to spend.

Gotham City candy store has 120 lb of taffy and sells 80 lb. How much does it have left?

```
    12
  120 lb
-  80 lb
   40 lb
```

It has 40 lb left.

Gotham City bakery orders 148 lb of sugar, 564 lb of salt, and 984 lb of butter. What is the total weight of the order?

Catwoman has to fill up with gas. After paying $42 for the gas, she has $145 left. How much did she have to start with??

Robin is saving up to buy a guitar that costs $169.99. If he already has $73.47, how much more does he need?

5¢ 5¢ 25¢ $10

The exercise yard in Gotham City penitentiary is 30 ft long and 20 ft wide. How much fence is needed to surround all four sides?

Decimal addition

Write in the answers to these problems.

$$\begin{array}{r} \overset{1}{4}7.\overset{1}{1}5 \\ + \ 19.36 \\ \hline 66.51 \end{array}$$

$$\begin{array}{r} 43.\overset{1}{9}\overset{1}{9} \\ + \ 12.76 \\ \hline 56.75 \end{array}$$

IT ALL ADDS UP! JUST FILL IN THE BOXES.

Write the answer to each problem.

63.72	85.17	28.46	24.76	73.49
+ 77.92	+ 68.21	+ 64.84	+ 89.14	+ 18.75

46.67	32.88	39.47	58.32	38.84
+ 12.99	+ 43.02	+ 81.70	+ 14.95	+ 22.65

Write the answer to each problem.

75.80	56.78	81.97	39.48	58.35
+ 22.98	+ 73.47	+ 23.59	+ 75.43	+ 28.67

85.78	65.37	53.75	85.74	73.76
+ 31.45	+ 28.99	+ 80.76	+ 39.47	+ 41.27

Write in the answer to each problem.

33.97 + 24.62 =   63.84 + 29.81 =   37.19 + 28.24 =

76.39 + 43.78 =   34.43 + 25.64 =   32.44 + 21.88 =

52.38 + 38.43 =   68.67 + 29.82 =   37.89 + 82.15 =

84.77 + 39.12 =   21.99 + 79.32 =   52.45 + 34.58 =

13

Decimal addition

Write in the answer to each problem. Remember to line up the decimal points and write zeros for place holders.

WHAT'S THE POINT?

$$
\begin{array}{r}
^{1\ \ 1}296.48 \\
+\ \ 131.70 \\
\hline
428.18 \\
\end{array}
$$

$$
\begin{array}{r}
^{1\ 1}73.00 \\
+\ 269.23 \\
\hline
342.23 \\
\end{array}
$$

Write in the answer to each problem.

$$
\begin{array}{r}
378.76 \\
+\ \ 25.84 \\
\hline
\end{array}
$$

$$
\begin{array}{r}
491.83 \\
+\ \ 37.84 \\
\hline
\end{array}
$$

$$
\begin{array}{r}
964.71 \\
+\ 321.20 \\
\hline
\end{array}
$$

$$
\begin{array}{r}
32.045 \\
+204.990 \\
\hline
\end{array}
$$

$$
\begin{array}{r}
306.00 \\
+\ 844.24 \\
\hline
\end{array}
$$

$$
\begin{array}{r}
471.932 \\
+\ 755.260 \\
\hline
\end{array}
$$

$$
\begin{array}{r}
842.010 \\
+\ \ 11.842 \\
\hline
\end{array}
$$

$$
\begin{array}{r}
675.82 \\
+\ 105.00 \\
\hline
\end{array}
$$

$$
\begin{array}{r}
37.82 \\
+\ 399.71 \\
\hline
\end{array}
$$

$$
\begin{array}{r}
65.24 \\
+\ 605.27 \\
\hline
\end{array}
$$

$$
\begin{array}{r}
178.935 \\
+599.410 \\
\hline
\end{array}
$$

$$
\begin{array}{r}
184.70 \\
+\ 372.81 \\
\hline
\end{array}
$$

$$
\begin{array}{r}
443.27 \\
+\ \ 75.00 \\
\hline
\end{array}
$$

$$
\begin{array}{r}
563.00 \\
+\ 413.98 \\
\hline
\end{array}
$$

$$
\begin{array}{r}
703.95 \\
+\ \ 85.22 \\
\hline
\end{array}
$$

$$
\begin{array}{r}
825.360 \\
+\ 249.857 \\
\hline
\end{array}
$$

Write in the sum for each problem.

527 + 134.8 =

85.42 + 321.75 =

501.8 + 361.93 =

558.32 + 137.945 =

27 + 142.07 =

75.31 + 105.37 =

421 + 136.25 =

92.31 + 241.73 =

153.3 + 182.02 =

491.445 + 105.37 =

Decimal subtraction

Write the difference for each problem.

$\begin{array}{r}62.95\\-\ 33.37\end{array}$	$\begin{array}{r}81.42\\-\ 25.04\end{array}$	$\begin{array}{r}48.52\\-\ 14.49\end{array}$	$\begin{array}{r}61.55\\-\ 13.26\end{array}$

$\begin{array}{r}45.76\\-\ 16.18\end{array}$	$\begin{array}{r}73.52\\-\ 39.27\end{array}$	$\begin{array}{r}98.98\\-\ 39.19\end{array}$	$\begin{array}{r}53.58\\-\ 14.39\end{array}$

$\begin{array}{r}92.63\\-\ 67.14\end{array}$	$\begin{array}{r}73.71\\-\ 19.24\end{array}$	$\begin{array}{r}64.21\\-\ 16.02\end{array}$	$\begin{array}{r}64.92\\-\ 26.35\end{array}$

$\begin{array}{r}81.94\\-\ 28.15\end{array}$	$\begin{array}{r}62.35\\-\ 13.16\end{array}$	$\begin{array}{r}21.74\\-\ 12.10\end{array}$	$\begin{array}{r}94.87\\-\ 65.28\end{array}$

Write the difference for each problem.

46.75 - 12.17 =   56.84 - 24.72 =

72.41 - 23.18 =   51.52 - 12.13 =

53.84 - 19.65 =   64.65 - 37.26 =

41.82 - 18.13 =   91.91 - 22.22 =

77.31 - 28.15 =   51.61 - 23.14 =

Decimal subtraction

Write the difference for each problem.

```
    7 11
  68.17          39.20
- 11.40        - 13.15
  56.77          26.05
```

NO ONE MESSES WITH THE JOKER.

Work out the difference for each problem.

```
  64.77          35.612          66.37          63.20
- 35.3         - 26.19         - 21.9         - 15.36
```

```
  63.14          35.612          99.235          55.492
- 32           - 13.207        - 33.70         - 27.66
```

```
  63.20          62.1           68             63.14
- 15.36        - 29.34        - 31.5         - 32
```

```
  55.492          85             53.64          95.15
- 27.66        - 26.32        - 23           - 31.356
```

Write the difference for each problem.

63.4 - 24.51   =   72.6 - 53.71   =

92.197 - 63.28   =   61.16 - 24.4   =

91.3 - 33   =   81.815 - 55.9   =

41.24 - 14.306   =   52.251 - 22.42   =

92.84 - 23   =   94.31 - 27.406   =

Multiplying larger numbers by ones

Write the product for each problem.

```
  1 3              1 31
  529             1.273
×    4          ×      5
─────          ─────────
2,116            6,365
```

Write the product for each problem.

```
  455          126          831          724
×   2        ×   3        ×   3        ×   4
─────        ─────        ─────        ─────


  105          253          282          349
×   4        ×   5        ×   5        ×   6
─────        ─────        ─────        ─────


  465          328          562          161
×   6        ×   6        ×   4        ×   4
─────        ─────        ─────        ─────
```

Write the product for each problem.

```
4,327        1,352        3,764        1,578
×    3       ×    3       ×    4       ×    4
──────       ──────       ──────       ──────


1,263        5,907        1,203        1,456
×    5       ×    5       ×    6       ×    6
──────       ──────       ──────       ──────


1,467        1,599        8,436        6,521
×    6       ×    6       ×    6       ×    6
──────       ──────       ──────       ──────


4,851        6,538        3,914        8,124
×    4       ×    5       ×    6       ×    6
──────       ──────       ──────       ──────
```

Multiplying larger numbers by ones

Write the answer to each problem.

$$\begin{array}{r} 14 \\ 417 \\ \times\ \ 7 \\ \hline 2,919 \end{array}$$

$$\begin{array}{r} 1\ 7\ 4 \\ 2,185 \\ \times\ \ \ \ 9 \\ \hline 19,665 \end{array}$$

TO THE BATCAVE! LET'S SPEED UP.

Write the answer to each problem.

604	413	682	327
× 7	× 7	× 8	× 7

436	171	715	254
× 8	× 9	× 8	× 8

235	319	581	999
× 8	× 9	× 9	× 9

Work out the answer to each problem.

2,816	4,331	2,617	1,439
× 7	× 7	× 8	× 8

4,022	3,104	2,591	4,361
× 8	× 8	× 9	× 9

4,361	3,002	2,567	1,514
× 9	× 8	× 7	× 8

4,624	3,894	2,993	1,710
× 7	× 8	× 8	× 9

Real-life multiplication problems

There are 157 apples in each box.
How many will there be in three boxes?

471 apples

$$\begin{array}{r} \overset{1\,2}{157} \\ \times\ \ 3 \\ \hline 471 \end{array}$$

Each of the Penguin's fish crates can hold 660 fish. How many fish will five crates hold?

A train on Gotham City transport system can take 425 passengers. How many can it take in five trips?

Officer Dan Foley puts $278 a month into the bank. How much will he have put in after 6 months?

Gotham City theater can seat 4,536 people. If a play runs for 7 days, what is the maximum number of people who will be able to see the play?

A Bat-Cycle costs $35,956. How much will it cost Batman to buy a bike for four of his friends?

The Batplane flies at a steady speed of 550 mph. How far will it travel in 6 hours?

Comparing and ordering decimals

Compare the decimals. Which decimal is greater?

2.2 and 3.1   0.45 and 0.6

Line them up vertically. Add zeros for place holders.

| 2.2 | 0.45 |
| 3.1 | 0.60 |

3 > 2, so 3.1 > 2.2   6 > 4, so 0.6 > 0.45

IT'S YOUR CHOICE.

Compare the decimals. Which decimal is greater?

8.9 and 8.1   0.4 and 0.52   3.6 and 0.94   0.5 and 0.68

1.5 and 1.8   0.41 and 4.10   8.6 and 6.8   5.45 and 5.41

Find the greatest decimal.

2.8 and 2.75 and 2.5   0.98 and 1.09 and 1.3   5.9 and 4.87 and 5.75

Write the decimals in order from greatest to least.

0.44   4.1   0.4   34.95   33.9   34.5   7.5   6.95   7.59

Find the answer to each problem.

Gotham City Weather Bureau reported 5.27 inches of rain in March, 6.54 inches in April, and 5.23 inches in May. Which month had the least rainfall?

Alfred walked 4.4 miles on Wednesday, 3.86 miles on Thursday, and 4.34 miles on Friday. Which day did he walk the farthest?

Converting units of measure

Convert 25 centimeters to millimeters.   Convert 200¢ to dollars.

25 x 10   = | 250 mm | 200 ÷ 100   = | $2 |

HOW LONG? HOW MUCH?

Convert these centimeters to millimeters.

30 cm		45 cm			
15 cm		24 cm			
53 cm		86 cm		106 cm	
93 cm		40 cm		376 cm	

Convert these millimeters to centimeters.

40 mm		100 mm		130 mm	
50 mm		80 mm		300 mm	
120 mm		10 mm		550 mm	

Convert these dollars to cents.

$45		$500		$25	
$12		$46		$95	
$82		$8		$250	

Convert these cents to dollars.

350¢		800¢		5,000¢	
250¢		300¢		450¢	

21

Converting units of measure

Convert 300 centimeters to meters.

$300 \div 100 =$ [3 m]

Convert 4 kilometers to meters.

$4 \times 1{,}000 =$ [4,000 m]

IT'S ALL A MATTER OF HUNDREDS AND THOUSANDS!

Convert these centimeters to meters.

400 cm		800 cm	
9,000 cm		5,000 cm	
7,800 cm		6,400 cm	
46,700 cm		85,200 cm	

Convert these meters to centimeters.

74 m		39 m		85 m	
59 m		24 m		48 m	
156 m		217 m		821 m	

Convert these meters to kilometers.

4,000 m		8,000 m		9,000 m	
25,000 m		37,000 m		71,000 m	
45,000 m		76,000 m		99,000 m	

Convert these kilometers to meters.

6 km		9 km		3 km	
23 km		56 km		84 km	

Areas of rectangles and squares

Find the area of this blue rectangle.

To find the area of a rectangle or square, we multiply length (l) by width (w).

Area = 800 in.²

(w) 25 in.

(l)

32 in.

$$\begin{array}{r} \overset{1}{32} \\ \times\ 25 \\ \hline {}^{1}160 \\ +\ 640 \\ \hline 800 \text{ in.}^2 \end{array}$$

Find the area of these rectangles and squares. You may need to do your work on a separate sheet.

NOW WHO'S LAUGHING?

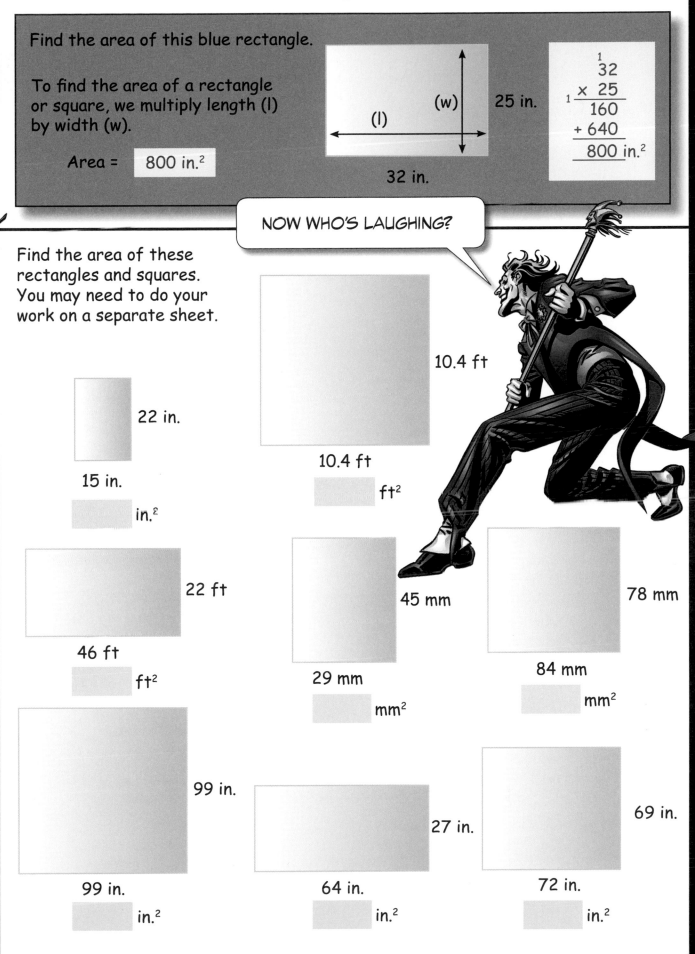

22 in.

15 in.

___ in.²

10.4 ft

10.4 ft

___ ft²

22 ft

46 ft

___ ft²

45 mm

29 mm

___ mm²

78 mm

84 mm

___ mm²

99 in.

99 in.

___ in.²

27 in.

64 in.

___ in.²

69 in.

72 in.

___ in.²

23

Perimeter of shapes

Find the perimeter of this brown rectangle.

To find the perimeter of a rectangle
or square, we add the two lengths and
the two widths together.

13.3 in.

25.4 in.

77.4 in.

$$\begin{array}{r} 1\ 1 \\ 13.3 \\ 13.3 \\ 25.4 \\ +25.4 \\ \hline 77.4 \end{array}$$ in.

Find the perimeter of these rectangles.
You may need to do your work on an extra sheet.

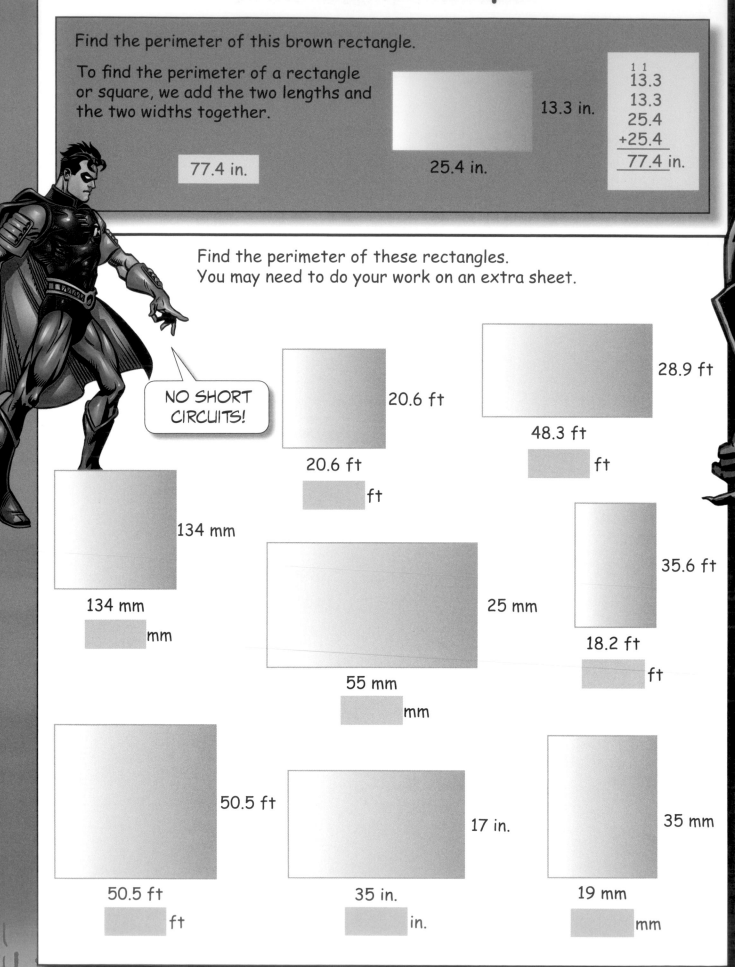

NO SHORT
CIRCUITS!

20.6 ft

20.6 ft

ft

28.9 ft

48.3 ft

ft

134 mm

134 mm

mm

25 mm

55 mm

mm

35.6 ft

18.2 ft

ft

50.5 ft

50.5 ft

ft

17 in.

35 in.

in.

35 mm

19 mm

mm

24

Decimal place value

Work out the answer to the problem.

2.385

What is the place value of the digit 8?

Ones	Tenths	Hundredths	Thousandths	Ten-thousandths
2.	3	8	5	0

2.3850
8 is in the hundredths place, so its value is 8 hundredths.

EVERY DIGIT COUNTS!

Name the place value of the digit 8 in each of the problems.

0.289	2.0548	1.108	5.86

Name the place value of the digit in **bold**.

5.3**9**47	7.56**4**	5.**4**08	0.51**2**4

8.356   1.062   4.622

Which number has a digit with the place value 6 tenths?

Which number has a digit with the place value 6 hundredths?

Which number has a digit with the place value 6 thousandths?

How much greater is the second decimal than the first?

7.46   7.56   3.171   3.172   0.751   0.761

Speed problems

How long will it take the Penguin to travel 36 mi on his pogo umbrella if he travels at a constant speed of 9 mi per hour?

| 4 hours |

Time = Distance ÷ Speed

If a car traveled 150 mi at a constant speed in 5 hours, at what speed was it traveling?

| 30 mph |

Speed = Distance ÷ Time

If a bus travels for 5 hours at 40 mph, how far does it travel?

5 x 40 = | 200 mi |

Distance = Speed x Time

The Batmobile cruises along a road at a steady speed of 60 mph. How far will it travel in 5 hours?

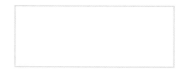

A train covers a distance of 560 mi in 8 hours. If it travels at a constant speed, how fast is it traveling?

Bruce Wayne walks at a steady speed of 3 mph. How long will it take him to travel 18 miles?

The old Batmobile had a top speed of 95 mph. What was the farthest it could travel in 3 hours?

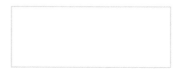

Robin has just done a long-distance training run, at an average speed of 6 mph. If it took him 4 hours, how far did he run?

The Penguin pogos 50 miles around Gotham City at a steady speed of 10 mph. If he started at 3:00 P.M., at what time did he finish his journey?

Conversion table

This is part of a conversion table that shows how to change dollars to euros, when 10 euros (10€) equal $1. To convert euros to dollars, divide by 10. To convert dollars to euros, multiply by 10.

U.S. Dollars	Euros (€)
1	10
2	20

How many euros would you get for $3?   3 x 10 = [30€]

How much is 15€ worth?   15 ÷ 10 = [$1.50]

How many dollars would you get for 40€?

How many dollars would you get for 75€?

How much is 1€ worth?

Change $55 into euros.

What is $4.50 in euros?

Change 250€ into dollars.

U.S. Dollars	Euros
1	10
2	20
3	30
4	40
5	50
6	60
7	70
8	80
9	90
10	100

The rate then changes to 8€ to the dollar. The conversion chart now looks like the one shown here.

How many euros are worth $5?

How many dollars can you get for 64€?

How many euros are worth $9.50?

How many euros can you get for $30?

How many dollars would you get for 120€?

What is the value of 4€?

U.S. Dollars	Euros
1	8
2	16
3	24
4	32
5	40
6	48
7	56
8	64
9	72
10	80

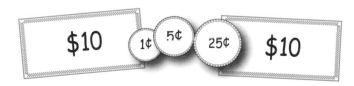

Interpreting circle graphs

48 children voted for their favorite ice cream flavor.
How many children voted for strawberry?

$48 \div 4 = 12$ so $\frac{1}{4}$ of 48 is 12

12 children voted for strawberry.

How many children voted for chocolate?

$48 \div 8 = 6$ $6 \times 3 = 18$ so $\frac{3}{8}$ of 48 = 18

18 children voted for chocolate.

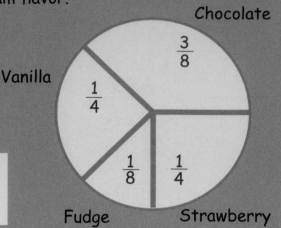

A class of 30 children voted for their favorite Batman character.

How many voted for Harley Quinn?

How many did not vote for Batman?

How many more children voted for Robin than for the Joker?

How many children altogether voted for Catwoman and Harley Quinn?

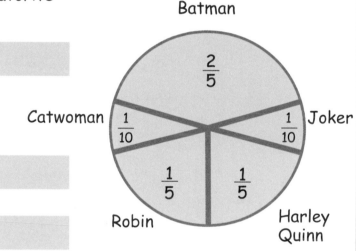

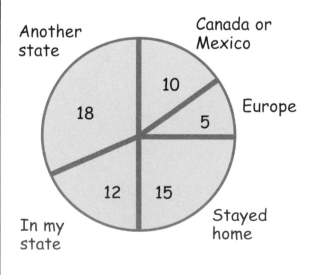

60 citizens of Gotham City were asked where they went on vacation last year. The circle graph shows the results.

What fraction of people vacationed in their own state?

What fraction of people vacationed in Canada or Mexico, or in Europe?

What fraction of people did not stay at home?

Probability scale 0 to 1

Look at this probability line.
Impossible = 0
Poor chance = 0.25
Fair = 0.5
Good chance = 0.75
Certain = 1

Write each letter in the correct place on the probability line.
a. It will be daylight in New Orleans at midnight.
b. The sun will come up tomorrow.
c. If I toss a coin it will come down heads.

```
a                        c                              b
↓                        ↓                              ↓
0          0.25         0.5          0.75              1
```

```
0          0.25         0.5          0.75              1
```

Write each letter in the correct place on the probability line.

a. If the Joker cuts a pack of cards he will get a red card.

b. If he cuts a pack of cards he will get a diamond.

c. If he cuts a pack of cards he will get a diamond, a spade, or a club.

d. If he cuts a pack of cards he will get a diamond, a spade, a club, or a heart.

e. If he cuts a pack of cards it will be a 15.

```
0          0.25         0.5          0.75              1
```

Write each letter in the correct place on the probability line.

a. Next week, Wednesday will be the day after Tuesday.

b. There will be 33 days in February next year.

c. It will snow in Miami in May.

d. It will snow in Chicago in January.

e. The next person to knock on the door will be female.

Likely outcomes

Throw one coin 20 times.

Put your results on a bar graph

Keep a tally.

| H | |
| T | |

What do you notice?

COIN THROWS

Heads and tails come up roughly the same number of times because there are only two possible outcomes and they are equally likely.

REMEMBER, LIFE IS NOT A GAMBLE IF YOU FIGURE IT OUT!

Predict what you think the outcome will be if you tossed two coins 48 times.

2 heads times   2 tails times   1 of each [ ] times

Now actually throw two coins 48 times and record your results on this tally chart.

2 heads	
2 tails	
1 of each	

Draw a bar graph to show your results.

 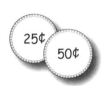

Which result comes up the most often?

COIN THROWS

Number of throws: 50 45 40 35 30 25 20 15 10 5 0

heads   tails   1 of each

Outcomes

Can you explain why some results are more probable than others?

Naming quadrilaterals

FAIR AND SQUARE?

Name this shape.

rhombus

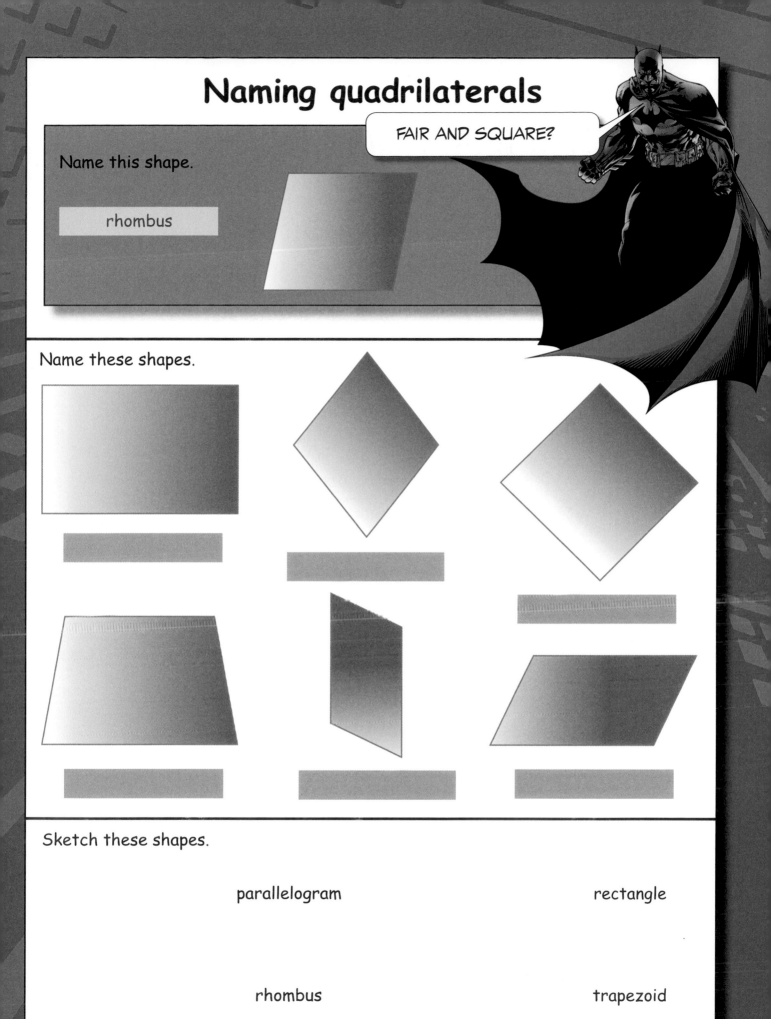

Name these shapes.

Sketch these shapes.

parallelogram   rectangle

rhombus   trapezoid

Speed trials

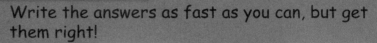

Write the answers as fast as you can, but get them right!

4 x 10 = | 40 | 8 x 2 = | 16

Write the answers as fast as you can, but get them right!

3 x 2 =	1 x 5 =	4 x 10 =	1 x 3 =
2 x 2 =	10 x 5 =	8 x 10 =	2 x 3 =
5 x 2 =	0 x 5 =	6 x 10 =	10 x 3 =
1 x 2 =	3 x 5 =	1 x 10 =	8 x 3 =
6 x 2 =	4 x 5 =	5 x 10 =	6 x 3 =
4 x 2 =	8 x 5 =	3 x 10 =	4 x 3 =
7 x 2 =	6 x 5 =	7 x 10 =	7 x 3 =
9 x 2 =	7 x 5 =	0 x 10 =	0 x 3 =
10 x 2 =	9 x 5 =	2 x 10 =	5 x 3 =
8 x 2 =	5 x 5 =	9 x 10 =	3 x 3 =
0 x 2 =	3 x 5 =	10 x 10 =	8 x 4 =
2 x 7 =	5 x 3 =	10 x 1 =	7 x 4 =
2 x 1 =	5 x 8 =	10 x 7 =	6 x 4 =
2 x 4 =	5 x 9 =	10 x 4 =	3 x 4 =
3 x 7 =	5 x 7 =	10 x 3 =	10 x 4 =
2 x 5 =	5 x 4 =	10 x 5 =	0 x 4 =
2 x 9 =	5 x 1 =	10 x 8 =	3 x 4 =
2 x 6 =	4 x 7 =	10 x 6 =	9 x 4 =
2 x 8 =	5 x 10 =	10 x 2 =	5 x 4 =
2 x 3 =	5 x 2 =	10 x 9 =	2 x 4 =

All the 3s

You will need to know these:

$1 \times 3 = 3$ $2 \times 3 = 6$ $3 \times 3 = 9$ $4 \times 3 = 12$
$5 \times 3 = 15$ $10 \times 3 = 30$

GET SOME PRACTICE!

How many altogether?

6 sets of three are ⬜   six threes are ⬜ $6 \times 3 =$ ⬜

How many altogether?

7 sets of three are ⬜   seven threes are ⬜ $7 \times 3 =$ ⬜

How many altogether?

8 sets of three are ⬜   eight threes are ⬜ $8 \times 3 =$ ⬜

How many altogether?

9 sets of three are ⬜   nine threes are ⬜ $9 \times 3 =$ ⬜

All the 3s again

You should know all of the three times table.

$1 \times 3 = 3$ $2 \times 3 = 6$ $3 \times 3 = 9$ $4 \times 3 = 12$ $5 \times 3 = 15$

$6 \times 3 = 18$ $7 \times 3 = 21$ $8 \times 3 = 24$ $9 \times 3 = 27$ $10 \times 3 = 30$

Say these to yourself a few times.

Cover the three times table with a sheet of paper so you can't see the numbers. Write the answers. Be as fast as you can, but get them right!

$1 \times 3 =$	$5 \times 3 =$	$6 \times 3 =$
$2 \times 3 =$	$7 \times 3 =$	$9 \times 3 =$
$3 \times 3 =$	$9 \times 3 =$	$4 \times 3 =$
$4 \times 3 =$	$4 \times 3 =$	$5 \times 3 =$
$5 \times 3 =$	$6 \times 3 =$	$3 \times 7 =$
$6 \times 3 =$	$8 \times 3 =$	$3 \times 4 =$
$7 \times 3 =$	$10 \times 3 =$	$2 \times 3 =$
$8 \times 3 =$	$1 \times 3 =$	$10 \times 3 =$
$9 \times 3 =$	$3 \times 3 =$	$3 \times 9 =$
$10 \times 3 =$	$2 \times 3 =$	$3 \times 6 =$
$3 \times 1 =$	$3 \times 5 =$	$3 \times 5 =$
$3 \times 2 =$	$3 \times 7 =$	$3 \times 8 =$
$3 \times 3 =$	$3 \times 9 =$	$7 \times 3 =$
$3 \times 4 =$	$3 \times 4 =$	$3 \times 2 =$
$3 \times 5 =$	$3 \times 6 =$	$3 \times 10 =$
$3 \times 6 =$	$3 \times 8 =$	$8 \times 3 =$
$3 \times 7 =$	$3 \times 10 =$	$3 \times 0 =$
$3 \times 8 =$	$3 \times 1 =$	$1 \times 3 =$
$3 \times 9 =$	$3 \times 0 =$	$3 \times 3 =$
$3 \times 10 =$	$3 \times 2 =$	$3 \times 9 =$

All the 4s

How many altogether?

6 sets of four are ⬜   six fours are ⬜   6 x 4 = ⬜

How many altogether?

7 sets of four are ⬜   seven fours are ⬜   7 x 4 = ⬜

How many altogether?

8 sets of four are ⬜   eight fours are ⬜   8 x 4 = ⬜

How many altogether?

9 sets of four are ⬜   nine fours are ⬜   9 x 4 = ⬜

All the 4s again

You should know all of the four times table by now.

1 x 4 = 4   2 x 4 = 8   3 x 4 = 12   4 x 4 = 16   5 x 4 = 20
6 x 4 = 24   7 x 4 = 28   8 x 4 = 32   9 x 4 = 36   10 x 4 = 40

Say these to yourself a few times.

OK, SO THAT'S ALL THE FOUR TIMES TABLE.

Cover the four times table with a sheet of paper so you can't see the numbers. Write the answers. Be as fast as you can, but get them right!

1 x 4 =	5 x 4 =	6 x 4 =
2 x 4 =	7 x 4 =	9 x 4 =
3 x 4 =	9 x 4 =	4 x 1 =
4 x 4 =	3 x 4 =	5 x 4 =
5 x 4 =	6 x 4 =	4 x 7 =
6 x 4 =	8 x 4 =	3 x 4 =
7 x 4 =	10 x 4 =	2 x 4 =
8 x 4 =	1 x 4 =	10 x 4 =
9 x 4 =	4 x 4 =	4 x 3 =
10 x 4 =	2 x 4 =	4 x 6 =
4 x 1 =	4 x 5 =	4 x 5 =
4 x 2 =	4 x 7 =	4 x 8 =
4 x 3 =	4 x 9 =	7 x 4 =
4 x 4 =	4 x 4 =	4 x 2 =
4 x 5 =	4 x 6 =	4 x 10 =
4 x 6 =	4 x 8 =	8 x 4 =
4 x 7 =	4 x 10 =	4 x 0 =
4 x 8 =	4 x 1 =	1 x 4 =
4 x 9 =	4 x 0 =	4 x 4 =
4 x 10 =	4 x 2 =	4 x 9 =

Speed trials

You should know all of the 1, 2, 3, 4, 5, and 10 times tables by now, but how quickly can you do them? Ask someone to time you as you do this page. Remember, you must be fast but also correct.

NOW LET'S MIX 'EM UP!

4 x 2 =	6 x 3 =	9 x 5 =
8 x 3 =	3 x 4 =	8 x 10 =
7 x 4 =	7 x 5 =	7 x 2 =
6 x 5 =	3 x 10 =	6 x 3 =
8 x 10 =	1 x 2 =	5 x 4 =
8 x 2 =	7 x 3 =	4 x 5 =
5 x 3 =	4 x 4 =	3 x 10 =
9 x 4 =	6 x 5 =	2 x 2 =
5 x 5 =	4 x 10 =	1 x 3 =
7 x 10 =	6 x 2 =	0 x 4 =
0 x 2 =	5 x 3 =	10 x 5 =
4 x 3 =	8 x 4 =	9 x 2 =
6 x 4 =	0 x 5 =	8 x 3 =
3 x 5 =	2 x 10 =	7 x 4 =
4 x 10 =	7 x 2 =	6 x 5 =
7 x 2 =	8 x 3 =	5 x 10 =
3 x 3 =	9 x 4 =	4 x 0 =
2 x 4 =	5 x 5 =	3 x 2 =
7 x 5 =	7 x 10 =	2 x 8 =
9 x 10 =	5 x 2 =	1 x 9 =

Some of the 6s

You should already know parts of the 6 times table because they are parts of the 1, 2, 3, 4, 5, and 10 times tables.

$1 \times 6 = 6$ $2 \times 6 = 12$ $3 \times 6 = 18$

$4 \times 6 = 24$ $5 \times 6 = 30$ $10 \times 6 = 60$

Find out if you can remember them quickly and correctly.

HEY, THIS
IS NEAT!

Cover the six times table with paper so you can't see the numbers. Write the answers as quickly as you can.

What are two sixes?

What are five sixes?

What are three sixes?

What are ten sixes?

What is one six?

What are four sixes?

Write the answers as quickly as you can.

How many sixes make 30?

How many sixes make 6?

How many sixes make 12?

How many sixes make 18?

How many sixes make 24?

How many sixes make 60?

Write the answers as quickly as you can.

Multiply six by three.

Multiply six by two.

Multiply six by five.

Multiply six by four.

Multiply six by one.

Multiply six by ten.

Write the answers as quickly as you can.

$2 \times 6 =$ $10 \times 6 =$ $4 \times 6 =$

$5 \times 6 =$ $3 \times 6 =$ $1 \times 6 =$

Each of Batman's utility belts contains 5 gas pellets. How many gas pellets will there be in 6 utility belts?

The rest of the 6s

You need to learn these:

$$6 \times 6 = 36 \qquad 7 \times 6 = 42$$

$$8 \times 6 = 48 \qquad 9 \times 6 = 54$$

NO SHORT CUTS. YOU'VE GOTTA LEARN THEM.

This work will help you remember the 6 times table.

Complete these sequences.

6   12   18   24   30

$5 \times 6 = 30$ so $6 \times 6 = 30$ plus another 6 =

18   24   30

$6 \times 6 = 36$ so $7 \times 6 = 36$ plus another 6 =

6   12   18   48   60

$7 \times 6 = 42$ so $8 \times 6 = 42$ plus another 6 =

6   12   18   24   30

$8 \times 6 = 48$ so $9 \times 6 = 48$ plus another 6 =

            24   42   60

Test yourself on the rest of the 6 times table.
Cover the above part of the page with a sheet of paper.

What are six sixes?   What are eight sixes?

What are seven sixes?   What are nine sixes?

$8 \times 6 =$ $7 \times 6 =$ $6 \times 6 =$ $9 \times 6 =$

Practice the 6s

1 x 6 =	2 x 6 =	7 x 6 =
2 x 6 =	4 x 6 =	3 x 6 =
3 x 6 =	6 x 6 =	9 x 6 =
4 x 6 =	8 x 6 =	6 x 4 =
5 x 6 =	10 x 6 =	1 x 6 =
6 x 6 =	1 x 6 =	6 x 2 =
7 x 6 =	3 x 6 =	6 x 8 =
8 x 6 =	5 x 6 =	0 x 6 =
9 x 6 =	7 x 6 =	6 x 3 =
10 x 6 =	9 x 6 =	5 x 6 =
6 x 1 =	6 x 3 =	6 x 7 =
6 x 2 =	6 x 5 =	2 x 6 =
6 x 3 =	6 x 7 =	6 x 9 =
6 x 4 =	6 x 9 =	4 x 6 =
6 x 5 =	6 x 2 =	8 x 6 =
6 x 6 =	6 x 4 =	10 x 6 =
6 x 7 =	6 x 6 =	6 x 5 =
6 x 8 =	6 x 8 =	6 x 0 =
6 x 9 =	6 x 10 =	6 x 1 =
6 x 10 =	6 x 0 =	6 x 6 =

Speed trials

You should know all of the 1, 2, 3, 4, 5, 6, and 10 times tables by now, but how quickly can you remember them?
Ask someone to time you as you do this page.
Remember, you must be fast but also correct.

CHECK THE TIME BEFORE YOU START!

4 x 6 =	6 x 3 =	9 x 6 =
5 x 3 =	8 x 6 =	6 x 8 =
7 x 3 =	6 x 6 =	3 x 7 =
6 x 5 =	3 x 10 =	6 x 6 =
6 x 10 =	6 x 2 =	5 x 4 =
8 x 2 =	7 x 3 =	4 x 6 =
5 x 3 =	4 x 6 =	3 x 6 =
9 x 6 =	6 x 5 =	2 x 6 =
5 x 5 =	6 x 10 =	6 x 3 =
7 x 6 =	6 x 2 =	0 x 6 =
0 x 2 =	5 x 3 =	10 x 5 =
6 x 3 =	8 x 4 =	6 x 2 =
6 x 6 =	0 x 6 =	8 x 3 =
3 x 5 =	5 x 10 =	7 x 6 =
4 x 10 =	7 x 6 =	6 x 5 =
7 x 10 =	8 x 3 =	5 x 10 =
3 x 6 =	9 x 6 =	6 x 0 =
2 x 4 =	5 x 5 =	3 x 10 =
6 x 9 =	7 x 10 =	2 x 8 =
9 x 10 =	5 x 6 =	1 x 8 =

Some of the 7s

You should already know parts of the 7 times table because they are parts of the 1, 2, 3, 4, 5, 6, and 10 times tables.

$1 \times 7 = 7$ $2 \times 7 = 14$ $3 \times 7 = 21$ $4 \times 7 = 28$

$5 \times 7 = 35$ $6 \times 7 = 42$ $10 \times 7 = 70$

Find out if you can remember them quickly and correctly.

Cover the six times table with paper so you can't see the numbers. Write the answers as quickly as you can.

What are three sevens?   What are four sevens?

What are two sevens?   What are six sevens?

What are five sevens?   What are ten sevens?

Write the answers as quickly as you can.

How many sevens make 14?   How many sevens make 28?

How many sevens make 35?   How many sevens make 21?

How many sevens make 70?   How many sevens make 42?

Write the answers as quickly as you can.

Multiply seven by three.   Multiply seven by six.

Multiply seven by five.   Multiply seven by two.

Multiply seven by four.   Multiply seven by ten.

Write the answers as quickly as you can.

$10 \times 7 =$ $4 \times 7 =$ $5 \times 7 =$

$3 \times 7 =$ $6 \times 7 =$ $2 \times 7 =$

Alfred spot-welds the rivets on six Bat gadgets. Each gadget needs seven welds. How many spot welds does Alfred make?

The rest of the 7s

You should now know all of the 1, 2, 3, 4, 5, 6, and 10 times tables. You need to learn only these parts of the seven times table.

7 x 7 = 49   7 x 8 = 56   7 x 9 = 63

ONLY THREE SUMS TO LEARN! TEE-HEE!

This work will help you remember the 7 times table.

Complete these sequences.

7   14   21   28   35

6 x 7 = 42   so   7 x 7 = 42 plus another 7 =

21   28   35

7 x 7 = 49   so   8 x 7 = 49 plus another 7 =

7   14   21   56   70

8 x 7 = 56   so   9 x 7 = 56 plus another 7 =

7   14   21   28   35

Test yourself on the rest of the 7 times table.
Cover the section above with a sheet of paper.

What are seven sevens?   What are eight sevens?

What are nine sevens?   What are six sevens?

8 x 7 =   7 x 7 =   9 x 7 =   6 x 7 =

How many days are there in eight weeks?

Color pens are sold in packs of seven. How many will there be in nine packets?

43

Practice the 7s

You should know all of the 7 times table now, but how quickly can you remember it? Ask someone to time you as you do this page. Remember, you must be fast but correct.

FEELING SMART? HAVE SOMEONE TIME YOU!

1 x 7 =	2 x 7 =	7 x 6 =
2 x 7 =	4 x 7 =	3 x 7 =
3 x 7 =	6 x 7 =	9 x 7 =
4 x 7 =	8 x 7 =	7 x 4 =
5 x 7 =	10 x 7 =	1 x 7 =
6 x 7 =	1 x 7 =	7 x 2 =
7 x 7 =	3 x 7 =	7 x 8 =
8 x 7 =	5 x 7 =	0 x 7 =
9 x 7 =	7 x 7 =	7 x 3 =
10 x 7 =	9 x 7 =	5 x 7 =
7 x 1 =	7 x 3 =	7 x 7 =
7 x 2 =	7 x 5 =	2 x 7 =
7 x 3 =	7 x 7 =	7 x 9 =
7 x 4 =	7 x 9 =	4 x 7 =
7 x 5 =	7 x 2 =	8 x 7 =
7 x 6 =	7 x 4 =	10 x 7 =
7 x 7 =	7 x 6 =	7 x 5 =
7 x 8 =	7 x 8 =	7 x 0 =
7 x 9 =	7 x 10 =	7 x 1 =
7 x 10 =	7 x 0 =	6 x 7 =

Speed trials

You should know the 7 times table now, but how quickly can you remember it?
Ask someone to time you as you do this page.
Remember, you must be fast but also correct.

CHECK THE CLOCK AS YOU DO THESE ONES. GET THEM RIGHT – QUICKLY!

4 x 7 =	7 x 3 =	9 x 7 =
5 x 10 =	8 x 7 =	7 x 6 =
7 x 5 =	6 x 6 =	8 x 3 =
6 x 5 =	5 x 10 =	6 x 6 =
8 x 7 =	6 x 3 =	7 x 4 =
5 x 8 =	7 x 5 =	4 x 6 =
9 x 6 =	4 x 6 =	3 x 7 =
5 x 7 =	6 x 5 =	2 x 8 =
7 x 6 =	7 x 10 =	7 x 3 =
0 x 5 =	6 x 7 =	0 x 6 =
6 x 3 =	5 x 7 =	10 x 7 =
6 x 7 =	8 x 4 =	6 x 2 =
3 x 5 =	0 x 7 =	8 x 7 =
4 x 7 =	5 x 8 =	7 x 7 =
7 x 10 =	7 x 6 =	6 x 5 =
7 x 8 =	8 x 3 =	5 x 10 =
2 x 7 =	9 x 6 =	7 x 0 =
4 x 9 =	7 x 7 =	3 x 10 =
9 x 10 =	7 x 10 =	2 x 7 =
6 x 10 =	5 x 6 =	7 x 8 =

Some of the 8s

You should already know some of the 8 times table because it is part of the 1, 2, 3, 4, 5, 6, 7, and 10 times tables.

$1 \times 8 = 8$ $2 \times 8 = 16$ $3 \times 8 = 24$ $4 \times 8 = 32$

$5 \times 8 = 40$ $6 \times 8 = 48$ $7 \times 8 = 56$ $10 \times 8 = 80$

Find out if you can remember them.

Cover the eight times table with paper so you can't see the numbers. Write the answers as quickly as you can.

What are three eights?   What are four eights?

What are two eights?   What are six eights?

What are five eights?   What are ten eights?

Write the answers as quickly as you can.

How many eights make 16?   How many eights make 24?

How many eights make 40?   How many eights make 56?

How many eights make 80?   How many eights make 48?

Write the answers as quickly as you can.

Multiply eight by three.   Multiply eight by six.

Multiply eight by five.   Multiply eight by two.

Multiply eight by four.   Multiply eight by ten.

Write the answers as quickly as you can.

$6 \times 8 =$ $2 \times 8 =$ $7 \times 8 =$

$4 \times 8 =$ $5 \times 8 =$ $3 \times 8 =$

The Penguin sells cans of soda in packs of eight. Robin buys seven packs. How many cans does he have?

46

The rest of the 8s

You need to learn only these parts of the eight times table.

8 x 8 = 64   9 x 8 = 72

This work will help you remember the 8 times table.

Complete these sequences.

8   16   24   32   40   48

7 x 8 = 56   so   8 x 8 = 56 plus another 8 =

24   32   40

8 x 8 = 64   so   9 x 8 = 64 plus another 8 =

8   16   24   64   80

8   24   40

Test yourself on the rest of the 8 times table.
Cover the section above with a sheet of paper.

What are seven eights?   What are eight eights?

What are nine eights?   What are six eights?

8 x 8 =   9 x 8 =   8 x 9 =   10 x 8 =

What number multiplied by 8 gives the answer 72?

A number multiplied by 8 gives the answer 64.
What is the number?

A shopkeeper arranges Batman sweatshirts
in piles of 8. How many sweatshirts will
there be in 10 piles?

How many 8s make 56?

Practice the 8s

THIS IS A RACE AGAINST TIME. GET YOUR SPEED UP!

You should know all of the 8 times table now, but how quickly can you remember it?
Ask someone to time you as you do this page.
Be fast but also correct.

1 x 8 =	2 x 8 =	8 x 6 =
2 x 8 =	4 x 8 =	3 x 8 =
3 x 8 =	6 x 8 =	9 x 8 =
4 x 8 =	8 x 8 =	8 x 4 =
5 x 8 =	10 x 8 =	1 x 8 =
6 x 8 =	1 x 8 =	8 x 2 =
7 x 8 =	3 x 8 =	7 x 8 =
8 x 8 =	5 x 8 =	0 x 8 =
9 x 8 =	7 x 8 =	8 x 3 =
10 x 8 =	9 x 8 =	5 x 8 =
8 x 1 =	8 x 3 =	8 x 8 =
8 x 2 =	8 x 5 =	2 x 8 =
8 x 3 =	8 x 7 =	8 x 9 =
8 x 4 =	8 x 9 =	4 x 8 =
8 x 5 =	8 x 2 =	8 x 6 =
8 x 6 =	8 x 4 =	10 x 8 =
8 x 7 =	8 x 6 =	8 x 5 =
8 x 8 =	8 x 8 =	8 x 0 =
8 x 9 =	8 x 10 =	8 x 1 =
8 x 10 =	8 x 0 =	6 x 8 =

Speed trials

You should know all of the 1, 2, 3, 4, 5, 6, 7, 8, and 10 times tables now, but how quickly can you remember them?
Ask someone to time you as you do this page.
Be fast but also correct.

QUICK! NO MISTAKES!

4 x 8 =	7 x 8 =	9 x 8 =
5 x 10 =	8 x 7 =	7 x 6 =
7 x 8 =	6 x 8 =	8 x 3 =
8 x 5 =	8 x 10 =	8 x 8 =
6 x 10 =	6 x 3 =	7 x 4 =
8 x 7 =	7 x 7 =	4 x 8 =
5 x 8 =	5 x 6 =	3 x 7 =
9 x 8 =	6 x 7 =	2 x 8 =
8 x 8 =	7 x 10 =	7 x 3 =
7 x 6 =	6 x 9 =	0 x 8 =
7 x 5 =	5 x 8 =	10 x 8 =
6 x 8 =	8 x 4 =	6 x 2 =
6 x 7 =	0 x 8 =	8 x 6 =
5 x 7 =	5 x 9 =	7 x 8 =
8 x 4 =	7 x 6 =	6 x 5 =
7 x 10 =	8 x 3 =	8 x 10 =
2 x 8 =	9 x 6 =	8 x 7 =
4 x 7 =	8 x 6 =	5 x 10 =
6 x 9 =	9 x 10 =	8 x 2 =
9 x 10 =	6 x 6 =	8 x 9 =

Some of the 9s

HAVE YOU GOT NINE LIVES? CAN YOU REMEMBER THEM ALL?

You should already know nearly all of the 9 times table because it is part of the 1, 2, 3, 4, 5, 6, 7, 8, and 10 times tables.

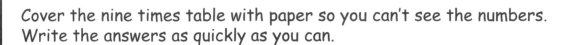

1 x 9 = 9	2 x 9 = 18	3 x 9 = 27
4 x 9 = 36	5 x 9 = 45	6 x 9 = 54
7 x 9 = 63	8 x 9 = 72	10 x 9 = 90

Cover the nine times table with paper so you can't see the numbers. Write the answers as quickly as you can.

What are three nines? 　　　What are four nines?

What are seven nines? 　　　What are five nines?

What are six nines? 　　　What are eight nines?

Write the answers as quickly as you can.

How many nines equal 18? 　　　How many nines equal 54?

How many nines equal 90? 　　　How many nines equal 63?

How many nines equal 72? 　　　How many nines equal 36?

Write the answers as quickly as you can.

Multiply nine by seven. 　　　Multiply nine by ten.

Multiply nine by two. 　　　Multiply nine by five.

Multiply nine by six. 　　　Multiply nine by four.

Multiply nine by three. 　　　Multiply nine by eight.

Write the answers as quickly as you can.

6 x 9 = 　　　2 x 9 = 　　　10 x 9 =

5 x 9 = 　　　3 x 9 = 　　　8 x 9 =

0 x 9 = 　　　7 x 9 = 　　　4 x 9 =

The rest of the 9s

You need to learn only this part of the nine times table.

9 × 9 = 81

YOU NEED ONLY LEARN ONE SUM. THAT'S SMART!

This work will help you remember the 9 times table.

Complete these sequences.

9   18   27   36   45   54

8 x 9 = 72   so   9 x 9 = 72 plus another 9 =

27   36   45

9   18   27   72   90

9   27   45

Look for a pattern in the nine times table.

1	x	9	=	09
2	x	9	=	18
3	x	9	=	27
4	x	9	=	36
5	x	9	=	45
6	x	9	=	54
7	x	9	=	63
8	x	9	=	72
9	x	9	=	81
10	x	9	=	90

Write down any patterns you can see. (There is more than one.)

_____
_____
_____
_____
_____
_____

Practice the 9s

You should know all of the 9 times table now, but how quickly can you remember it?
Ask someone to time you as you do this page.
Be fast and correct.

BEAT ME OR I'LL MAKE YOU EAT CROW!

$1 \times 9 =$

$2 \times 9 =$

$3 \times 9 =$

$4 \times 9 =$

$5 \times 9 =$

$6 \times 9 =$

$7 \times 9 =$

$8 \times 9 =$

$9 \times 9 =$

$10 \times 9 =$

$9 \times 1 =$

$9 \times 2 =$

$9 \times 3 =$

$9 \times 4 =$

$9 \times 5 =$

$9 \times 6 =$

$9 \times 7 =$

$9 \times 8 =$

$9 \times 9 =$

$9 \times 10 =$

$2 \times 9 =$

$4 \times 9 =$

$6 \times 9 =$

$8 \times 9 =$

$10 \times 9 =$

$1 \times 9 =$

$3 \times 9 =$

$5 \times 9 =$

$7 \times 9 =$

$9 \times 9 =$

$9 \times 3 =$

$9 \times 5 =$

$9 \times 7 =$

$9 \times 2 =$

$9 \times 4 =$

$9 \times 6 =$

$9 \times 8 =$

$9 \times 10 =$

$9 \times 0 =$

$9 \times 9 =$

$9 \times 6 =$

$3 \times 9 =$

$9 \times 9 =$

$9 \times 4 =$

$1 \times 9 =$

$9 \times 2 =$

$7 \times 9 =$

$0 \times 9 =$

$9 \times 3 =$

$5 \times 9 =$

$9 \times 9 =$

$2 \times 9 =$

$8 \times 9 =$

$4 \times 9 =$

$9 \times 7 =$

$10 \times 9 =$

$9 \times 5 =$

$9 \times 0 =$

$9 \times 1 =$

$6 \times 9 =$

Speed trials

You should know all of the times tables now, but how quickly can you remember them? Ask someone to time you as you do this page. Be fast and correct.

NOW GET GOING – BUT GET THEM RIGHT!

6 x 8 =	4 x 8 =	8 x 10 =
9 x 10 =	9 x 8 =	7 x 9 =
5 x 8 =	6 x 6 =	8 x 5 =
7 x 5 =	8 x 9 =	8 x 7 =
6 x 4 =	6 x 4 =	7 x 4 =
8 x 8 =	7 x 3 =	4 x 9 =
5 x 10 =	5 x 9 =	6 x 7 =
9 x 8 =	6 x 8 =	4 x 6 =
8 x 3 =	7 x 7 =	7 x 8 =
7 x 7 =	6 x 9 =	6 x 9 =
9 x 5 =	7 x 8 =	10 x 8 =
4 x 8 =	8 x 4 =	6 x 5 =
6 x 7 =	0 x 9 =	8 x 8 =
2 x 9 =	10 x 10 =	7 x 6 =
8 x 4 =	7 x 6 =	6 x 8 =
7 x 10 =	8 x 7 =	9 x 10 =
2 x 8 =	9 x 6 =	8 x 4 =
4 x 7 =	8 x 6 =	7 x 10 =
6 x 9 =	9 x 9 =	5 x 8 =
9 x 9 =	6 x 7 =	8 x 9 =

Times tables for division

DIVIDE AND DEFEAT YOUR ENEMIES!

Knowing the times tables can also help with division problems.
Look at these examples.
3 x 6 = 18 which means that 18 ÷ 3 = 6 and 18 ÷ 6 = 3
4 x 5 = 20 which means that 20 ÷ 4 = 5 and 20 ÷ 5 = 4
9 x 3 = 27 which means that 27 ÷ 3 = 9 and 27 ÷ 9 = 3

Use your knowledge of the times tables to work these division problems.

4 x 8 = 32   which means that 32 ÷ 4 =   and that 32 ÷ 8 =

4 x 7 = 28   which means that 28 ÷ 4 =   and that 28 ÷ 7 =

3 x 9 = 27   which means that 27 ÷ 3 =   and that 27 ÷ 9 =

4 x 3 = 12   which means that 12 ÷ 4 =   and that 12 ÷ 3 =

3 x 10 = 30 which means that 30 ÷ 3 =   and that 30 ÷ 10 =

3 x 5 = 15   which means that 15 ÷ 3 =   and that 15 ÷ 5 =

3 x 8 = 24   which means that 24 ÷ 3 =   and that 24 ÷ 8 =

4 x 10 = 40 which means that 40 ÷ 4 =   and that 40 ÷ 10 =

These division problems help practice the 3 and 4 times tables.

24 ÷ 4 =   15 ÷ 3 =   16 ÷ 4 =

20 ÷ 4 =   18 ÷ 3 =   27 ÷ 3 =

12 ÷ 3 =   21 ÷ 3 =   28 ÷ 4 =

24 ÷ 3 =   32 ÷ 4 =   9 ÷ 3 =

How many fours in 28?   How many sevens in 35?

Divide 36 by four.   Divide 27 by nine.

How many threes in 21?   How many eights in 48?

Times tables for division

This page will help you remember times tables by dividing by 2, 3, 4, 5, and 10.

20 ÷ 5 = [4]   18 ÷ 3 = [6]   60 ÷ 10 = [6]

Complete the problems.

50 ÷ 10 =	28 ÷ 4 =	32 ÷ 4 =
20 ÷ 4 =	21 ÷ 3 =	16 ÷ 4 =
24 ÷ 4 =	14 ÷ 2 =	12 ÷ 2 =
45 ÷ 5 =	35 ÷ 5 =	12 ÷ 3 =
10 ÷ 2 =	40 ÷ 10 =	12 ÷ 4 =
20 ÷ 10 =	20 ÷ 2 =	20 ÷ 2 =
6 ÷ 2 =	18 ÷ 3 =	20 ÷ 4 =
24 ÷ 3 =	32 ÷ 4 =	20 ÷ 5 =
30 ÷ 5 =	40 ÷ 5 =	20 ÷ 10 =
30 ÷ 10 =	80 ÷ 10 =	18 ÷ 2 =
40 ÷ 5 =	6 ÷ 2 =	18 ÷ 3 =
21 ÷ 3 =	15 ÷ 3 =	15 ÷ 3 =
14 ÷ 2 =	24 ÷ 4 =	40 ÷ 10 =
27 ÷ 3 =	15 ÷ 5 =	24 ÷ 3 =
90 ÷ 10 =	10 ÷ 10 =	24 ÷ 4 =
15 ÷ 5 =	4 ÷ 2 =	50 ÷ 5 =
15 ÷ 3 =	4 ÷ 4 =	50 ÷ 10 =
20 ÷ 5 =	10 ÷ 5 =	30 ÷ 3 =
20 ÷ 4 =	100 ÷ 10 =	30 ÷ 5 =
16 ÷ 2 =	9 ÷ 3 =	30 ÷ 10 =

Times tables for division

This page will help you remember times tables by dividing by 2, 3, 4, 5, 6, and 10.

$30 \div 6$ [5] $12 \div 6 =$ [2] $60 \div 10 =$ [6]

Complete the problems.

$18 \div 3 =$	$27 \div 3 =$	$48 \div 6 =$
$30 \div 5 =$	$18 \div 6 =$	$35 \div 5 =$
$21 \div 3 =$	$20 \div 2 =$	$36 \div 4 =$
$18 \div 3 =$	$24 \div 6 =$	$24 \div 3 =$
$20 \div 4 =$	$24 \div 3 =$	$20 \div 2 =$
$15 \div 5 =$	$24 \div 4 =$	$30 \div 6 =$
$8 \div 2 =$	$30 \div 10 =$	$25 \div 5 =$
$15 \div 3 =$	$18 \div 2 =$	$32 \div 4 =$
$16 \div 4 =$	$18 \div 3 =$	$27 \div 3 =$
$25 \div 5 =$	$36 \div 4 =$	$16 \div 2 =$
$6 \div 6 =$	$36 \div 6 =$	$42 \div 6 =$
$10 \div 10 =$	$40 \div 5 =$	$5 \div 5 =$
$42 \div 6 =$	$100 \div 10 =$	$4 \div 4 =$
$24 \div 4 =$	$16 \div 4 =$	$28 \div 4 =$
$54 \div 6 =$	$42 \div 6 =$	$14 \div 2 =$
$90 \div 10 =$	$48 \div 6 =$	$24 \div 6 =$
$30 \div 6 =$	$32 \div 4 =$	$18 \div 6 =$
$90 \div 10 =$	$60 \div 6 =$	$54 \div 6 =$
$36 \div 6 =$	$60 \div 10 =$	$60 \div 6 =$
$50 \div 5 =$	$30 \div 6 =$	$40 \div 5 =$

Times tables for division

This page will help you remember times tables by dividing by 2, 3, 4, 5, 6, 7, and 10.

$14 \div 7 =$ 2 $28 \div 7 =$ 4 $70 \div 7 =$ 10

Complete the problems.

$21 \div 7 =$	$40 \div 5 =$	$49 \div 7 =$
$35 \div 5 =$	$18 \div 6 =$	$35 \div 5 =$
$14 \div 2 =$	$28 \div 7 =$	$35 \div 7 =$
$18 \div 6 =$	$24 \div 6 =$	$24 \div 6 =$
$20 \div 5 =$	$24 \div 4 =$	$21 \div 3 =$
$15 \div 3 =$	$24 \div 2 =$	$70 \div 7 =$
$36 \div 4 =$	$21 \div 7 =$	$42 \div 7 =$
$56 \div 7 =$	$42 \div 7 =$	$32 \div 4 =$
$18 \div 2 =$	$18 \div 3 =$	$27 \div 3 =$
$15 \div 5 =$	$49 \div 7 =$	$16 \div 4 =$
$49 \div 7 =$	$36 \div 4 =$	$42 \div 6 =$
$25 \div 5 =$	$36 \div 6 =$	$45 \div 5 =$
$7 \div 7 =$	$70 \div 7 =$	$40 \div 4 =$
$63 \div 7 =$	$24 \div 3 =$	$24 \div 3 =$
$42 \div 7 =$	$42 \div 6 =$	$14 \div 7 =$
$24 \div 6 =$	$48 \div 6 =$	$18 \div 3 =$
$54 \div 6 =$	$54 \div 6 =$	$56 \div 7 =$
$28 \div 7 =$	$60 \div 6 =$	$63 \div 7 =$
$30 \div 6 =$	$63 \div 7 =$	$48 \div 6 =$
$35 \div 7 =$	$25 \div 5 =$	$24 \div 3 =$

Times tables for division

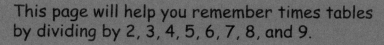

This page will help you remember times tables
by dividing by 2, 3, 4, 5, 6, 7, 8, and 9.

16 ÷ 8 = ⟦ 2 ⟧   35 ÷ 7 = ⟦ 5 ⟧   27 ÷ 9 = ⟦ 3 ⟧

MORE NUMBERS! THIS IS TOO
TOUGH FOR THE JOKER!

Complete the problems.

48 ÷ 6 =	81 ÷ 9 =	56 ÷ 7 =
24 ÷ 8 =	56 ÷ 7 =	45 ÷ 5 =
14 ÷ 7 =	72 ÷ 8 =	35 ÷ 7 =
18 ÷ 9 =	32 ÷ 8 =	18 ÷ 9 =
63 ÷ 7 =	27 ÷ 9 =	21 ÷ 3 =
72 ÷ 9 =	72 ÷ 9 =	28 ÷ 7 =
72 ÷ 8 =	42 ÷ 6 =	64 ÷ 8 =
56 ÷ 7 =	27 ÷ 3 =	32 ÷ 8 =
18 ÷ 6 =	14 ÷ 7 =	27 ÷ 9 =
81 ÷ 9 =	36 ÷ 4 =	16 ÷ 8 =
63 ÷ 9 =	36 ÷ 6 =	42 ÷ 6 =
45 ÷ 5 =	48 ÷ 8 =	45 ÷ 9 =
54 ÷ 9 =	21 ÷ 7 =	40 ÷ 4 =
70 ÷ 7 =	24 ÷ 3 =	24 ÷ 8 =
42 ÷ 7 =	40 ÷ 8 =	63 ÷ 7 =
30 ÷ 5 =	45 ÷ 9 =	24 ÷ 6 =
54 ÷ 6 =	54 ÷ 6 =	18 ÷ 6 =
56 ÷ 8 =	42 ÷ 7 =	56 ÷ 8 =
30 ÷ 5 =	63 ÷ 9 =	63 ÷ 9 =
35 ÷ 7 =	50 ÷ 5 =	48 ÷ 8 =

Times tables practice grids

This is a times tables grid.

X	3	4	5	6
7	21	28	35	42
8	24	32	40	48

CHECK OUT THE GRIDS IN THE BATCAVE.

Complete each times tables grid.

X	1	3	5	7	9
2					
3					

X	4	6
6		
7		
8		

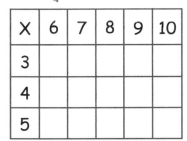

X	6	7	8	9	10
3					
4					
5					

X	10	7	8	4	2
3					
5					
7					

X	6	2	4	7
5				
10				

X	8	7	9	6
9				
7				

Times tables practice grids

Here are more times tables grids.

X	2	4	6
3			
7			

X	8	3	7	2
5				
6				
7				

X	2	3	4	5
8				
9				

X	10	9	8	7
6				
5				
4				

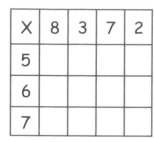

THESE BATS
ARE TOO
CLEVER FOR ME!

X	3	6
2		
3		
4		
5		
6		
7		

X	2	4	6	8
1				
3				
5				
7				
9				
0				

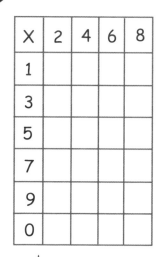

Times tables practice grids

Here are some other times tables grids.

DON'T GET GRID LOCK!

X	7	8	9	10
7				
8				

X	9	8	7	6	5	4
9						
8						
7						

X	2	5	7	9
4				
6				
8				

X	2	3	4	5	7
4					
6					
8					

X	3	5	7
2			
8			
6			
0			
4			
7			

X	8	7	9	6
7				
9				
0				
10				
8				
6				

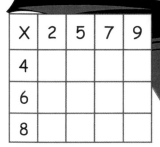
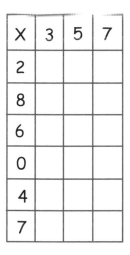

Speed trials

THESE ARE TRICKY – LIKE ME! WATCH OUT FOR THE SIGNS!

Try this final test.

42 ÷ 6 =	4 x 9 =	14 ÷ 2 =
7 x 4 =	18 ÷ 2 =	9 x 9 =
64 ÷ 8 =	6 x 8 =	15 ÷ 3 =
90 ÷ 10 =	21 ÷ 3 =	8 x 8 =
3 x 7 =	9 x 7 =	24 ÷ 4 =
6 x 8 =	36 ÷ 4 =	7 x 8 =
48 ÷ 6 =	4 x 6 =	30 ÷ 5 =
7 x 7 =	45 ÷ 5 =	6 x 6 =
9 x 5 =	8 x 5 =	27 ÷ 3 =
45 ÷ 9 =	42 ÷ 6 =	9 x 5 =
3 x 9 =	7 x 9 =	49 ÷ 7 =
56 ÷ 8 =	35 ÷ 7 =	8 x 6 =
36 ÷ 4 =	9 x 3 =	72 ÷ 8 =
24 ÷ 3 =	24 ÷ 8 =	9 x 7 =
36 ÷ 9 =	8 x 2 =	54 ÷ 9 =
6 x 7 =	36 ÷ 9 =	7 x 6 =
4 x 4 =	6 x 10 =	10 ÷ 10 =
32 ÷ 8 =	80 ÷ 10 =	7 x 7 =
49 ÷ 7 =	6 x 9 =	16 ÷ 8 =
25 ÷ 5 =	16 ÷ 2 =	7 x 9 =
56 ÷ 7 =	54 ÷ 9 =	63 ÷ 7 =

Line of symmetry

If a plane figure is divided into two congruent (matching) parts, the line that divides the two parts is called a line of symmetry.

Draw as many lines of symmetry as you can find on each of these shapes.

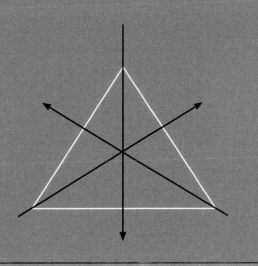

Draw a line of symmetry on each of these shapes.

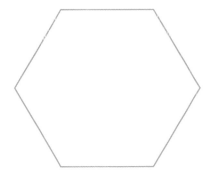

Draw as many lines of symmetry as you can find on each of these shapes.

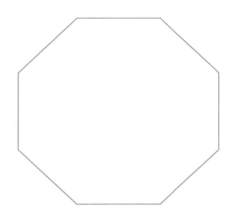

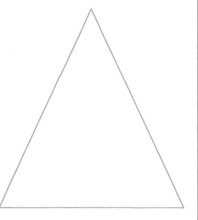

Ordering large numbers

Write these numbers in order, starting with the least.

256	9,644,327	39,214	9,631
256	9,613	39,214	9,644,327

YOU'RE OUT OF ORDER!

Write these numbers in order, starting with the least.

327,914	3,654, 212	47,900	3,825	416

72,463	8,730,241	261	5,247	643,292

6,436	643	64,370	6,430	643,000

593,102	761	374,239	91,761	1,425

9,641,471	260,453	59,372	657,473	4,290

5,600,200	500,200	5,200	50,200	52,000

9,900	999	900,200	920,200	9,200,000

At the Gotham City elections
The Penguin got 900,540 votes,
The Joker got 830,580 votes,
Robin got 8,305,800 votes,
Batman got 9,764,201 votes,
and the Riddler got
849,999 votes.

Place the candidates in order.

1st _____
2nd _____
3rd _____
4th _____
5th _____

Rounding whole numbers

Round these numbers to the nearest hundred.

529 | 500 | 1,687 | 1,700

If the place to the right of the place you are rounding is 5 or more, round the previous number up.

652 | 700

ROUND 'EM ALL UP – OR DOWN!

Round to the nearest hundred.

687		234		8,467		3,561	
16,543		4,855		769		1,300	
22,751		227		792		354	

Round to the nearest ten-thousand.

23,478		618,600		58,473		452,899	
209,544		32,059		67,414		33,500	
89,388		801,821		134,800		45,010	

Round to the nearest ten.

77		386		53		65	
1,392		15		12,489		2,861	
75		715		34		18,149	

Round to the nearest thousand.

3,284		112,810		10,518		83,477	
8,499		225,500		4,500		6,112	
1,059		93,606		6,752		2,550	

Choosing units of measure

Circle the units that are the closest estimate.

The amount of orange juice in a full glass.

(6 fluid ounces)   4 pints   2 gallons

USE YOUR BRAIN. MAKE A GOOD GUESS!

Circle the units that are the closest estimate.

The weight of a box of cereal	15 ounces	3 pounds	2 tons
The length of a football field	20 feet	100 yards	1 mile
The area of a rug	90 sq. inches	108 sq. feet	1 sq. mile
The amount of cough medicine in a bottle	3 fluid ounces	2 cups	1 quart
The distance from home plate to first base	120 inches	90 feet	6 yards
The weight of a package of sugar	7 ounces	5 pounds	$\frac{1}{2}$ ton
The length of an airport runway	2 miles	50 yards	500 feet
The amount of water in a full pail	8 fluid ounces	2 pints	3 gallons
The area of a place mat	144 sq. inches	6 sq. feet	1 sq. mile

Comparing fractions

Which is greater, $\dfrac{2}{3}$ or $\dfrac{3}{4}$? $\boxed{\dfrac{3}{4}}$

The common denominator of 3 and 4 is 12.

$\dfrac{2}{3}\overset{\times 4 = 8}{\underset{\times 4 = 12}{}}$ So $\dfrac{2}{3}$ = $\dfrac{8}{12}$ $\qquad$ $\dfrac{3}{4}\overset{\times 3 = 9}{\underset{\times 3 = 12}{}}$ So $\dfrac{3}{4}$ = $\dfrac{9}{12}$

Since $\dfrac{9}{12}$ is greater than $\dfrac{8}{12}$, then $\dfrac{3}{4}$ must be greater than $\dfrac{2}{3}$.

Which is greater?

$\dfrac{1}{2}$ or $\dfrac{5}{8}$ $\qquad$ $\dfrac{1}{4}$ or $\dfrac{1}{3}$ $\qquad$ $\dfrac{5}{6}$ or $\dfrac{7}{9}$ $\qquad$ $\dfrac{1}{3}$ or $\dfrac{4}{9}$

$\dfrac{7}{10}$ or $\dfrac{8}{9}$ $\qquad$ $\dfrac{2}{5}$ or $\dfrac{3}{8}$ $\qquad$ $\dfrac{7}{8}$ or $\dfrac{8}{10}$ $\qquad$ $\dfrac{2}{3}$ or $\dfrac{7}{12}$

$\dfrac{5}{8}$ or $\dfrac{2}{3}$ $\qquad$ $\dfrac{3}{5}$ or $\dfrac{2}{3}$ $\qquad$ $\dfrac{4}{15}$ or $\dfrac{1}{3}$ $\qquad$ $\dfrac{1}{4}$ or $\dfrac{3}{8}$

Which two fractions in each row are equal?

$\dfrac{5}{8}$ $\qquad$ $\dfrac{1}{4}$ $\qquad$ $\dfrac{7}{8}$ $\qquad$ $\dfrac{3}{8}$ $\qquad$ $\dfrac{3}{12}$ $\qquad$ $\dfrac{4}{12}$

$\dfrac{7}{10}$ $\qquad$ $\dfrac{6}{9}$ $\qquad$ $\dfrac{5}{8}$ $\qquad$ $\dfrac{9}{12}$ $\qquad$ $\dfrac{1}{2}$ $\qquad$ $\dfrac{3}{4}$

$\dfrac{9}{12}$ $\qquad$ $\dfrac{4}{8}$ $\qquad$ $\dfrac{3}{8}$ $\qquad$ $\dfrac{7}{14}$ $\qquad$ $\dfrac{6}{14}$ $\qquad$ $\dfrac{7}{12}$

$\dfrac{4}{7}$ $\qquad$ $\dfrac{9}{10}$ $\qquad$ $\dfrac{6}{7}$ $\qquad$ $\dfrac{2}{6}$ $\qquad$ $\dfrac{3}{9}$ $\qquad$ $\dfrac{3}{8}$

$\dfrac{3}{10}$ $\qquad$ $\dfrac{5}{15}$ $\qquad$ $\dfrac{2}{10}$ $\qquad$ $\dfrac{3}{15}$ $\qquad$ $\dfrac{4}{10}$ $\qquad$ $\dfrac{7}{15}$

LET'S GO! THERE'S MORE WORK TO BE DONE.

Put these fractions in order, starting with the least.

$\dfrac{1}{2}$ $\qquad$ $\dfrac{5}{6}$ $\qquad$ $\dfrac{2}{3}$

$\dfrac{2}{3}$ $\qquad$ $\dfrac{8}{15}$ $\qquad$ $\dfrac{3}{5}$

Converting fractions to decimals

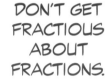

Convert these fractions to decimals.

$\frac{3}{10}$ = 0.3

(because the three goes in the tenths column)

$\frac{7}{100}$ = 0.07

(because the seven goes in the hundredths column)

DON'T GET FRACTIOUS ABOUT FRACTIONS.

Convert these fractions to decimals.

$\frac{4}{100}$ =

$\frac{6}{100}$ =

$\frac{1}{10}$ =

$\frac{3}{100}$ =

$\frac{6}{10}$ =

$\frac{2}{10}$ =

$\frac{8}{10}$ =

$\frac{9}{10}$ =

$\frac{4}{10}$ =

$\frac{5}{10}$ =

$\frac{1}{100}$ =

$\frac{3}{100}$ =

$\frac{2}{100}$ =

$\frac{8}{100}$ =

$\frac{7}{10}$ =

$\frac{5}{100}$ =

Convert $\frac{1}{4}$ to a decimal.

To do this we have to divide the bottom number into the top.

When we run out of numbers we put in the decimal point and enough zeros to finish the sum. Be careful to keep the decimal point in your answer above the decimal point in the sum.

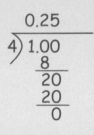

Convert these fractions to decimals.

$\frac{1}{4}$ =

$\frac{1}{2}$ =

$\frac{4}{5}$ =

$\frac{1}{5}$ =

$\frac{1}{8}$ =

$\frac{3}{4}$ =

$\frac{3}{8}$ =

$\frac{3}{5}$ =

Adding fractions

Find the sum of each problem.

$$\frac{1}{5} + \frac{3}{5} = \boxed{\frac{4}{5}}$$

$$\frac{4}{9} + \frac{2}{9} = \frac{^2\cancel{6}}{\cancel{9}_3} = \boxed{\frac{2}{3}}$$

Add the numerators but keep the denominators the same.
Remember to reduce to simplest form if you need to.

I'M KEEPING AN EYE ON THE ANSWERS!

Find the sum of each problem.

$$\frac{2}{9} + \frac{5}{9} = \frac{\boxed{}}{9}$$

$$\frac{2}{7} + \frac{3}{7} = \frac{\boxed{}}{7}$$

$$\frac{1}{3} + \frac{1}{3} = \frac{\boxed{}}{3}$$

$$\frac{2}{9} + \frac{3}{9} = \boxed{}$$

$$\frac{2}{8} + \frac{1}{8} = \boxed{}$$

$$\frac{3}{10} + \frac{6}{10} = \boxed{}$$

$$\frac{4}{20} + \frac{5}{20} = \boxed{}$$

$$\frac{1}{100} + \frac{16}{100} = \boxed{}$$

$$\frac{7}{10} + \frac{2}{10} = \boxed{}$$

$$\frac{2}{5} + \frac{1}{5} = \boxed{}$$

$$\frac{1}{7} + \frac{3}{7} = \boxed{}$$

$$\frac{4}{9} + \frac{1}{9} = \boxed{}$$

$$\frac{1}{6} + \frac{2}{6} = \boxed{} = \boxed{}$$

$$\frac{19}{100} + \frac{31}{100} = \boxed{} = \boxed{}$$

$$\frac{5}{20} + \frac{10}{20} = \boxed{} = \boxed{}$$

$$\frac{4}{10} + \frac{4}{10} = \boxed{} = \boxed{}$$

$$\frac{3}{12} + \frac{6}{12} = \boxed{} = \boxed{}$$

$$\frac{2}{6} + \frac{2}{6} = \boxed{} = \boxed{}$$

$$\frac{3}{8} + \frac{3}{8} = \boxed{} = \boxed{}$$

$$\frac{1}{8} + \frac{3}{8} = \boxed{} = \boxed{}$$

$$\frac{5}{12} + \frac{1}{12} = \boxed{} = \boxed{}$$

$$\frac{1}{4} + \frac{1}{4} = \boxed{} = \boxed{}$$

$$\frac{4}{20} + \frac{1}{20} = \boxed{} = \boxed{}$$

$$\frac{1}{6} + \frac{3}{6} = \boxed{} = \boxed{}$$

$$\frac{3}{7} + \frac{3}{7} = \boxed{}$$

$$\frac{2}{9} + \frac{2}{9} = \boxed{}$$

$$\frac{13}{20} + \frac{5}{20} = \boxed{} = \boxed{}$$

$$\frac{81}{100} + \frac{9}{100} = \boxed{} = \boxed{}$$

$$\frac{5}{20} + \frac{8}{20} = \boxed{}$$

$$\frac{2}{8} + \frac{3}{8} = \boxed{}$$

$$\frac{6}{10} + \frac{2}{10} = \boxed{} = \boxed{}$$

$$\frac{28}{100} + \frac{47}{100} = \boxed{} = \boxed{}$$

$$\frac{72}{100} + \frac{18}{100} = \boxed{} = \boxed{}$$

Subtracting fractions

Find the difference of each problem.

$$\frac{4}{5} - \frac{2}{5} = \boxed{\frac{2}{5}} \qquad \frac{8}{9} - \frac{5}{9} = \boxed{\frac{{}^1\cancel{3}}{\cancel{9}_3}} = \boxed{\frac{1}{3}}$$

Add the numerators but keep the denominators the same. Remember to reduce to simplest form if you need to.

EVERYTHING'S A RIDDLE TO ME!

Find the difference of each problem.

$$\frac{4}{5} - \frac{1}{5} = \frac{\boxed{}}{5} \qquad\qquad \frac{5}{7} - \frac{2}{7} = \frac{\boxed{}}{7}$$

$$\frac{5}{10} - \frac{4}{10} = \boxed{} \qquad\qquad \frac{6}{9} - \frac{2}{9} = \boxed{}$$

$$\frac{7}{8} - \frac{3}{8} = \boxed{} = \boxed{} \qquad \frac{14}{20} - \frac{8}{20} = \boxed{} = \boxed{} \qquad \frac{4}{6} - \frac{1}{6} = \boxed{} = \boxed{}$$

$$\frac{11}{12} - \frac{7}{12} = \boxed{} = \boxed{} \qquad \frac{17}{20} - \frac{12}{20} = \boxed{} = \boxed{} \qquad \frac{8}{12} - \frac{2}{12} = \boxed{} = \boxed{}$$

$$\frac{8}{9} - \frac{2}{9} = \boxed{} = \boxed{} \qquad \frac{12}{12} - \frac{2}{12} = \boxed{} = \boxed{} \qquad \frac{8}{10} - \frac{3}{10} = \boxed{} = \boxed{}$$

$$\frac{6}{10} - \frac{4}{10} = \boxed{} = \boxed{} \qquad \frac{6}{8} - \frac{4}{8} = \boxed{} = \boxed{} \qquad \frac{9}{12} - \frac{5}{12} = \boxed{} = \boxed{}$$

$$\frac{3}{4} - \frac{2}{4} = \boxed{} \qquad\qquad \frac{6}{8} - \frac{1}{8} = \boxed{} \qquad\qquad \frac{18}{20} - \frac{4}{20} = \boxed{} = \boxed{}$$

$$\frac{4}{6} - \frac{2}{6} = \boxed{} = \boxed{} \qquad \frac{7}{12} - \frac{6}{12} = \boxed{} \qquad\qquad \frac{5}{8} - \frac{2}{8} = \boxed{}$$

$$\frac{5}{7} - \frac{1}{7} = \boxed{} \qquad\qquad \frac{5}{16} - \frac{1}{16} = \boxed{} = \boxed{} \qquad \frac{70}{100} - \frac{60}{100} = \boxed{} = \boxed{}$$

Adding fractions

Find the sum of each problem.

$$\frac{3}{8} + \frac{5}{8} = \boxed{\frac{8}{8}} = \boxed{1}$$

$$\frac{3}{4} + \frac{3}{4} = \boxed{\frac{^3\cancel{6}}{\cancel{4}_2}} = \boxed{\frac{3}{2}} = \boxed{1\frac{1}{2}}$$

Add the numerators but keep the denominators the same. Remember to reduce to simplest form if you need to.

> YOU'D BETTER NOT GIVE PENGUIN ANY FISHY ANSWERS!

Find the sum of each problem.

$$\frac{7}{10} + \frac{6}{10} = \frac{}{10} = 1\frac{}{10}$$

$$\frac{6}{10} + \frac{5}{10} = \frac{}{} = \frac{}{}$$

$$\frac{6}{13} + \frac{7}{13} = = $$

$$\frac{4}{8} + \frac{11}{8} = \frac{}{} = \frac{}{}$$

$$\frac{3}{8} + \frac{7}{8} = \frac{}{} = \frac{}{} = \frac{}{}$$

$$\frac{2}{5} + \frac{3}{5} = \frac{}{} = $$

$$\frac{5}{8} + \frac{7}{8} = \frac{}{} = \frac{}{} = \frac{}{}$$

$$\frac{10}{20} + \frac{15}{20} = \frac{}{} = \frac{}{} = \frac{}{}$$

$$\frac{5}{12} + \frac{8}{12} = \frac{}{} = \frac{}{}$$

$$\frac{9}{10} + \frac{5}{10} = \frac{}{} = \frac{}{} = \frac{}{}$$

$$\frac{10}{20} + \frac{12}{20} = \frac{}{} = \frac{}{} = \frac{}{}$$

$$\frac{7}{10} + \frac{3}{10} = \frac{}{} = $$

$$\frac{75}{100} + \frac{75}{100} = \frac{}{} = \frac{}{} = \frac{}{}$$

$$\frac{5}{6} + \frac{3}{6} = \frac{}{} = \frac{}{} = \frac{}{}$$

$$\frac{2}{3} + \frac{1}{3} = \frac{}{} = $$

$$\frac{5}{6} + \frac{5}{6} = \frac{}{} = \frac{}{} = \frac{}{}$$

$$\frac{10}{20} + \frac{16}{20} = \frac{}{} = \frac{}{} = \frac{}{}$$

$$\frac{4}{5} + \frac{4}{5} = = \frac{}{}$$

$$\frac{11}{21} + \frac{17}{21} = \frac{}{} = \frac{}{} = \frac{}{}$$

Adding fractions

Find the sum of each problem. Remember to find the common denominator and reduce if you need to.

$$\frac{2}{3} + \frac{1}{6} = \frac{4}{6} + \frac{1}{6} = \frac{5}{6}$$

$$\frac{3}{4} + \frac{5}{6} = \frac{9}{12} + \frac{10}{12} = \frac{19}{12} = 1\frac{7}{12}$$

MIX AND MATCH ... BUT KEEP YOUR HEAD SCREWED ON.

Find the sum of each problem.

$$\frac{5}{10} + \frac{3}{5} = \underline{} + \underline{} = \underline{} = \underline{}$$

$$\frac{9}{10} + \frac{3}{4} = \underline{} + \underline{} = \underline{} = \underline{}$$

$$\frac{5}{6} + \frac{1}{4} = \underline{} + \underline{} = \underline{} = \underline{}$$

$$\frac{7}{8} + \frac{3}{4} = \underline{} + \underline{} = \underline{} = \underline{}$$

$$\frac{1}{4} + \frac{2}{3} = \underline{} + \underline{} = \underline{}$$

$$\frac{1}{6} + \frac{11}{12} = \underline{} + \underline{} = \underline{} = \underline{}$$

$$\frac{3}{14} + \frac{3}{7} = \underline{} + \underline{} = \underline{}$$

$$\frac{7}{10} + \frac{7}{8} = \underline{} + \underline{} = \underline{} = \underline{}$$

$$\frac{3}{5} + \frac{3}{4} = \underline{} + \underline{} = \underline{} = \underline{}$$

$$\frac{5}{9} + \frac{1}{2} = \underline{} + \underline{} = \underline{} = \underline{}$$

$$\frac{1}{3} + \frac{8}{9} = \underline{} + \underline{} = \underline{} = \underline{}$$

$$\frac{1}{3} + \frac{7}{8} = \underline{} + \underline{} = \underline{} = \underline{}$$

$$\frac{1}{6} + \frac{3}{8} = \underline{} + \underline{} = \underline{}$$

$$\frac{3}{5} + \frac{2}{3} = \underline{} + \underline{} = \underline{} = \underline{}$$

$$\frac{5}{6} + \frac{4}{5} = \underline{} + \underline{} = \underline{} = \underline{}$$

$$\frac{1}{3} + \frac{5}{10} = \underline{} + \underline{} = \underline{}$$

Subtracting fractions

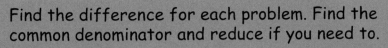

Find the difference for each problem. Find the common denominator and reduce if you need to.

$$\frac{7}{9} - \frac{1}{3} = \frac{7}{9} - \frac{3}{9} = \frac{4}{9}$$

$$\frac{7}{10} - \frac{3}{8} = \frac{28}{40} - \frac{15}{40} = \frac{13}{40}$$

SUBLIME SUBTRACTION! CAN YOU FIGURE THEM ALL OUT?

Find the difference for each problem.

$$\frac{7}{8} - \frac{1}{2} = \underline{} - \underline{} = \underline{}$$

$$\frac{5}{6} - \frac{1}{4} = \underline{} - \underline{} = \underline{}$$

$$\frac{7}{10} - \frac{1}{8} = \underline{} - \underline{} = \underline{}$$

$$\frac{3}{7} - \frac{1}{5} = \underline{} - \underline{} = \underline{}$$

$$\frac{11}{12} - \frac{1}{6} = \underline{} - \underline{} = \underline{} = \underline{}$$

$$\frac{9}{10} - \frac{3}{4} = \underline{} - \underline{} = \underline{} = \underline{}$$

$$\frac{7}{9} - \frac{1}{3} = \underline{} - \underline{} = \underline{}$$

$$\frac{5}{9} - \frac{1}{4} = \underline{} - \underline{} = \underline{}$$

$$\frac{9}{16} - \frac{1}{8} = \underline{} - \underline{} = \underline{}$$

$$\frac{7}{12} - \frac{1}{3} = \underline{} - \underline{} = \underline{} = \underline{}$$

$$\frac{6}{7} - \frac{2}{5} = \underline{} - \underline{} = \underline{}$$

$$\frac{3}{10} - \frac{1}{7} = \underline{} - \underline{} = \underline{}$$

$$\frac{5}{8} - \frac{1}{6} = \underline{} - \underline{} = \underline{}$$

$$\frac{4}{5} - \frac{1}{4} = \underline{} - \underline{} = \underline{}$$

$$\frac{2}{3} - \frac{1}{2} = \underline{} - \underline{} = \underline{}$$

$$\frac{3}{5} - \frac{1}{4} = \underline{} - \underline{} = \underline{}$$

Adding mixed numbers

Find the sum of each problem.

$8\frac{10}{30} + 1\frac{3}{30} = \boxed{9\frac{13}{30}}$

$3\frac{1}{4} + 1\frac{1}{6} = \boxed{3\frac{3}{12}} + \boxed{1\frac{2}{12}} = \boxed{4\frac{5}{12}}$

OK. JUST GIVE ME ALL THE ANSWERS!

Find the sum of each problem.

$3\frac{1}{8} + 2\frac{5}{8} = \boxed{} = \boxed{}$

$1\frac{1}{6} + 3\frac{3}{8} = \boxed{} + \boxed{} = \boxed{}$

$2\frac{1}{6} + 4\frac{7}{10} = \boxed{} + \boxed{} = \boxed{} = \boxed{}$

$3\frac{2}{3} + 1\frac{1}{9} = \boxed{} + \boxed{} = \boxed{}$

$5\frac{1}{4} + 4\frac{1}{5} = \boxed{} + \boxed{} = \boxed{}$

$3\frac{1}{6} + 6\frac{2}{9} = \boxed{} + \boxed{} = \boxed{}$

$6\frac{1}{2} + 3\frac{1}{4} = \boxed{} + \boxed{} = \boxed{}$

$4\frac{7}{12} + 3\frac{1}{12} = \boxed{} = \boxed{}$

$3\frac{1}{4} + 5\frac{1}{6} = \boxed{} + \boxed{} = \boxed{}$

$6\frac{2}{3} + 2\frac{1}{10} = \boxed{} + \boxed{} = \boxed{}$

$6\frac{1}{4} + 2\frac{1}{4} = \boxed{} = \boxed{}$

$3\frac{1}{4} + 5\frac{3}{16} = \boxed{} + \boxed{} = \boxed{}$

$1\frac{2}{9} + 7\frac{1}{3} = \boxed{} + \boxed{} = \boxed{}$

$1\frac{7}{10} + 2\frac{1}{5} = \boxed{} + \boxed{} = \boxed{}$

Subtracting mixed numbers

Find the difference.

$$2\frac{7}{8} - 1\frac{5}{8} = 1\frac{2}{8} = 1\frac{1}{4}$$

$$9\frac{9}{10} - 6\frac{5}{8} = 9\frac{36}{40} - 6\frac{25}{40} = 3\frac{11}{40}$$

Find the difference for each problem. Always reduce.

$6\frac{3}{8} - 3\frac{1}{8} = \boxed{} = \boxed{}$

$4\frac{14}{15} - 1\frac{4}{9} = \boxed{} - \boxed{} = \boxed{}$

$4\frac{1}{3} - 2\frac{1}{6} = \boxed{} - \boxed{} = \boxed{}$

$5\frac{3}{5} - 2\frac{1}{2} = \boxed{} - \boxed{} = \boxed{}$

$3\frac{5}{7} - 1\frac{1}{3} = \boxed{} - \boxed{} = \boxed{}$

$7\frac{11}{12} - 3\frac{5}{12} = \boxed{} = \boxed{}$

$9\frac{7}{9} - 2\frac{4}{6} = \boxed{} - \boxed{} = \boxed{} = \boxed{}$

$3\frac{7}{8} - 2\frac{1}{8} = \boxed{} = \boxed{}$

$3\frac{2}{3} - 1\frac{1}{6} = \boxed{} - \boxed{} = \boxed{} = \boxed{}$

$5\frac{5}{8} - 2\frac{1}{2} = \boxed{} - \boxed{} = \boxed{}$

$5\frac{2}{3} - 1\frac{2}{3} = \boxed{} = \boxed{}$

$9\frac{8}{9} - 8\frac{3}{4} = \boxed{} - \boxed{} = \boxed{}$

$3\frac{7}{15} - 2\frac{1}{3} = \boxed{} - \boxed{} = \boxed{}$

$3\frac{7}{9} - 1\frac{1}{5} = \boxed{} - \boxed{} = \boxed{}$

Adding mixed numbers and fractions

Find the sum of each problem. Remember to find the common denominator and reduce if you need to.

$$4 \frac{3}{4} + \frac{3}{4} = 4 \frac{6}{4} = 5 \frac{2}{4} = 5 \frac{1}{2}$$

$$3 \frac{1}{2} + \frac{2}{3} = 3 \frac{3}{6} + \frac{4}{6} = 3 \frac{7}{6} = 4 \frac{1}{6}$$

IT'S GETTING TRICKY! FIGURE IT OUT!

Find the sum of each problem.

$6 \frac{3}{4} + \frac{3}{4} =$ =   = $3 \frac{3}{4} + \frac{7}{8} =$ +   =   =

$3 \frac{3}{8} + \frac{7}{8} =$ = $7 \frac{7}{10} + \frac{1}{2} =$ +   =

$3 \frac{3}{7} + \frac{6}{7} =$ = $4 \frac{3}{4} + \frac{4}{5} =$ +   =   =

$4 \frac{5}{6} + \frac{2}{3} =$ +   =   = $2 \frac{1}{2} + \frac{3}{4} =$ +   =   =

$4 \frac{7}{8} + \frac{1}{4} =$ +   =   = $4 \frac{5}{7} + \frac{3}{4} =$ +   =   =

$3 \frac{7}{8} + \frac{1}{2} =$ +   =   = $4 \frac{2}{3} + \frac{3}{8} =$ +   =   =

$2 \frac{9}{10} + \frac{2}{5} =$ +   =   = $3 \frac{5}{6} + \frac{4}{5} =$ +   =   =

Simple use of parentheses

Work out these problems.

$(4 + 6) - (2 + 1) =$ $10 - 3 = 7$

$(2 \times 5) + (10 - 4) =$ $10 + 6 = 16$

Work out these problems.

$(3 + 5) - (7 - 2) =$

$(6 - 2) + (2 - 1) =$

$(3 + 8) - (4 + 2) =$

$(7 - 4) + (3 + 2) =$

$(4 - 2) + (8 - 2) =$

$(7 + 6) - (6 - 3) =$

$(10 - 5) - (2 + 3) =$

$(14 + 16) - (12 + 11) =$

Work out these problems.

$(12 - 2) + (9 - 5) + (2 + 7) =$

$(10 + 5) - (2 + 3) + (4 - 1) =$

$(19 + 3) + (4 - 3) + (2 + 6) =$

$(15 + 3) + (7 - 2) - (3 + 2) =$

... AND NOW TRY THESE LONGER PROBLEMS.

Now try these. Be careful, the parentheses now have multiplication problems.

$(3 \times 2) + (2 \times 5) =$

$(2 \times 7) - (3 \times 3) =$

$(12 \times 4) - (3 \times 8) =$

$(4 \times 3) + (6 \times 6) =$

$(5 \times 9) - (6 \times 4) =$

$(4 \times 7) + (2 \times 8) =$

If the answer is 24, which of these problems gives the correct answer?

a $(3 + 5) - (7 \times 1)$ c $(5 \times 2) + (2 \times 6)$ e $(3 \times 5) + (3 \times 3)$

b $(3 \times 5) + (2 \times 3)$ d $(7 \times 5) - (2 \times 5)$ f $(6 + 8) + (3 \times 4)$

Simple use of parentheses

Work out these problems.

(3 + 2) x (4 +1) = $\boxed{5 \times 5 = 25}$

(10 x 5) ÷ (10 - 5) = $\boxed{50 \div 5 = 10}$

Remember to work out the problems inside the parentheses first.

NOW TRY THESE. NO JOKES!

Work out these problems.

(5 - 2) x (8 - 2) =

(9 + 5) ÷ (2 + 5) =

(7 + 3) x (8 - 4) =

(14 - 6) x (3 + 4) =

(14 + 4) ÷ (13 - 7) =

(10 + 10) ÷ (2 + 3) =

(11 - 5) x (9 - 2) =

(8 + 20) ÷ (12 - 10) =

(9 + 21) ÷ (8 - 5) =

(14 - 3) x (6 + 1) =

(9 + 3) x (6 + 1) =

(6 + 9) ÷ (8 - 3) =

Work out these problems.

(5 x 4) ÷ (2 x 2) =

(8 x 5) ÷ (4 x 1) =

(6 x 4) ÷ (3 x 4) =

(2 x 4) x (2 x 3) =

(4 x 3) ÷ (1 x 2) =

(3 x 5) x (1 x 2) =

(6 x 4) ÷ (4 x 2) =

(8 x 4) ÷ (2 x 2) =

If the answer is 30, which of these problems gives the correct answer?

a   (3 x 5) x (2 x 2)   c   (12 x 5) ÷ (8 ÷ 4)   e   (5 x 12) ÷ (2 x 5)

b   (4 x 5) x (5 x 2)   d   (20 ÷ 2) x (12 ÷ 3)   f   (9 x 5) ÷ (10 ÷2)

If the answer is 8, which of these problems gives the correct answer?

a   (10 ÷ 2) x (4 ÷ 4)   c   (12 x 4) ÷ (6 x 2)   e   (8 ÷ 4) x (8 ÷ 1)

b   (9 ÷ 3) x (3 x 2)   d   (24 ÷ 6) x (8 ÷ 4)   f   (16 ÷4) x (20 ÷ 4)

Simple use of parentheses

Work out these problems.

(5 + 3) + (9 - 2) = | 8 + 7 = 15

(5 + 2) - (4 - 1) = | 7 - 3 = 4

(4 + 2) x (3 + 1) = | 6 x 4 = 24

(3 x 5) ÷ (9 - 6) = | 15 ÷ 3 = 5

Remember to work out the parentheses first.

YOU'VE GOTTA FIND ALL THE LITTLE PIECES FIRST TO GET THE BIG PICTURE.

Work out these problems.

(9 - 2) + (6 + 4) =   (7 + 3) - (9 - 2) =

(15 - 5) + (2 + 3) =   (11 x 2) - (3 x 2) =

(15 ÷ 3) + (8 x 2) =   (12 x 2) - (3 x 3) =

(15 ÷ 5) + (3 x 4) =   (9 x 3) - (7 x 3) =

(6 ÷ 2) + (9 x 2) =   (20 ÷ 5) - (8 ÷ 2) =

(5 x 10) - (12 x 4) =   (5 + 4) + (7 - 3) =

Now try these.

(4 + 8) ÷ (3 x 2) =   (6 x 4) ÷ (3 x 2) =

(9 + 5) ÷ (2 x 1) =   (7 x 4) ÷ (3 + 4) =

(3 + 6) x (3 x 3) =   (5 x 5) ÷ (10 ÷ 2) =

(24 ÷ 2) x (3 x 2) =   (8 x 6) ÷ (2 x 12) =

Write down the letters of all the problems that make 25.

a (2 x 5) x (3 x 2)   c (40 ÷ 2) + (10 ÷ 2)   e (6 x 5) - (10 ÷ 2)

b (5 x 5) + (7 - 2)   d (10 x 5) - (5 x 5)   f (10 x 10) ÷ (10 - 6)

Write down the letters of all the problems that make 20.

a (10 ÷ 2) x (4 ÷ 4)   c (8 x 4) - (6 x 2)   e (10 ÷ 2) + (20 ÷ 2)

b (7 x 3) - (3 ÷ 3)   d (20 ÷ 4) x (8 + 2)   f (14 ÷ 2) + (2 x 7)

Multiplying decimals

Work out these problems.

$$\begin{array}{r} \overset{1}{4}.6 \\ \times\ \ 3 \\ \hline 13.8 \end{array}$$

$$\begin{array}{r} \overset{4}{3}.9 \\ \times\ \ 5 \\ \hline 19.5 \end{array}$$

$$\begin{array}{r} \overset{3}{8}.4 \\ \times\ \ 8 \\ \hline 67.2 \end{array}$$

I'VE GOT ALL THE ANSWERS! CAN YOU FIND THESE ONES?

Work out these problems.

7.4	3.6	6.5	4.2	3.8
× 2	× 4	× 4	× 2	× 2

4.7	9.1	5.6	1.7	5.1
× 3	× 3	× 3	× 2	× 2

4.2	4.7	1.8	3.4	3.7
× 4	× 4	× 5	× 5	× 5

2.5	2.3	5.3	7.3	5.1
× 5	× 6	× 7	× 8	× 9

7.9	8.4	8.7	7.5	9.9
× 9	× 9	× 8	× 8	× 6

6.8	5.6	6.8	7.4	8.3
× 7	× 6	× 7	× 9	× 9

7.4	2.9	3.8	7.7	9.4
× 8	× 7	× 8	× 7	× 9

Multiplying decimals

Work out these problems.

$$\begin{array}{r} \overset{1\ 1}{37.5} \\ \times\quad 2 \\ \hline 75.0 \end{array}$$

$$\begin{array}{r} \overset{3\ 1}{26.2} \\ \times\quad 5 \\ \hline 131.0 \end{array}$$

$$\begin{array}{r} \overset{4\ 2}{65.3} \\ \times\quad 9 \\ \hline 587.7 \end{array}$$

I GIVE UP! CAN YOU FIGURE OUT THESE PROBLEMS?

Work out these problems.

54.3 × 2	93.1 × 2	34.6 × 2	55.3 × 3	35.4 × 3
46.7 × 4	25.6 × 4	16.5 × 3	51.4 × 5	37.3 × 5
12.3 × 5	46.3 × 5	17.6 × 6	36.5 × 6	73.4 × 7
37.5 × 7	20.3 × 7	73.5 × 7	92.4 × 6	47.9 × 6
53.9 × 8	75.7 × 8	28.2 × 8	79.4 × 8	99.9 × 9
37.8 × 9	14.8 × 9	36.5 × 9	46.7 × 8	27.3 × 7
39.6 × 6	84.3 × 9	68.5 × 8	73.5 × 9	57.6 × 6

Real-life problems

Robin earns $3.50 a day on his paper route. How much does he earn in a week?

$24.50

$$\begin{array}{r} \overset{3}{\$3.50} \\ \times \quad 7 \\ \hline \$24.50 \end{array}$$

When Poison Ivy subtracts the width of her closet from the length of her bedroom wall she finds she has 3.65 m of wall space left. If the closet is 0.87 m wide, what is the length of her bedroom wall?

4.52 m

$$\begin{array}{r} \overset{1}{0.8}\overset{1}{7} \\ + \ 3.65 \\ \hline 4.52 \end{array}$$

The Joker buys Harley Quinn a bunch of flowers for $15.95 and some candy for $3.76. If he has $5.84 left, how much did he start with?

Alfred is making some shelves for the Batcave. Each shelf has to be 75.5 cm long. If the wood he is using is 160 cm long, how many pieces will he need to make six shelves?

Gotham City transit station uses 78.5 barrels of oil a day. If they have a weekly delivery of 480 barrels, how much will they have left after six days?

Alfred is preparing food for a banquet at Wayne Manor. He needs 20.5 lbs of flour to make pastry, 13.6 lbs of flour to make cakes, and 2.4 lbs for sauces. How much flour does Alfred need altogether?

Real-life problems

A comic-book writer writes 8.5 pages of his book a day. How many pages will he write in nine days?

76.5 pages

$$
\begin{array}{r}
{}^{4}\ \\
8.5 \\
\times\ \ 9 \\
\hline
76.5
\end{array}
$$

After driving 147.7 mi Batman stops at a service station. If he has another 115.4 mi to go, how long will his trip be?

263.1 mi

$$
\begin{array}{r}
{}^{1\ 1}\ \\
147.7 \\
+\ 115.4 \\
\hline
263.1
\end{array}
$$

The Penguin divides his money equally among four separate banks. If he has $78.55 in each bank, what is the total of his savings?

Batgirl buys two bottles of perfume; one contains 48.5 ml and the other contains 125.5 ml. How much more perfume is in the larger of the two bottles?

In Bruce Wayne's bathroom, seven tiles, each 15.75 cm wide, fit exactly across the width of the shower. How wide is the shower?

The Joker spends 6.25 minutes telling a joke. How long would it take to tell eight jokes?

Real-life problems

In a class of 30 children, 6 children are painting. What percent of children are painting?

$\frac{6}{30}$ of the children are painting.   **20%**
  To change a fraction to a percent we multiply by 100.

$$\frac{\overset{1}{\cancel{6}}}{\underset{5}{\cancel{30}}} \times \frac{100}{1} =$$

$$\frac{1}{\underset{1}{\cancel{5}}} \times \frac{\overset{20}{\cancel{100}}}{1} = \frac{20}{1} = 20$$

40% of a class is made up of girls. If there are 12 girls, how many children are in the class?

If 12 girls are 40% of the class, we divide 12 by 40 to find 1% . Then we multiply by 100 to find 100%.

$$\frac{\overset{3}{\cancel{12}}}{\underset{10}{\cancel{40}}} \times \frac{100}{1} =$$

$$\frac{3}{\underset{1}{\cancel{10}}} \times \frac{\overset{10}{\cancel{100}}}{1} = \frac{30}{1} = 30$$

30 children

A shop has 60 new Batman comic books in stock. If the shop sells 45 books, what percent does it sell?

Gotham high school sells 65% of its prom tickets. If it had 120 tickets to start with, how many has it sold?

A shop sells 150 Batman outfits, but 12 are returned because they are faulty. What percent of the outfits was faulty?

A group of 120 children are asked their favorite colors.

15% like red. How many children like red?

20% like green. How many children like green?

35% like yellow. How many children like yellow?

Conversions: length

Units of length	
12 inches	1 foot
3 feet	1 yard
5,280 feet	1 mile
1,760 yards	1 mile

This conversion table shows how to convert inches, feet, yards, and miles.

Batman's jumpline is 3 yards long. How many feet is it?

3 x 3 = 9
9 x 12 = 108

9 feet long

Robin's jumpline is 120 inches long. How many feet is it?

120 ÷ 12 = 10

10 feet long

IT'S EASY ONCE YOU KNOW HOW!

Convert each measurement to feet.

36 inches	12 inches	48 inches

Convert each measurement to yards.

6 feet	12 feet	27 feet	36 feet

Convert each measurement to inches.

4 feet	12 feet	8 feet	5 feet

Convert each measurement.

4 yards	5 yards	4 miles	1 mile
inches	inches	feet	inches

15,840 feet	31,680 feet	1,760 yards	3,520 yards
miles	miles	mile	miles

Conversions: capacity

Units of length	
8 fluid ounces	1 cup
2 cups	1 pint
2 pints	1 quart
4 quarts	1 gallon

Alfred's pitcher holds 8 pints. How many cups does it hold?

8 x 2 = 16	16 cups

This conversion table shows how to convert ounces, cups, pints, quarts, and gallons.

Robin's pitcher holds 6 cups. How many pints does it hold?

6 ÷ 2 = 3	3 pints

DON'T CONFUSE CUPS AND QUARTS OR YOU'LL GET IN A MESS!

Convert each measurement to cups.

32 fluid ounces	16 fluid ounces	96 fluid ounces

Convert each measurement to pints.

6 cups	12 cups	30 quarts	6 quarts

Convert each measurement to gallons.

16 quarts	32 quarts	100 quarts	20 quarts

Convert each measurement.

3 gallons	5 quarts	36 cups	72 pints
pints	cups	quarts	gallons
1 quart	240 fluid ounces	7 quarts	11 gallons
fluid ounces	pints	cups	pints

Fraction of a number

Work out to find the fraction of the number. Write the answer in the box.

$\dfrac{1}{6}$ of 42

$\dfrac{1}{6} \times 42 = \dfrac{42}{6} = 7$

$1 \times 7 = 7$

so $\boxed{\dfrac{1}{6} \text{ of } 42 = 7}$

$\dfrac{1}{4}$ of 100 $= \dfrac{100}{4} = \boxed{25}$

$\dfrac{3}{5}$ of 35

$\dfrac{1}{5} \times 35 = \dfrac{35}{5} = 7$

$3 \times 7 = 21$

so $\boxed{\dfrac{3}{5} \text{ of } 35 = 21}$

$\dfrac{1}{3}$ of 69 $= \dfrac{69}{3} = \boxed{23}$

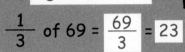

WE'RE BACK TO FRACTIONS AGAIN NOW. MOTOR ON!

Work out to find the fraction of the number. Write the answer in the box.

$\dfrac{1}{8}$ of 72

$\dfrac{1}{9}$ of 54

$\dfrac{1}{4}$ of 52

$\dfrac{1}{5}$ of 175

$\dfrac{1}{6}$ of 300

$\dfrac{1}{10}$ of 100

$\dfrac{3}{4}$ of 100

$\dfrac{2}{5}$ of 25

$\dfrac{5}{9}$ of 36

$\dfrac{3}{4}$ of 56

$\dfrac{4}{5}$ of 100

$\dfrac{2}{3}$ of 210

$\dfrac{1}{5}$ of 250

$\dfrac{1}{2}$ of 84

$\dfrac{1}{7}$ of 140

$\dfrac{1}{8}$ of 64

$\dfrac{1}{9}$ of 81

$\dfrac{1}{5}$ of 55

$\dfrac{2}{3}$ of 75

$\dfrac{5}{8}$ of 40

$\dfrac{2}{3}$ of 225

$\dfrac{5}{7}$ of 133

$\dfrac{2}{10}$ of 100

$\dfrac{4}{9}$ of 90

$\dfrac{1}{2}$ of 38

$\dfrac{1}{6}$ of 72

$\dfrac{1}{3}$ of 36

$\dfrac{1}{4}$ of 100

$\dfrac{1}{2}$ of 114

$\dfrac{1}{7}$ of 140

$\dfrac{4}{7}$ of 42

$\dfrac{2}{3}$ of 27

$\dfrac{5}{6}$ of 120

$\dfrac{2}{3}$ of 180

$\dfrac{3}{8}$ of 64

$\dfrac{7}{8}$ of 72

Showing decimals

Write the decimals on the number line.

0.4, 0.5, 0.6, 0.8, 0.9, 0.25, 0.45, 0.63

0   [0.25]   [0.45]   [0.63]   1

0.1 0.2 0.3 [0.4] [0.5] [0.6] 0.7 [0.8] [0.9]

IT'S EASY TO DEAL WITH DECIMALS IF YOU PUT THEM ALONG THE LINE!

Write the decimals on the number line.

0.56, 0.2, 0.87, 0.45, 0.98, 0.6, 0.1

0   0.25   0.5   0.75   1

Write the decimals on the number line.

1.41, 1.8, 1.3, 1.98, 1.68, 1.2

1   1.25   1.5   1.75   0

Write the decimals on the number line.

2.5, 3.75, 2.25, 3.1, 3.68, 4.2

2   3   4

Area of right-angled triangles

Find the area of this right-angled triangle.

Because the area of this triangle is half the area of the rectangle shown, we can find the area of the rectangle and then divide it by two to find the area of the triangle.

So the area = (8 cm x 4 cm) ÷ 2
= 32 cm² ÷ 2 = 16cm²

Area = 16 cm²

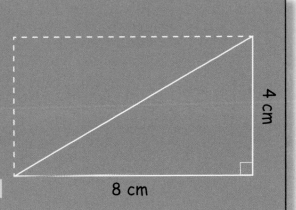

4 cm

8 cm

Find the area of these right-angled triangles.

IT'S EASY TO FIND THE AREA
IF THE ANGLE IS RIGHT!

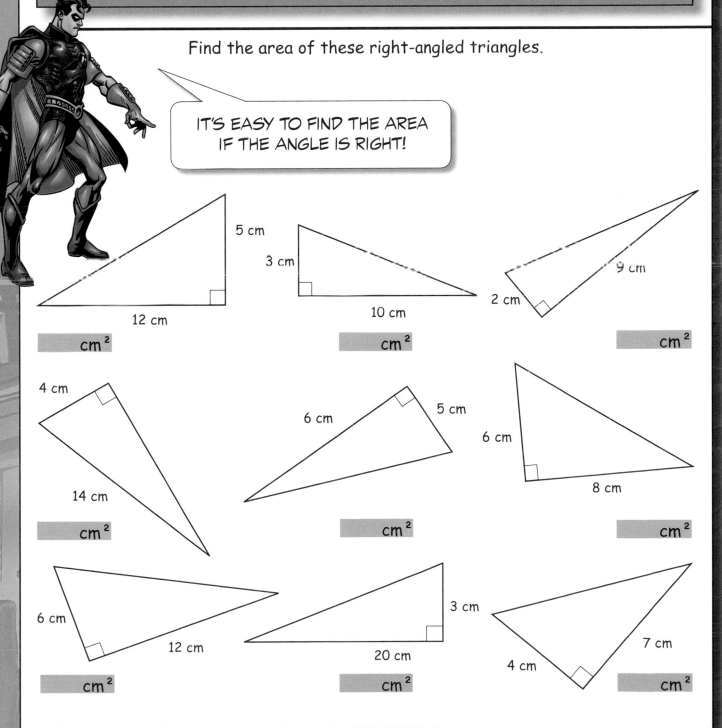

5 cm

3 cm

9 cm

2 cm

12 cm

10 cm

cm²

cm²

cm²

4 cm

6 cm

5 cm

6 cm

14 cm

8 cm

cm²

cm²

cm²

6 cm

3 cm

12 cm

20 cm

7 cm

4 cm

cm²

cm²

cm²

Speed problems

How long would it take to travel
120 mi at 8 mph?
(Time = Distance ÷ Speed)

15 hours

$$\begin{array}{r} 15 \\ 8\overline{)120} \end{array}$$

If a bus takes 3 hours to travel
150 mi, how fast is it going?
(Speed = Distance ÷ Time)

50 mph

$$\begin{array}{r} 50 \\ 3\overline{)150} \end{array}$$

If a car travels at 60 mph for
2 hours, how far has it gone?
(Distance = Speed x Time)

120 mi

$$\begin{array}{r} 60 \\ \times\ 2 \\ \hline 120 \end{array}$$

If the Penguin walks for 6 miles at a steady
speed of 3 mph, how long will it take him?

Batman travels 120 mi in 3 hours. If he went
at a steady speed, how fast was he going.

Robin drives at a steady speed of 40 mph.
How far will he travel in 4 hours?

Catwoman walks 10 mi at 4 mph. Robin walks 12 mi
at 5 mph. Which of them will take the longest?

A bat flies for 30 minutes at 10 mph and for 1 hour
at 15 mph. How far has it traveled altogether?

Catwoman rides her bike 340 mi in 120
minutes. What speed is she traveling at?

Conversion tables

Draw a table to convert dollars to cents.

$	cents
1	100
2	200
3	300

Weeks	Days
1	7
2	
	28
10	70

Complete the conversion table.
Hint: look for a pattern.

CONVERTING IS EASY FOR ME...JUST LIKE TOSSING A COIN!

If there are 60 minutes in 1 hour, make a conversion chart for up to 10 hours.

TIME'S TICKING AWAY!

Hours	Minutes

Reading bar graphs

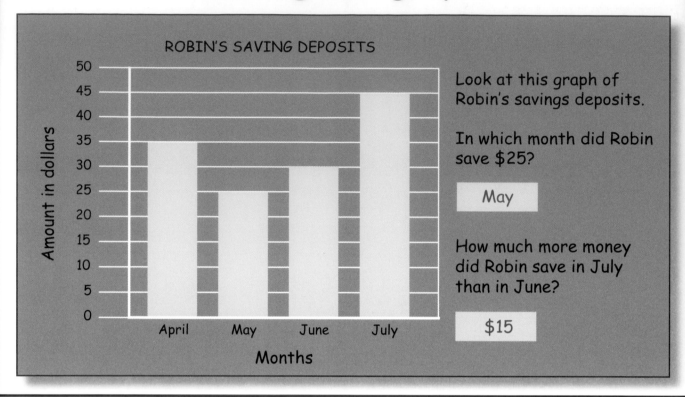

ROBIN'S SAVING DEPOSITS

Look at this graph of Robin's savings deposits.

In which month did Robin save $25?

| May |

How much more money did Robin save in July than in June?

| $15 |

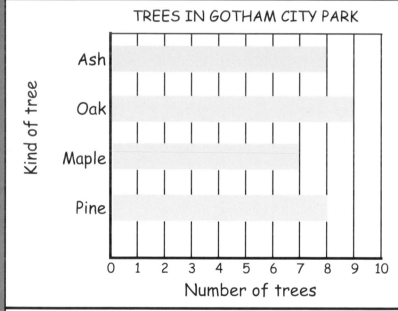

TREES IN GOTHAM CITY PARK

How many maple trees were planted?

The same number of ash trees were planted as what other kind of tree?

How many more oak trees were planted than maple trees?

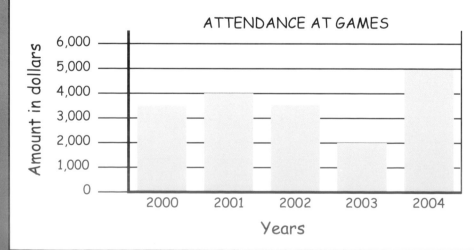

ATTENDANCE AT GAMES

In which year did 5,000 people attend the games?

How many people attended the games in 2001?

The biggest increase in attendance was between which years?

Expanded form

POSITION MEANS VALUE!

What is the value of 3 in 2,308?   **300**

Write 32,804 in expanded form.   **30,000 + 2,000 + 800 + 4**

What is the value of 7 in these numbers?

37	872		56,870	
13,704	62,740		467,834	
3,576	12,907		16,792	

What is the value of 5 in these numbers?

14,532	853		8,657	
22,458	256,784		75,783	
6,045	86,548		875	

Circle the numbers that have a 7 with the value of seventy thousand.

457,682	67,924	870,234	372,987
171,345	767,707	79,835	16,757

Write the numbers in expanded form.

42,573

208,967

8,794

50,735

Cubes of small numbers

What is 2^3 ?

$2 \times 2 \times 2 = 8$

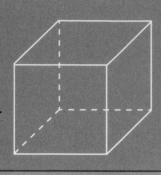

2 in.

What is the volume of this cube?

$2 \text{ in.} \times 2 \text{ in.} \times 2 \text{ in.} = 8 \text{ in}^3$

You find the volume of a cube in the same way as you find out the cube of a number.

Use extra paper if you need to here. What is...

1^3

5^3

6^3

3^3

4^3

2^3

What are the volumes of these cubes?

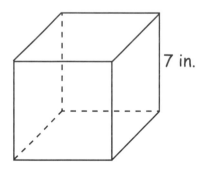

7 in.

in.³

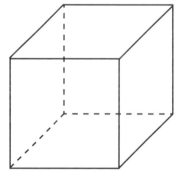

8 in.

in.³

TO THE POWER OF 3!

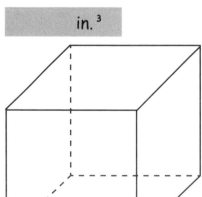

9 in.

in.³

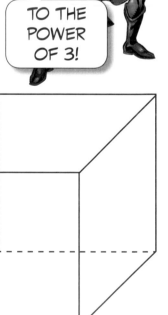

10 in.

in.³

Multiplying fractions

To find the product, multiply the numerators, multiply the denominators, then reduce answer to the simplest form.

$$\frac{3}{8} \times \frac{4}{7} = \frac{12 \div 4}{56 \div 4} = \boxed{\frac{3}{14}}$$

DON'T GIVE UP... YOU CAN DO IT!

Write the product.

$\dfrac{1}{2} \times \dfrac{1}{2} = $ ⬜

$\dfrac{4}{10} \times \dfrac{3}{8} = $ ⬜

$6 \times \dfrac{3}{4} = $ ⬜ $=$ ⬜

$6 \times \dfrac{1}{3} = $ ⬜

$\dfrac{3}{5} \times \dfrac{5}{7} = $ ⬜

$\dfrac{3}{5} \times \dfrac{5}{6} = $ ⬜

$\dfrac{2}{3} \times \dfrac{2}{5} = $ ⬜

$4 \times \dfrac{1}{16} = $ ⬜

$10 \times \dfrac{5}{8} = $ ⬜ $=$ ⬜

$\dfrac{1}{4} \times 16 = $ ⬜

$\dfrac{4}{9} \times \dfrac{1}{4} = $ ⬜

$\dfrac{3}{4} \times \dfrac{4}{9} = $ ⬜

$\dfrac{1}{3} \times \dfrac{9}{10} = $ ⬜

$\dfrac{3}{4} \times \dfrac{2}{9} = $ ⬜

$12 \times \dfrac{7}{10} = $ ⬜ $=$ ⬜

$\dfrac{1}{3} \times \dfrac{2}{3} = $ ⬜

$\dfrac{1}{8} \times 7 = $ ⬜

$\dfrac{1}{4} \times \dfrac{3}{4} = $ ⬜

$8 \times \dfrac{5}{6} = $ ⬜ $=$ ⬜

$\dfrac{1}{8} \times \dfrac{4}{9} = $ ⬜

$\dfrac{1}{6} \times \dfrac{5}{6} = $ ⬜

$25 \times \dfrac{1}{2} = $ ⬜ $=$ ⬜

$\dfrac{5}{9} \times \dfrac{9}{10} = $ ⬜

$\dfrac{3}{4} \times \dfrac{4}{5} = $ ⬜

More complex fraction problems

Find $\frac{3}{5}$ of $30.00.

| Find $\frac{1}{5}$: $30 ÷ 5 = $6 |
| $6 × 3 = $18 |
| So $\frac{3}{5}$ of $30 is $18 |

Find $\frac{7}{10}$ of 60 in.

| Find $\frac{1}{10}$: 60in. ÷ 10 = 6 in. |
| 6 in. × 7 = 42 in. |
| So $\frac{7}{10}$ of 60 in. is 42 in. |

LOOK, THERE'S PLENTY OF SPACE FOR YOU TO WORK IT OUT!

Find $\frac{3}{5}$ of these amounts.

45 in.

$70

$10.50

60 yd

35 oz

25 lb

Find $\frac{7}{10}$ of these amounts.

48 yd

$76

85 mi

Find $\frac{2}{3}$ of these amounts.

51 in.

180 lb

$27.00

Finding percentages

Find 30% of 140.

$$\frac{14\cancel{0}}{10\cancel{0}} \times 3\cancel{0} = 42$$

(Divide by 100 to find 1% and then multiply by 30 to find 30%.)

Find 12% of 75.

$$\frac{\cancel{75}^{3}}{\cancel{100}_{\,4}\,_1} \times \cancel{12}^{\,3} = 9$$

(Divide by 100 to find 1% and then multiply by 12 to find 12%.)

Find 30% of these numbers.

420   260

30   160

Find 60% of these numbers.

50   270

120   540

Find 45% of these numbers.

60 oz   600 mi

80 yd   220 yd

Find 12% of these numbers.

$125   600 ft

$775   150 yd

FRACTIONS? PERCENTAGES? WHO NEEDS THEM? YOU!

Addition

Work out the answer to each problem.

$$\begin{array}{r} \scriptstyle 1\ 1\ 1 \\ 645 \\ 4{,}823 \\ +\ 1{,}433 \\ \hline \boxed{6{,}901} \end{array}$$

$$\begin{array}{r} \scriptstyle 1\ 31 \\ 1{,}472 \\ 96 \\ 8{,}391 \\ +\ 564 \\ \hline \boxed{10{,}523} \end{array}$$

Remember to regroup if you need to.

THESE SUMS ARE GETTING LONGER.

Find each sum.

$$\begin{array}{r} 6{,}931 \\ 8{,}174 \\ +\ 219 \\ \hline \end{array}$$

$$\begin{array}{r} 7{,}694 \\ 3{,}722 \\ +\ 612 \\ \hline \end{array}$$

$$\begin{array}{r} 486 \\ 8{,}560 \\ +\ 7{,}924 \\ \hline \end{array}$$

$$\begin{array}{r} 532 \\ 8{,}420 \\ +\ 348 \\ \hline \end{array}$$

$$\begin{array}{r} 2{,}560 \\ 6{,}548 \\ +\ 499 \\ \hline \end{array}$$

$$\begin{array}{r} 382 \\ 6{,}582 \\ +\ 3{,}291 \\ \hline \end{array}$$

$$\begin{array}{r} 7{,}154 \\ 532 \\ +\ 287 \\ \hline \end{array}$$

$$\begin{array}{r} 6{,}492 \\ 378 \\ +\ 2{,}436 \\ \hline \end{array}$$

Find each sum.

$$\begin{array}{r} 8{,}562 \\ 629 \\ 9{,}432 \\ +\ 312 \\ \hline \end{array}$$

$$\begin{array}{r} 6{,}329 \\ 845 \\ 4{,}328 \\ +\ 27 \\ \hline \end{array}$$

$$\begin{array}{r} 324 \\ 8{,}265 \\ 27 \\ +\ 4{,}620 \\ \hline \end{array}$$

$$\begin{array}{r} 5{,}268 \\ 93 \\ 2{,}076 \\ +\ 398 \\ \hline \end{array}$$

$$\begin{array}{r} 8{,}794 \\ 659 \\ 3{,}212 \\ +\ 961 \\ \hline \end{array}$$

$$\begin{array}{r} 6{,}526 \\ 5{,}209 \\ 38 \\ +\ 124 \\ \hline \end{array}$$

$$\begin{array}{r} 459 \\ 1{,}560 \\ 7{,}643 \\ +\ 154 \\ \hline \end{array}$$

$$\begin{array}{r} 84 \\ 146 \\ 2{,}362 \\ +\ 9{,}268 \\ \hline \end{array}$$

More addition

Work out the answer to each problem.

```
  1 1   1
 23,714
  9,024
+   348
 33,086
```

```
   1 2 1
 11,541
    861
 29,652
+     5
 42,059
```

Remember to regroup if you need to.

> I THINK WE ALL NEED TO REGROUP?

Find each sum.

```
 18,342
    133
+ 4,609
```

```
 49,568
  2,425
+    32
```

```
    978
 23,476
+ 4,385
```

```
    371
 42,747
+    42
```

```
 84,119
     27
+ 2,643
```

```
    200
 72,654
+ 9,220
```

```
    274
  8,542
+ 9,762
```

Find each sum.

```
 24,679
  4,308
     65
+   217
```

```
     78
  2,001
 62,472
+   123
```

```
 67,592
  4,374
     22
+ 8,465
```

```
 61,320
    314
     62
+ 5,732
```

```
 63,473
    267
 35,306
+    43
```

```
  2,785
     29
    812
+ 5,228
```

```
      6
    205
 32,428
+ 4,620
```

```
 34,629
  4,572
    843
+     4
```

Dividing by ones

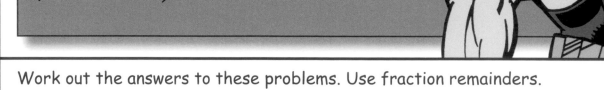

477 ÷ 2 can be written in two ways:

238 1/2   or   238 r 1
2)477   2)477

NOW TRY THESE.

Work out the answers to these problems. Use fraction remainders.

2)589   3)847   5)638   7)870

2)189   5)274   9)374   7)531

Work out the answers to these problems. Use unit remainders.

2)703   5)438   4)647   7)922

Dividing by tens

361 ÷ 20 can be written in two ways:

 18 $\frac{1}{20}$

20) 361

or

18 r 1

20) 361

YOU CAN DO IT!

Work out the answers to these problems. Use fraction remainders.

40) 360

70) 420

80) 347

90) 548

10) 506

20) 457

10) 953

30) 351

Work out the answers to these problems. Use unit remainders.

50) 427

90) 720

30) 323

40) 367

20) 953

70) 743

60) 737

10) 357

Dividing by larger numbers

589 ÷ 15 can be written in two ways:

$$39 \frac{4}{15}$$ or $$39 \text{ r } 4$$

$$15\overline{)589}$$ $$15\overline{)589}$$

DIVIDE AND RULE!

Work out the answers to these problems. Use fraction remainders.

$$46\overline{)369}$$ $$70\overline{)493}$$ $$22\overline{)139}$$ $$57\overline{)463}$$

$$32\overline{)937}$$ $$65\overline{)799}$$ $$17\overline{)259}$$ $$51\overline{)379}$$

Work out the answers to these problems. Use unit remainders.

$$96\overline{)797}$$ $$24\overline{)113}$$ $$85\overline{)379}$$ $$26\overline{)257}$$

$$12\overline{)379}$$ $$80\overline{)999}$$ $$17\overline{)489}$$ $$45\overline{)673}$$

Everyday problems

Alfred has 6 m of copper tubing. If he uses 2.36 m, how much will he have left?

3.64 m

$$\begin{array}{r} \overset{9}{\underset{}{5\,\cancel{10}}} \\ 6.\cancel{0}\cancel{0} \\ -\ 2.36 \\ \hline 3.64 \end{array}$$

If he buys another 4.5 m of copper tubing, how much will he now have?

8.14 m

$$\begin{array}{r} \overset{1}{}\ \\ 3.64 \\ +\ 4.50 \\ \hline 8.14 \end{array}$$

The Penguin spends $36.65, $103.43, $68.99 and $35.60 in four different stores. How much money did he spend altogether?

Batman has the following amounts of gasoline delivered to the Batcave in each year: 10,400 gallons in 2001; 13,350 gal in 2002; 14,755 gal in 2003; 9,656 gal in 2004 and 15,975 gal in 2005. How much did he have delivered over the five years?

If he had used 59,248 gallons in that time, how much gasoline did he have left at the end of 2005?

Batgirl runs 22.56 km to get away from the Joker. The Joker gives up – he runs 8,420 m less. How far did the Joker run?

What is the combined distance run by Batgirl and the Joker?

Robin is 4ft 10 in. tall. Catwoman is 5 ft 1 in. tall. How much taller is Catwoman?

103

Real-life problems

A man walks 18.34 km on Saturday and 16.57 km on Sunday. How far did he walk that weekend?

34.91 km

$$\begin{array}{r} \overset{1}{1}\overset{1}{8}.34 \\ +\ 16.57 \\ \hline 34.91 \end{array}$$

How much farther did he walk on Sunday?

1.77 km

$$\begin{array}{r} 7\ \overset{12}{\overset{2}{1}}\overset{14}{8}.\overset{}{3}\overset{}{4} \\ -\ 16.57 \\ \hline 1.77 \end{array}$$

Lockhaven Penitentiary exercise yard is rectangular. It measures 102.7 m by 95.6 m. What is the perimeter of the yard?

When Batman and Robin stand on a scale it reads $236\frac{1}{2}$ lb. When Batman steps off it reads $68\frac{1}{4}$ lb. How much does Batman weigh?

A rectangular room in the Batcave has an area of 32.58 m². When a carpet is put down, there is still 6.99 m² of floor showing. What is the area of the carpet?

Echo and Query's combined height is $124\frac{3}{4}$ in. If Echo is $66\frac{1}{2}$ in, how tall is Query?

Four highways radiate from Gotham City. Route 1 is 1,246 mi long; Rte 2 is 399 mi long; Rte 3 is 1,327 mi long, and Rte 4 is 56 mi long. What is the total length of the four highways?

The reserve gas tank in the Batmobile holds $25\frac{1}{2}$ quarts of gasoline. Alfred replaces it with a new one that holds 35 quarts. How much extra emergency gas is there?

Real-life problems

Echo's weekend bag weighs $22\frac{1}{2}$ lb.
Query's weighs $24\frac{1}{2}$ lb.
How much more does Query's weigh than Echo's?

2 lb

$$\begin{array}{r} 24\frac{1}{2} \\ -\ 22\frac{1}{2} \\ \hline 2 \end{array}$$

What is the total weight of the two bags?

47 lb

$$\begin{array}{r} 24\frac{1}{2} \\ +\ 22\frac{1}{2} \\ \hline 47 \end{array}$$

Alfred is renovating Wayne Manor. He needs to put weather stripping around four sides of the front door. The door is 100 in. high and 60 in. wide. How many inches of weather stripping does he need?

In a series of crime capers, the Joker steals $24,632, Catwoman steals $34,321, and Harley Quinn steals $22,971. How much do they steal altogether?

How much more than the Joker does Catwoman steal?

How much more than Harley Quinn does the Joker steal?

An elevator says "Maximum weight 1,400 lb." If four people get in, weighing 198 lb, 132 lb, 254 lb, and 172 lb, how much more weight will the elevator hold?

Multiplication by 2-digit numbers

Work out the answer to each problem.

```
    527          834
  x  76        x  58
  -----        -----
  3,162        6,672
+36,890      +41,700
  ------      -------
 40,052       48,372
```

THIS SENDS ME INTO A SPIN! YOU'VE GOTTA WORK IT OUT!

Work out the answer to each problem.

```
    573          795          582          788
  x  74        x  68        x  29        x  38
  -----        -----        -----        -----


    587          995          653          757
  x  42        x  37        x  84        x  85
  -----        -----        -----        -----


    489          158          257          175
  x  96        x  61        x  88        x  43
  -----        -----        -----        -----


    386          539          492          783
  x  85        x  73        x  29        x  63
  -----        -----        -----        -----
```

Division by ones

47 ÷ 2 can be written in two ways:

$$23 \frac{1}{2}$$

$$\begin{array}{r} 23 \\ 2\overline{)47} \\ 4 \\ \hline 7 \\ 6 \\ \hline 1 \end{array}$$

$$23 \text{ r } 1$$

$$\begin{array}{r} 23 \\ 2\overline{)47} \\ 4 \\ \hline 7 \\ 6 \\ \hline 1 \end{array}$$

HMM! QUANTITIES OF QUOTIENTS...

Write the quotients for these problems with fraction remainders.

$2\overline{)19}$ $4\overline{)17}$ $3\overline{)17}$ $4\overline{)35}$

$3\overline{)28}$ $2\overline{)47}$ $5\overline{)81}$ $5\overline{)53}$

Write the quotients for these problems with unit remainders.

$2\overline{)95}$ $2\overline{)83}$ $2\overline{)49}$ $4\overline{)67}$

$4\overline{)73}$ $4\overline{)81}$ $5\overline{)72}$ $5\overline{)99}$

Dividing larger numbers

645 ÷ 13 can be written in two ways:

$$49 \frac{8}{13}$$

or

$$49 \text{ r } 8$$

$$13 \overline{)645}$$

$$13 \overline{)645}$$

THIS DIVISION IS AS DEVILISH AS ME!

Work out the answer to each problem.
Use fraction remainders.

$$45 \overline{)367}$$ $$21 \overline{)179}$$ $$16 \overline{)139}$$ $$43 \overline{)378}$$

$$50 \overline{)193}$$ $$93 \overline{)583}$$ $$13 \overline{)354}$$ $$15 \overline{)769}$$

Work out the answer to each problem. Use unit remainders.

$$70 \overline{)467}$$ $$84 \overline{)733}$$ $$44 \overline{)367}$$ $$62 \overline{)459}$$

$$52 \overline{)983}$$ $$35 \overline{)751}$$ $$43 \overline{)948}$$ $$31 \overline{)843}$$

Division of 3-digit decimal numbers

Work out these division sums.

```
      0.89           0.74
      0.89           0.74
   3) 2.67        4) 2.96
      2.4            2.8
       27             16
       27             16
        0              0
```

```
2) 5.72
```

```
4) 8.64
```

```
4) 7.32
```

```
2) 9.78
```

```
3) 4.68
```

```
4) 5.36
```

```
5) 8.75
```

```
4) 3.28
```

NOW DO YOU GET THE POINT?

```
4) 5.88
```

```
3) 9.36
```

```
3) 8.43
```

Division of 3-digit decimals

Work out these division problems.

$$\begin{array}{r} 1.99 \\ 5{\overline{)9.95}} \\ 5 \\ \hline 49 \\ 45 \\ \hline 45 \\ 45 \\ \hline 0 \end{array}$$

1.99

$$\begin{array}{r} 1.61 \\ 6{\overline{)9.66}} \\ 6 \\ \hline 36 \\ 36 \\ \hline 6 \\ 6 \\ \hline 0 \end{array}$$

1.61

PROBLEMS NEED TO BE FIGURED OUT.

Work out these division problems.

$5{\overline{)8.35}}$

$5{\overline{)9.75}}$

$5{\overline{)5.85}}$

$6{\overline{)9.12}}$

$6{\overline{)2.34}}$

$7{\overline{)8.82}}$

$7{\overline{)8.33}}$

$8{\overline{)5.84}}$

$8{\overline{)8.56}}$

$9{\overline{)8.73}}$

$9{\overline{)5.31}}$

$9{\overline{)3.78}}$

Real-life problems

A builder uses 1,600 lb of sand a day. How much will he use in 5 days?

8,000 lb

$$\begin{array}{r} 1,600 \\ \times\ \ \ \ 5 \\ \hline 8,000 \end{array}$$

If he uses 9,500 lb the next week, how much more has he used than the week before?

1,500 lb

$$\begin{array}{r} 9,500 \\ -\ 8,000 \\ \hline 1,500 \end{array}$$

Alfred is rewiring four rooms in the Batcave. He uses 196 ft of cable altogether. If he uses the same amount in each room, how much does he use for each room?

Harley Quinn is going on vacation and looks at two different resorts. The first one costs $847.95. The second costs $931. How much will she save if she chooses the cheaper resort?

If she decides to go on both holidays, how much will it cost her?

The Penguin is collecting money from people who owe him cash. He collects $15.95 from Mr. Black, $8.36 from Mr. White, $12.45 from Mr. Green, and $25.75 from Mr. Brown. How much does he collect altogether?

A Batmobile holds 16.4 gallons of gasoline. If Batman has 9 Batmobiles, and fills all the tanks, how many gallons will he need?

Rounding money

Round to the nearest dollar.

$2.70 rounds to $1.75 rounds to

$9.65 rounds to $6.95 rounds to

$4.15 rounds to $3.39 rounds to $7.14 rounds to

$7.75 rounds to $4.30 rounds to $2.53 rounds to

Round to the nearest ten dollars.

$38.35 rounds to $32.75 rounds to $85.05 rounds to

$22.75 rounds to $66.70 rounds to $24.55 rounds to

$56.85 rounds to $14.95 rounds to $15.00 rounds to

Round to the nearest hundred dollars.

$407.25 rounds to $357.85 rounds to $115.99 rounds to

$870.45 rounds to $524.45 rounds to $650.15 rounds to

$849.75 rounds to $728.55 rounds to $467.25 rounds to

Estimating sums of money

Round to the leading digit. Estimate the sum.

$3.26 → $3
+ $4.82 → + $5
is about $8

$68.53 → $70
+ $34.60 → + $30
is about $100

IT'S HELPFUL TO THINK ABOUT IT...

Round to the leading digit. Estimate the sum.

$53.64 →
+ $28.40 → _____
is about _____

$18.45 →
+ $23.05 → _____
is about _____

$28.95 →
+ $34.22 → _____
is about _____

$35.95 →
+ $12.70 → _____
is about _____

$63.40 →
+ $47.80 → _____
is about _____

$25.75 →
+ $32.20 → _____
is about _____

$47.30 →
+ $23.85 → _____
is about _____

$28.73 →
+ $32.60 → _____
is about _____

$72.30 →
+ $10.40 → _____
is about _____

$560.70 →
+ $332.40 → _____
is about _____

$382.60 →
+ $238.50 → _____
is about _____

$780.75 →
+ $98.75 → _____
is about _____

Round to the leading digit. Estimate the sum.

$17.95 + $75.95 → _____

$20.35 + $32.87 → _____

$51.19 + $39.50 → _____

$875.90 + $103.20 → _____

$517.75 + $291.50 → _____

$48.87 + $90.34 → _____

$83.40 + $12.30 → _____

$90.34 + $16.20 → _____

Estimating differences of money

KEEP COUNTING THE CASH!

Round to the leading digit. Estimate the difference.

$27.80 →
- $11.90 →
is about _____

$48.35 →
- $32.25 →
is about _____

$89.20 →
- $22.40 →
is about _____

$37.40 →
- $31.20 →
is about _____

$58.20 →
- $17.30 →
is about _____

$326.30 →
- $178.90 →
is about _____

$54.10 →
- $33.80 →
is about _____

$87.40 →
- $8.75 →
is about _____

$783.90 →
- $417.60 →
is about _____

Round to the leading digit. Estimate the difference.

$8.12 - $3.78

→   = _____

$49.60 - $21.80

→   = _____

$7.70 - $3.20

→   = _____

$84.20 - $39.80

→   = _____

$5.95 - $4.60

→   = _____

$675.80 - $267.50

→   = _____

$32.85 - $21.90

→   = _____

$829.90 - $516.20

→   = _____

$56.78 - $38.90

→   = _____

$679.20 - $211.10

→   = _____

114

Estimating sums and differences

Round to the leading digit. Estimate the sum or difference.

$$3,762 \rightarrow 4,000$$
$$- \ 1,204 \rightarrow + \ 1,000$$
is about **5,000**

$$287,257 \rightarrow 300,000$$
$$- \ \ 98,592 \rightarrow - \ 100,000$$
is about **200,000**

Round to the leading digit. Estimate the sum or difference.

$587 \rightarrow$
$+ \ 496 \rightarrow$ _____
is about _____

$22,945 \rightarrow$
$- \ 12,352 \rightarrow$ _____
is about _____

$8,265 \rightarrow$
$+ \ 2,156 \rightarrow$ _____
is about _____

$685,271 \rightarrow$
$+ \ 213,876 \rightarrow$ _____
is about _____

$57,998 \rightarrow$
$- \ 22,135 \rightarrow$ _____
is about _____

$492,076 \rightarrow$
$+ \ 237,631 \rightarrow$ _____
is about _____

$23,957 \rightarrow$
$+ \ 14,702 \rightarrow$ _____
is about _____

$8,752 \rightarrow$
$- \ 2,398 \rightarrow$ _____
Is about _____

$62,973 \rightarrow$
$+ \ 21,482 \rightarrow$ _____
is about _____

$5,294 \rightarrow$
$+ \ 3,813 \rightarrow$ _____
is about _____

$736 \rightarrow$
$+ \ 829 \rightarrow$ _____
is about _____

$33,729 \rightarrow$
$- \ 19,372 \rightarrow$ _____
is about _____

Write > or < for each problem.

I'M GREATER THAN ALL OF THESE!

$567 + 295$ ▢ 800

$467 - 307$ ▢ 100

$11,987 - 5,424$ ▢ $6,000$

$41,925 - 12,354$ ▢ $40,000$

$8,183 - 6,875$ ▢ $1,000$

$19,885 + 12,681$ ▢ $30,000$

$645,900 + 183,650$ ▢ $800,000$

$753 - 347$ ▢ 300

$913,312 - 432,667$ ▢ $500,000$

Estimating products

Round to the leading digit. Estimate the product.

3,465 x 6   72 x 58
3,000 x 6 = 18,000   70 x 60 = 4,200

Round to the leading digit. Estimate the product.

1,907 x 7   6 x 4,220
      x 7 =   6 x

8 x 2,407   5,120 x 8
8 x   =   x 8 =

82 x 47   21 x 63
  x =   x =

78 x 32   92 x 18
  x =   x =

THESE SHORTCUTS
DO THE TRICK!

Estimate the product.

7 x 6,820	8 x 2,873	3 x 8,325
8 x 6,230	3,987 x 9	7,890 x 5
6,887 x 9	3,823 x 4	5 x 4,807
8,320 x 9	6 x 2,874	3,972 x 9
75 x 21	67 x 22	34 x 58
52 x 58	16 x 32	23 x 75
18 x 81	17 x 74	59 x 52
77 x 46	31 x 91	38 x 87

Estimating quotients

Round to the leading digit. Estimate the product.

2,934 ÷ 6   2,356 ÷ 5
3,000 ÷ 6 = [500]   2,500 ÷ 5 = [500]

Round to compatible numbers. Estimate the quotient.

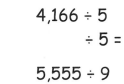
DO YOU THINK I'M A
COMPATIBLE NUMBER?

1,895 ÷ 8
   ÷ 8 =

2,120 ÷ 4
   ÷ 4 =

4,998 ÷ 6
   ÷ 6 =

1,689 ÷ 3
   ÷ 3 =

4,166 ÷ 5
   ÷ 5 =

5,555 ÷ 9
   ÷ 9 =

5,587 ÷ 7
   ÷ 7 =

1,580 ÷ 2
   ÷ 2 =

Estimate the quotient.

4,942 ÷ 7		8,208 ÷ 9		5,124 ÷ 5	
3,712 ÷ 4		5,602 ÷ 6		2,275 ÷ 8	
1,651 ÷ 3		4,143 ÷ 4		4,867 ÷ 9	
7,153 ÷ 8		1,775 ÷ 2		3,294 ÷ 7	
3,572 ÷ 6		2,896 ÷ 5		3,175 ÷ 4	
1,472 ÷ 3		4,379 ÷ 6		2,987 ÷ 8	
1,972 ÷ 4		3,672 ÷ 7		4,486 ÷ 9	
2,687 ÷ 5		6,500 ÷ 8		2,895 ÷ 3	

Rounding mixed numbers

Round to the closest whole number

$2\frac{5}{6}$

$\frac{5}{6}$ is more than $\frac{1}{2}$

$2\frac{5}{6}$ rounds up to 3

$3\frac{2}{5}$

$\frac{2}{5}$ is less than $\frac{1}{2}$

$3\frac{2}{5}$ rounds down to 3

DON'T FIDDLE WITH FRACTIONS!

Circle the fractions that are more than $\frac{1}{2}$.

$\frac{1}{7}$ $\frac{3}{8}$ $\frac{5}{9}$ $\frac{7}{10}$ $\frac{2}{9}$ $\frac{3}{8}$ $\frac{6}{7}$ $\frac{2}{3}$

$\frac{5}{6}$ $\frac{1}{3}$ $\frac{2}{5}$ $\frac{4}{7}$ $\frac{5}{8}$ $\frac{1}{7}$ $\frac{5}{6}$ $\frac{3}{5}$

Circle the fractions that are less than $\frac{1}{2}$.

$\frac{2}{5}$ $\frac{2}{7}$ $\frac{3}{4}$ $\frac{3}{10}$ $\frac{6}{7}$ $\frac{2}{5}$ $\frac{5}{8}$ $\frac{1}{8}$

$\frac{2}{3}$ $\frac{4}{9}$ $\frac{1}{5}$ $\frac{1}{4}$ $\frac{6}{10}$ $\frac{3}{7}$ $\frac{3}{8}$ $\frac{6}{9}$

Round to the closest whole number.

$6\frac{3}{4}$ ☐ $1\frac{1}{3}$ ☐ $5\frac{3}{8}$ ☐ $3\frac{2}{9}$ ☐

$2\frac{4}{5}$ ☐ $4\frac{7}{8}$ ☐ $4\frac{1}{4}$ ☐ $5\frac{1}{7}$ ☐

$5\frac{2}{5}$ ☐ $3\frac{2}{7}$ ☐ $7\frac{1}{3}$ ☐ $6\frac{9}{13}$ ☐

$7\frac{3}{9}$ ☐ $1\frac{1}{4}$ ☐ $3\frac{3}{5}$ ☐ $5\frac{7}{12}$ ☐

$4\frac{3}{5}$ ☐ $2\frac{2}{3}$ ☐ $1\frac{3}{8}$ ☐ $6\frac{5}{7}$ ☐

Calculate the mean

What is the mean of 6 and 10?

$(6 + 10) \div 2 = 8$

Tim, Tom, and Joe are Batman fans. Tim is 9, Tom is 10, and Joe is 5. What is their mean age?

$(9 + 10 + 5) \div 3 = 8$

Calculate the mean of these amounts.

8 and 4

9 and 3

6 and 12

CALCULATE THE MEAN? WHO'S MEAN AROUND HERE?

13 and 15

17 and 21

20 and 60

Calculate the mean of these amounts.

3, 5, and 7

5, 9, and 13

4, 8, and 12

4, 10, and 16

20, 35, and 65

$1, $1.50, $2.50, and $3

3¢, 9¢, 12¢, and 16¢

5 g, 7 g, 8 g, and 8 g

The mean of two numbers is 9. If one of the numbers is 8, what is the other number?

The mean of three numbers is 4. If two of the numbers are 3 and 4, what is the other number?

The mean of three numbers is 5. If two of the numbers are 5 and 7, what is the other number?

The mean of four numbers is 7. If three of the numbers are 6, 5, and 12, what is the other number?

Mean, median, and mode

Harley Quinn thows a dice 7 times. Here are her results: 4, 2, 1, 2, 4, 2, 6

What is the mean? $(4 + 2 + 1 + 2 + 4 + 2 + 6) \div 7 = 3$

What is the median? Put the numbers in order of size and find the middle number, example: 1, 2, 2, 2, 4, 4, 6.

The median is 2.

What is the mode?   The most common result, which is 2.

In 11 spelling tests, Robin scored the following:
15, 12, 15, 17, 11, 16, 19, 11, 3, 11, 13

What is his mean score?

What is his median score?

Write down the mode for his scores.

Gotham City soccer team scores the following number of goals in their first 9 matches: 2, 2, 1, 3, 2, 1, 2, 4, 1

What is the mean score?

What is the median score?

Write down the mode for their scores.

The Joker sets out cards in 11 piles.
The numbers of cards in each piles is: 17, 15, 19, 17, 18, 19, 21, 17, 16, 22, 17

What is the mean number?   What is the median number in a pile?

What is the mode number of cards?

Line graphs

Look at this graph.

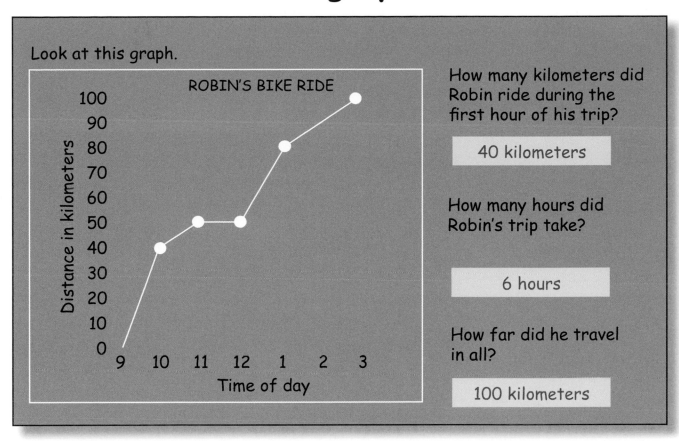

ROBIN'S BIKE RIDE

Distance in kilometers

100
90
80
70
60
50
40
30
20
10
0

9   10   11   12   1   2   3

Time of day

How many kilometers did Robin ride during the first hour of his trip?

40 kilometers

How many hours did Robin's trip take?

6 hours

How far did he travel in all?

100 kilometers

Robin stopped for lunch for one hour. What time did he stop?

Did Robin cover more distance between 12 and 1 or between 1 and 2?

Between which two hours did Robin travel 10 kilometers?

Did Robin travel farther before or after his lunch break?

How much longer did it take Robin to ride 50 kilometers after lunch?

During which hours did Robin ride the fastest?

I'VE GOTTA GET TO THE CRIME SCENE IN TIME...

Coordinates

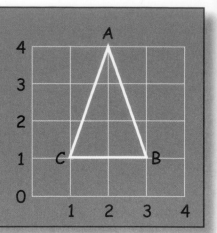

Write the coordinates of:

A (2,4)

B (3,1)

C (1,1)

KEEP COORDINATED!

Write the coordinates of:

A	B	C	D	E
F	G	H	I	J
K	L	M	N	O
P	Q	R	S	T

Plot these points on the grid, and connect them up in the right order.

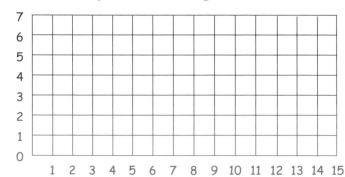

(0,1) (1,3) (3,3) (5,1) (0,1)
What shape does this make?

(3,6) (5,7) (9,2) (8,1) (3,6)
What shape does this make?

(11,3) (13,5) (15,3) (13,1) (11,3)
What shape does this make?

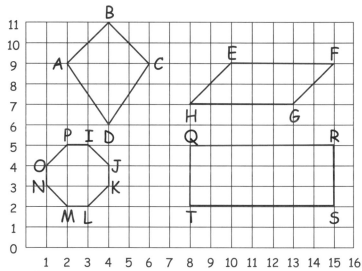

Drawing angles

Acute angles are between 0° and 90°.   Obtuse angles are between 90° and 180°.

When you get to 180° you have a straight line.

Use a protractor to draw these angles.

ACUTE OR OBTUSE? THERE'S SOME OF EACH!

110°	10°
45°	135°
150°	20°

123

Reading and writing numbers

275,346 in words is Two hundred seventy-five thousand, three hundred forty-six

One million, four hundred eleven thousand, five hundred two is 1,411,502

Write each of these numbers in words.

326,208

807,692

350,904

297,461

Write each of these words in numbers.

Five hundred seventeen thousand, forty-two

Eight hundred sixty-four thousand, four hundred eleven

Three hundred seven thousand, two hundred eight

Seven hundred thousand, four hundred four

Write each of these numbers in words.

8,405,013

4,052,434

8,904,152

7,500,632

Write each of these words in numbers.

Six million, three hundred sixty-one

Three million, fifty thousand, five hundred five

Seven million, three hundred forty-nine thousand, seven

Multiplying and dividing by 10

Write the answer in the box.

27 x 10 = 270

40 ÷ 10 = 4

PRACTICE MAKES PERFECT!

Write the product in the box.

84 x 10 = ⬜   35 x 10 = ⬜   72 x 10 = ⬜

77 x 10 = ⬜   18 x 10 = ⬜   56 x 10 = ⬜

156 x 10 = ⬜   274 x 10 = ⬜   372 x 10 = ⬜

387 x 10 = ⬜   928 x 10 = ⬜   495 x 10 = ⬜

Write the quotient in the box.

30 ÷ 10 = ⬜   60 ÷ 10 = ⬜   40 ÷ 10 = ⬜

70 ÷ 10 = ⬜   100 ÷ 10 = ⬜   360 ÷ 10 = ⬜

420 ÷ 10 = ⬜   930 ÷ 10 = ⬜   750 ÷ 10 = ⬜

840 ÷ 10 = ⬜   270 ÷ 10 = ⬜   470 ÷ 10 = ⬜

Write the product in the box.

⬜ x 10 = 720   ⬜ x 10 = 120   ⬜ x 10 = 370

⬜ x 10 = 650   ⬜ x 10 = 830   ⬜ x 10 = 290

⬜ x 10 = 3,720   ⬜ x 10 = 1,650   ⬜ x 10 = 8,140

⬜ x 10 = 8,460   ⬜ x 10 = 9,320   ⬜ x 10 = 6,350

Write the quotient in the box.

⬜ ÷ 10 = 6   ⬜ ÷ 10 = 1   ⬜ ÷ 10 = 20

⬜ ÷ 10 = 49   ⬜ ÷ 10 = 94   ⬜ ÷ 10 = 78

Identifying patterns

Continue each pattern.

Steps of 9:	5	14	23	32	41	50
Steps of 14:	20	34	48	62	76	90

Continue each pattern.

4	34	64				
10	61	112				
48	100	152				
20	37	54				
25	100	175		400		
25	45	65				165
8	107	206				
7	25	43				
22	72	122	222			
60	165	270				
13	37	61		133		
11	30	49				
32	48	64				
36	126	216		486		
32	54	76				186
26	127	228				
12	72	132				432
32	50	68				

Recognizing multiples of 6, 7, and 8

Multiples are found by multiplying one number by another.
Circle all the multiples of 6.

8   (12)   15   (18)   20   (24)

Circle all the multiples of 6.

20	32	62	6	42	34
24	10	38	72	16	60
14	22	44	8	30	18
66	64	52	25	54	28

Circle all the multiples of 7.

27	34	49	36	47	35
21	60	58	19	56	26
28	73	40	46	23	63
18	25	14	37	69	27

Circle all the multiples of 8.

50	32	62	12	16	25
56	18	38	28	60	24
34	72	48	44	82	14
22	54	70	40	64	80

Circle the number that is a multiple of 6 and 7.

24	35	42	62	70	72

Circle all the numbers that are multiples of both 6 and 8.

16	24	28	48	54	60

THE MULTIPLES
KEEP
MULTIPLYING!

Factors of numbers from 1 to 30

The factors of 10 are the numbers that divide evenly into 10:

| 1 | 2 | 5 | 10 |

Circle the factors of 4:

(1) (2) 3 (4)

Write all the factors of each number.

The factors of 15 are

The factors of 12 are

The factors of 9 are

The factors of 20 are

The factors of 30 are

The factors of 22 are

The factors of 24 are

The factors of 26 are

YOUR TURN NOW.

Circle all the factors of each number.

Which numbers are factors of 14?   1 2 3 5 7 9 12 14

Which numbers are factors of 13?   1 3 4 5 6 7 8 9 10 12 13

Which numbers are factors of 7?   1 2 3 4 5 6 7

Which numbers are factors of 11?   1 2 3 4 5 6 7 8 9 10 11

Which numbers are factors of 6?   1 2 3 4 5 6

Which numbers are factors of 8?   1 2 3 4 5 6 7 8

Which numbers are factors of 17?   1 2 5 7 8 9 11 17

Which numbers are factors of 18?   1 2 3 4 5 6 8 9 10 12 18

Some numbers only have factors of 1 and themselves; they are called prime numbers. Write down all the prime numbers that are less than 30.

Recognizing equivalent fractions

Make each pair of fractions equal by writing a number in the box.

$$\frac{1^{\times 2}}{2_{\times 2}} = \frac{2}{4} \qquad \frac{1^{\times 3}}{3_{\times 3}} = \frac{3}{9}$$

NOW THE FRACTIONS ARE MULTIPLYING!

Make each pair of fractions equal by writing a number in the box.

$$\frac{1}{2} = \frac{\boxed{}}{6} \qquad \frac{3}{4} = \frac{\boxed{}}{12} \qquad \frac{1}{3} = \frac{\boxed{}}{12}$$

$$\frac{2}{3} = \frac{\boxed{}}{9} \qquad \frac{6}{12} = \frac{\boxed{}}{4} \qquad \frac{4}{8} = \frac{\boxed{}}{2}$$

$$\frac{1}{5} = \frac{\boxed{}}{20} \qquad \frac{4}{12} = \frac{\boxed{}}{6} \qquad \frac{3}{5} = \frac{\boxed{}}{10}$$

$$\frac{1}{4} = \frac{\boxed{}}{8} \qquad \frac{6}{18} = \frac{\boxed{}}{9} \qquad \frac{3}{12} = \frac{\boxed{}}{4}$$

$$\frac{3}{9} = \frac{6}{\boxed{}} \qquad \frac{4}{10} = \frac{2}{\boxed{}} \qquad \frac{3}{4} = \frac{15}{\boxed{}}$$

$$\frac{4}{16} = \frac{2}{\boxed{}} \qquad \frac{9}{12} = \frac{3}{\boxed{}} \qquad \frac{6}{12} = \frac{2}{\boxed{}}$$

$$\frac{3}{5} = \frac{6}{\boxed{}} \qquad \frac{2}{6} = \frac{1}{\boxed{}} \qquad \frac{9}{12} = \frac{3}{\boxed{}}$$

Make each pair of fractions equal by writing a number in the box.

$$\frac{1}{2} = \frac{\boxed{}}{4} = \frac{3}{\boxed{}} = \frac{\boxed{}}{8} = \frac{\boxed{}}{10} = \frac{6}{\boxed{}}$$

$$\frac{1}{4} = \frac{2}{\boxed{}} = \frac{\boxed{}}{12} = \frac{4}{\boxed{}} = \frac{5}{\boxed{}} = \frac{\boxed{}}{24}$$

$$\frac{3}{4} = \frac{6}{\boxed{}} = \frac{\boxed{}}{12} = \frac{12}{\boxed{}} = \frac{\boxed{}}{20} = \frac{18}{\boxed{}}$$

$$\frac{1}{3} = \frac{\boxed{}}{6} = \frac{3}{\boxed{}} = \frac{4}{\boxed{}} = \frac{\boxed{}}{15} = \frac{6}{\boxed{}}$$

$$\frac{1}{5} = \frac{\boxed{}}{10} = \frac{\boxed{}}{15} = \frac{4}{\boxed{}} = \frac{5}{\boxed{}} = \frac{\boxed{}}{30}$$

$$\frac{2}{3} = \frac{\boxed{}}{6} = \frac{\boxed{}}{9} = \frac{8}{\boxed{}} = \frac{10}{\boxed{}} = \frac{12}{\boxed{}}$$

Rounding decimals

Round each decimal to the nearest whole number.

3.4	3
5.7	6
4.5	5

REMEMBER, IF THE WHOLE NUMBER IS FOLLOWED BY 5, ROUND IT UP.

Round each decimal to the nearest whole number.

1.1		6.2		7.3		4.8	
2.8		5.8		8.6		3.7	
1.3		3.2		8.5		6.4	
6.5		4.7		0.9		2.1	

Round each decimal to the nearest whole number.

22.2		14.8		27.5		33.8	
56.2		37.8		48.2		56.7	
75.4		81.8		66.5		71.6	
98.3		42.1		19.9		36.4	

Round each decimal to the nearest whole number.

110.4		126.3		107.1		111.9	
275.3		352.7		444.4		398.7	
359.8		276.8		348.3		599.8	
673.4		785.6		543.2		987.4	
867.2		686.8		743.2		845.5	

130

Real-life problems

Write the answers in the box.

Robin has $4.50 and he is given another $3.20
How much money does she have?

$7.70

$$\begin{array}{r} 4.50 \\ +\ 3.20 \\ \hline 7.70 \end{array}$$

The Joker has 120 cards.
He divides them equally among five people.
How many cards does each person get?

24

$$\begin{array}{r} 24 \\ 5\overline{)120} \\ \underline{10} \\ 2 \\ 20 \\ \underline{20} \end{array}$$

Write the answers in the box.

The Penguin buys a top hat for
$5.50 and an umbrella for $6.65.
How much does he spend?

How much does he have left
from $20?

The 32 children in a class bring in $5 each for a school trip.
What is the total of the amount brought in?

A set of 5 shelves can be made from a piece of wood 4 yards long.
What fraction of a yard will each shelf be?

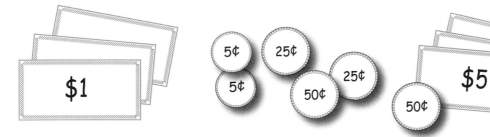

Each of 5 children has $18.
How much do they have altogether?

If the above total were shared among 9 children, how much would
each child have?

Real-life problems

A box is 16 in. wide. How wide will six boxes side by side be?

96 in.

$$\begin{array}{r} \overset{3}{16} \\ \times\ \ 6 \\ \hline 96 \end{array}$$

Robin is 1.20 m tall. His friend is 1.55 m tall. How much taller than Robin is his friend?

0.35 m

$$\begin{array}{r} 1.55 \\ -\ 1.20 \\ \hline 0.35 \end{array}$$

A pitcher contains 800 ml of lemonade. If 320 ml is poured into a glass, how much is left in the pitcher?

A giant bat weighs 280 g. A smaller bat weighs 130 g. How much heavier is the giant bat than the smaller bat?

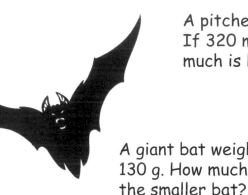

There are 7 shelves of comics. 5 shelves are 1.2 m long. 2 shelves are 1.5 m long. What is the total length of the 7 shelves.

Robin has read 5 pages of a 20-page comic book. If it has taken him 9 minutes, how long is it likely to take him to read the whole comic book?

Bruce Wayne is signing letters at his office in Wayne Enterprises. If he can sign 36 letters in a minute, how many can he sign in 30 seconds?

Problems involving time

Find the answer to this problem.

A train leaves the station at 7:30 A.M. and arrives at the end of the line at 10:45 A.M. How long did the journey take?

3 hours 15 minutes

7:30 → 10:30 = 3 h

10:30 → 10:45 = 15 min

Total = 3 h 15 min

Find the answer to each problem

Alfred's cake takes 2 hours 25 minutes to bake. If he began to bake it at 1:35 P.M. at what time was the cake cooked?

A film starts at 7:00 P.M. and finishes at 8:45 P.M. How long is the film?

Commissioner Gordon takes his car in for a repair at 7:00 A.M. It is finished at 1:50 P.M. How long did the repair take?

Robin needs to clean the Bat-Costume vault in the Batcave and wash the Batmobile. It takes him 1 hour 10 minutes to clean the vault and 45 minutes to wash the Batmobile. If he starts at 10:00 A.M., at what time will he finish?

Bruce Wayne has to be at work by 8:50 A.M. If he takes 1 hour 30 minutes to get ready, and the trip takes 35 minutes, at what time does he need to get up?

Elapsed time

Write the answer in the box.

10:40		11:40		12:40		1:20

1 hr → 1 hr → 40 mins →

Catwoman burgles an art gallery. She enters the building at 10:40 P.M. and leaves at 1:20 A.M. How long is she in the gallery?

2 hours 40 minutes

Write the answer in the box.

The ferry leaves Gotham City at 11:00 A.M. and docks across the river at 2:00 P.M. How long is the ride?

The movie starts at 6:05 P.M. and ends at 9:17 P.M. How long is it?

Commissioner Gordon works a 9-hour shift at the police department. If he starts work at 9 A.M., at what time is he finished?

Alfred wants to videotape a program that starts at 11:30 P.M. It lasts 1 hour and 55 minutes. What time will it end?

HOW MUCH TIME DOES A CRIME CAPER TAKE?

134

Recognizing multiples

Multiples are found by multiplying a number by another.
Circle all the multiples of 10.

14   (20)   25   (30)   47   (60)

TENS ARE THE
EASY ONES!

Circle all the multiples of 6.

20	24	56	72	26	35
1	3	6	16	32	36

Circle all the multiples of 7.

14	17	35	27	47	49
63	42	52	37	64	71

Circle all the multiples of 8.

18	54	64	35	72	8
25	31	48	84	32	28

Circle all the multiples of 9.

64	81	36	35	33	98
45	53	27	18	92	106

Circle all the multiples of 10.

44	37	30	29	50	100
15	35	60	46	90	45

Circle all the multiples of 11.

45	33	87	98	99	87
24	44	65	54	66	121

Circle all the multiples of 12.

23	34	48	74	24	60
72	66	29	109	108	132

Bar graphs

Use this bar graph to answer each question.

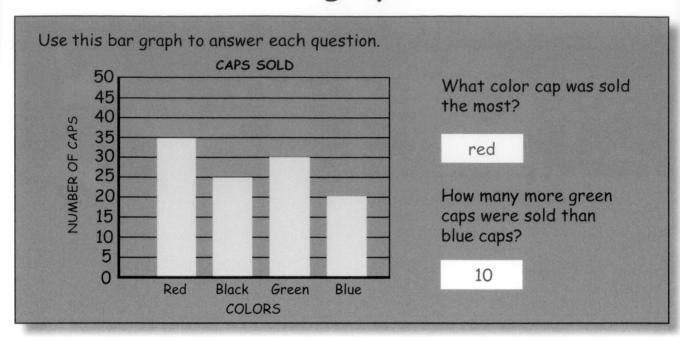

What color cap was sold the most?

red

How many more green caps were sold than blue caps?

10

Use the bar graphs to answer the questions.

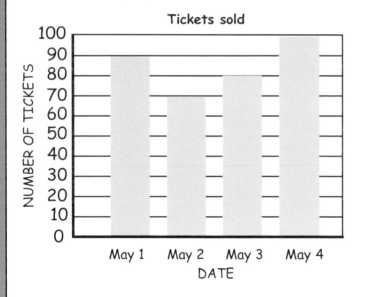

How many tickets were sold on May 4

How many more tickets were sold on May 3 than on May 2?

On which date were 90 tickets sold?

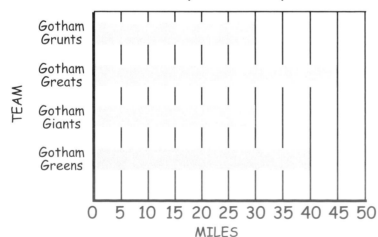

Which team ran 40 miles?

Which team ran the same distance as the Grunts?

How much farther did the Greats run than the Greens?

Triangles

Look at these different triangles.

Equilateral
(all sides equal;
is also isosceles)

Isosceles
(at least two sides
are of equal length)

Scalene
(all sides
different)

Right angle
(may be isosceles or
scalene, but one angle
must be a right angle)

1	2	3	4
5	6	7	8
9	10	11	12

List the triangles that are:

Equilateral _____

Isoceles _____

Scalene _____

Right Angle _____

LOTS OF TRIANGLES. (I PREFER
DIAMONDS, MYSELF.)

137

Place value to 10,000,000

| How many hundreds are there in 7,000? | 70 | hundreds (70 x 100 = 7,000) |
| What is the value of the 9 in 694? | 90 | (because the 9 is in the tens column) |

Write how many tens there are in:

200	tens	800	tens	400	tens
500	tens	1,400	tens	4,600	tens
5,300	tens	1,240	tens	1,320	tens
2,700	tens	5,930	tens	4,530	tens

What is the value of the 8 in these numbers?

| 86 | | 820 | | 138 | |
| 8,122 | | 84,301 | | 124,382 | |

What is the value of the 3 in these numbers?

| 324,126 | | 3,927,142 | | 214,623 | |
| 8,254,320 | | 3,711,999 | | 124,372 | |

How many hundreds are there in:

| 6,500 | hundreds | 524,600 | hundreds |
| 18,800 | hundreds | 712,400 | hundreds |

What is the value of the 9 in these numbers?

| 9,214,631 | | 2,389,147 | | 463,946 | |
| 297,034 | | 9,110,827 | | 105,429 | |

Multiplying and dividing by 10

To multiply by 10, add a zero. To divide by 10, move the decimal point one place to the left. Write the answer in the box.

42 x 10 = [420]

68 ÷ 10 = [6.8]

Write the product in the box.

SOMETIMES, ALL YOU NEED IS A ZERO...

84 x 10 =

13 x 10 =

36 x 10 =

58 x 10 =

54 x 10 =

256 x 10 =

412 x 10 =

836 x 10 =

4,700 x 10 =

687 x 10 =

2,145 x 10 =

Write the quotient in the box.

82 ÷ 10 =

58 ÷ 10 =

38 ÷ 10 =

19 ÷ 10 =

79 ÷ 10 =

82 ÷ 10 =

245 ÷ 10 =

367 ÷ 10 =

279 ÷ 10 =

379 ÷ 10 =

924 ÷ 10 =

674 ÷ 10 =

Find the missing factor.

x 10 = 240

x 10 = 750

x 10 = 990

x 10 = 370

x 10 = 140

x 10 = 350

x 10 = 550

x 10 = 870

x 10 = 760

Find the dividend.

÷ 10 = 4.7

÷ 10 = 7.8

÷ 10 = 4.7

÷ 10 = 25.7

÷ 10 = 9.9

÷ 10 = 80.7

÷ 10 = 40.9

÷ 10 = 67.9

÷ 10 = 26.9

Appropriate units of measure

Choose the best units to measure the length of each item.

inches	feet	yards

notebook	car	swimming pool
inches	feet	yards

Choose the best units to measure the length of each item.

inches	feet	yards

TV set	bicycle	toothbrush	football field

shoe	backyard	canoe	fence

The height of a door is about 7 _____

The length of a pencil is about 7 _____

The height of a flagpole is about 7 _____

Choose the best units to measure the weight of each item.

ounces	pounds	tons

kitten	train	tomato

hamburger	elephant	refrigerator	sweatshirt

The weight of a tennis ball is about 2 _____

The weight of a bag of potatoes is about 5 _____

The weight of a truck is about 4 _____

HOW DO YOU MEASURE UP?

140

Identifying patterns

Continue each pattern.

Intervals of 6:	1	7	13	19	25	31
Intervals of 3:	27	24	21	18	15	12

Continue each pattern.

0	10	20				
5	10	15				
3	5	7				
3	10	17				
4	7	10			19	
1	9	17		33		

Continue each pattern.

46	42	38				
33	29	25				
65	60	55				
50	43	36			15	
28	25	22				
49	42	35				7

Continue each pattern.

5	7	9		13		
56	53	50				
3	8	13				
47	40	33			12	
1	4	7				
81	72	63				

JUST FOLLOW THE PATTERN!

141

Factors of numbers from 31 to 65

Factors are numbers that divide evenly into another number.

The factors of 40 are: | 1 | 2 | 4 | 5 | 8 | 10 | 20 | 40

Circle the factors of 56:

(1) (2) 3 (4) 5 6 (7) (8) (14) (28) 32 (56)

Find all the factors of each number.

The factors of 31 are

The factors of 47 are

The factors of 35 are

The factors of 50 are

The factors of 42 are

The factors of 52 are

The factors of 48 are

The factors of 60 are

YOU NEED A SYSTEM!

Circle all the factors of each number.

Which numbers are factors of 39?

1   2   3   4   5   6   7   8   10   11   12   13   14   39

Which numbers are factors of 45?

1   3   4   5   8   9   12   15   16   21   24   36   40   44   45

Which numbers are factors of 61?

1   3   4   5   6   10   15   16   18   20   24   29   30   61

Which numbers are factors of 65?

1   2   4   5   6   8   9   10   12   13   14   15   30   60   65

Some numbers have only factors of 1 and themselves. They are called prime numbers. Write all the prime numbers between 31 and 65 in the box.

Greatest common factor

Circle the common factors. Find the greatest common factor (GCF).

24: 1, 2, 3, 4, 6, 8, 12, 24

60: 1, 2, 3, 4, 5, 6, 8, 10, 12, 60

42: 1, 2, 3, 6, 7, 14   The GCF is 6

HA! HA! YOU CAN RUN RINGS AROUND THEM!

Circle the common factors.

45:

1, 3, 5, 9, 15, 45

36:

1, 2, 3, 4, 6, 9, 12, 18, 36

28:

1, 2, 4, 7, 14, 28

54:

1, 2, 3, 6, 9, 18, 27, 54

Circle the common factors. Write the GCF .

35:

1, 5, 7, 35

The GCF is

80:

1, 2, 4, 5, 8, 10, 16, 20, 40, 80

32:

1, 2, 4, 8, 16, 32

The GCF is

64:

1, 2, 4, 8, 16, 32, 64

Circle the common factors. Write the GCF.

12:

1, 2, 3, 4, 6, 12

The GCF is

48:

1, 2, 3, 4, 6, 8, 12, 24, 48

15:

1, 3, 5, 15

18:

1, 2, 3, 6, 9, 18

The GCF is

72:

1, 2, 3, 4, 6, 8,

9, 12, 18, 24, 36, 72

54:

1, 2, 3, 6, 9, 18,

27, 54

Writing equivalent fractions

Make these fractions equal by writing in the missing number.

$$\frac{20^{\div 10}}{200_{\div 10}} = \frac{2^{\div 2}}{10_{\div 2}} = \frac{1}{5} \qquad\qquad \frac{1^{\times 2}}{4_{\times 2}} = \frac{2}{8}$$

Make these fractions equal by writing in the missing number.

$\dfrac{10}{100} = \dfrac{\boxed{}}{10}$ $\qquad$ $\dfrac{3}{5} = \dfrac{\boxed{}}{10}$ $\qquad$ $\dfrac{5}{100} = \dfrac{\boxed{}}{20}$

$\dfrac{2}{20} = \dfrac{\boxed{}}{10}$ $\qquad$ $\dfrac{2}{3} = \dfrac{\boxed{}}{12}$ $\qquad$ $\dfrac{2}{8} = \dfrac{\boxed{}}{4}$

$\dfrac{11}{12} = \dfrac{\boxed{}}{24}$ $\qquad$ $\dfrac{5}{6} = \dfrac{\boxed{}}{18}$ $\qquad$ $\dfrac{6}{20} = \dfrac{\boxed{}}{10}$

$\dfrac{2}{12} = \dfrac{\boxed{}}{6}$ $\qquad$ $\dfrac{9}{15} = \dfrac{\boxed{}}{5}$ $\qquad$ $\dfrac{5}{8} = \dfrac{10}{\boxed{}}$

$\dfrac{7}{8} = \dfrac{28}{\boxed{}}$ $\qquad$ $\dfrac{5}{20} = \dfrac{1}{\boxed{}}$ $\qquad$ $\dfrac{6}{24} = \dfrac{1}{\boxed{}}$

$\dfrac{5}{25} = \dfrac{1}{\boxed{}}$ $\qquad$ $\dfrac{25}{100} = \dfrac{5}{\boxed{}}$ $\qquad$ $\dfrac{1}{5} = \dfrac{2}{\boxed{}}$

$\dfrac{5}{30} = \dfrac{1}{\boxed{}}$ $\qquad$ $\dfrac{12}{14} = \dfrac{6}{\boxed{}}$ $\qquad$ $\dfrac{25}{30} = \dfrac{5}{\boxed{}}$

$\dfrac{9}{18} = \dfrac{1}{\boxed{}}$ $\qquad$ $\dfrac{40}{100} = \dfrac{2}{\boxed{}}$ $\qquad$ $\dfrac{1}{3} = \dfrac{5}{\boxed{}}$

$\dfrac{3}{8} = \dfrac{9}{\boxed{}}$ $\qquad$ $\dfrac{4}{100} = \dfrac{1}{\boxed{}}$

$\dfrac{1}{8} = \dfrac{\boxed{}}{16} = \dfrac{3}{\boxed{}} = \dfrac{\boxed{}}{32} = \dfrac{\boxed{}}{40} = \dfrac{6}{\boxed{}}$

$\dfrac{20}{100} = \dfrac{\boxed{}}{25} = \dfrac{2}{\boxed{}} = \dfrac{1}{\boxed{}} = \dfrac{\boxed{}}{50} = \dfrac{\boxed{}}{200}$

$\dfrac{2}{5} = \dfrac{6}{\boxed{}} = \dfrac{\boxed{}}{20} = \dfrac{4}{\boxed{}} = \dfrac{\boxed{}}{50} = \dfrac{40}{\boxed{}}$

$\dfrac{1}{6} = \dfrac{\boxed{}}{12} = \dfrac{3}{\boxed{}} = \dfrac{4}{\boxed{}} = \dfrac{5}{\boxed{}} = \dfrac{6}{\boxed{}}$

$\dfrac{2}{3} = \dfrac{\boxed{}}{24} = \dfrac{\boxed{}}{36} = \dfrac{\boxed{}}{21} = \dfrac{6}{\boxed{}} = \dfrac{\boxed{}}{300}$

Fraction models

Write the missing numbers to show
what part is shaded.

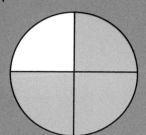

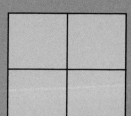

$$\frac{4}{4} = \boxed{1} \qquad \frac{2}{4} = \frac{1}{2}$$

$$\boxed{3} \text{ shaded parts} \over \boxed{4} \text{ parts} = \frac{3}{4}$$

So, shaded part = $1\frac{1}{\boxed{2}}$

Write the missing numbers to show what part is shaded.

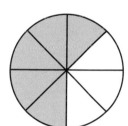

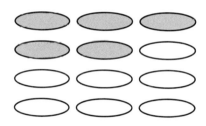

$$\frac{}{9} \qquad \frac{2}{}$$

Write the fraction for the part that is shaded.

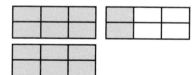

$$\square \text{ or } \square \qquad \square\square \text{ or } \square\square \qquad \square\square \text{ or } \square\square$$

Write the fraction for the part that is shaded.

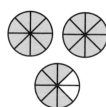

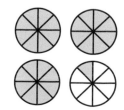

$$\square\square \text{ or } \square\square \qquad \square\square \text{ or } \square\square \qquad \square\square$$

Multiplying by one-digit numbers

Find each product. Remember to regroup.

$$
\begin{array}{r}
{\scriptstyle 1\ 1}\\
465\\
\times\quad 3\\
\hline
\boxed{1{,}395}
\end{array}
\qquad
\begin{array}{r}
{\scriptstyle 3}\\
391\\
\times\quad 4\\
\hline
\boxed{1{,}564}
\end{array}
\qquad
\begin{array}{r}
{\scriptstyle 3\ 4}\\
278\\
\times\quad 5\\
\hline
\boxed{1{,}390}
\end{array}
$$

ARE YOU GETTING FASTER?

Find each product.

$$
\begin{array}{r}
573\\
\times\ 3\\
\hline
\end{array}
\qquad
\begin{array}{r}
920\\
\times\ 2\\
\hline
\end{array}
\qquad
\begin{array}{r}
438\\
\times\ 3\\
\hline
\end{array}
\qquad
\begin{array}{r}
813\\
\times\ 2\\
\hline
\end{array}
$$

$$
\begin{array}{r}
582\\
\times\ 4\\
\hline
\end{array}
\qquad
\begin{array}{r}
832\\
\times\ 3\\
\hline
\end{array}
\qquad
\begin{array}{r}
405\\
\times\ 5\\
\hline
\end{array}
\qquad
\begin{array}{r}
396\\
\times\ 6\\
\hline
\end{array}
$$

Find each product.

$$
\begin{array}{r}
317\\
\times\ 3\\
\hline
\end{array}
\qquad
\begin{array}{r}
224\\
\times\ 3\\
\hline
\end{array}
\qquad
\begin{array}{r}
543\\
\times\ 4\\
\hline
\end{array}
\qquad
\begin{array}{r}
218\\
\times\ 3\\
\hline
\end{array}
$$

$$
\begin{array}{r}
128\\
\times\ 4\\
\hline
\end{array}
\qquad
\begin{array}{r}
276\\
\times\ 5\\
\hline
\end{array}
\qquad
\begin{array}{r}
798\\
\times\ 6\\
\hline
\end{array}
\qquad
\begin{array}{r}
365\\
\times\ 6\\
\hline
\end{array}
$$

$$
\begin{array}{r}
100\\
\times\ 5\\
\hline
\end{array}
\qquad
\begin{array}{r}
373\\
\times\ 4\\
\hline
\end{array}
\qquad
\begin{array}{r}
882\\
\times\ 4\\
\hline
\end{array}
\qquad
\begin{array}{r}
954\\
\times\ 3\\
\hline
\end{array}
$$

Solve each problem.

Gotham middle school has 255 students. The high school has 6 times as many students. How many students are there at the high school?

A train can carry 375 passengers. How many can it carry on four trips?

six trips?

Multiplying by one-digit numbers

Find each product. Remember to regroup.

$$\begin{array}{r} \overset{3\ 3}{465} \\ \times\ \ 6 \\ \hline 2{,}790 \end{array}$$

$$\begin{array}{r} \overset{1\ 2}{823} \\ \times\ \ 8 \\ \hline 6{,}584 \end{array}$$

$$\begin{array}{r} \overset{4\ 4}{755} \\ \times\ \ 9 \\ \hline 6{,}795 \end{array}$$

BIGGER AND BETTER!

Find each product.

$$\begin{array}{r} 395 \\ \times\ \ 7 \\ \hline \end{array}$$
$$\begin{array}{r} 734 \\ \times\ \ 8 \\ \hline \end{array}$$
$$\begin{array}{r} 826 \\ \times\ \ 8 \\ \hline \end{array}$$
$$\begin{array}{r} 943 \\ \times\ \ 9 \\ \hline \end{array}$$

$$\begin{array}{r} 643 \\ \times\ \ 7 \\ \hline \end{array}$$
$$\begin{array}{r} 199 \\ \times\ \ 6 \\ \hline \end{array}$$
$$\begin{array}{r} 823 \\ \times\ \ 7 \\ \hline \end{array}$$
$$\begin{array}{r} 546 \\ \times\ \ 8 \\ \hline \end{array}$$

Find each product.

$$\begin{array}{r} 502 \\ \times\ \ 7 \\ \hline \end{array}$$
$$\begin{array}{r} 377 \\ \times\ \ 8 \\ \hline \end{array}$$
$$\begin{array}{r} 845 \\ \times\ \ 8 \\ \hline \end{array}$$
$$\begin{array}{r} 222 \\ \times\ \ 9 \\ \hline \end{array}$$

$$\begin{array}{r} 473 \\ \times\ \ 9 \\ \hline \end{array}$$
$$\begin{array}{r} 224 \\ \times\ \ 8 \\ \hline \end{array}$$
$$\begin{array}{r} 606 \\ \times\ \ 6 \\ \hline \end{array}$$
$$\begin{array}{r} 514 \\ \times\ \ 7 \\ \hline \end{array}$$

$$\begin{array}{r} 500 \\ \times\ \ 9 \\ \hline \end{array}$$
$$\begin{array}{r} 800 \\ \times\ \ 9 \\ \hline \end{array}$$
$$\begin{array}{r} 900 \\ \times\ \ 9 \\ \hline \end{array}$$
$$\begin{array}{r} 200 \\ \times\ \ 9 \\ \hline \end{array}$$

Solve each problem.

A crate holds 230 oxygen cylinders. How many cylinders are there in 8 crates?

Commissioner Gordon drives 457 miles a month on patrol. How many miles does he drive on patrol in 6 months?

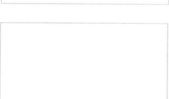

Real-life problems

Harley Quinn spent $4.68 at the store and had
$4.77 left. How much did she start with?

$9.45

$$\begin{array}{r} \overset{1\ 1}{4.77} \\ +\ 4.68 \\ \hline 9.45 \end{array}$$

Azrael receives a weekly allowance of $3.00 a week.
How much will he have if he saves all of it
for 8 weeks?

$24.00

$$\begin{array}{r} 3.00 \\ \times\ \ 8 \\ \hline 24.00 \end{array}$$

Gotham City theater charges $4 for
each matinee ticket. If the theater sells
560 tickets for a matinee performance,
how much does it take in?

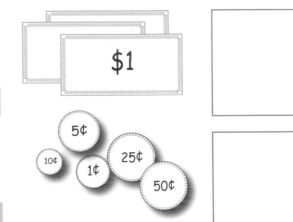

Robin has saved $9.69. His friend has
saved $3.24 less. How much does his
friend have?

The cost for 9 children to go to see a Batman film is $54.
How much does each child pay? If only 6 children go, what
will the cost be?

Harley Quinn has $2.95. The Joker
gives her another $5.25, and she goes
out and buys a coffee for $3.25. How
much does she have left?

Nightwing has $60 in savings. He
decides to spend $\frac{1}{4}$ of it. How much
will he have left?

THIS IS THE REAL WORLD!

Real-life problems

A boy has an hour to do his homework. He plans to spend $\frac{1}{3}$ of his time on math. How many minutes will he spend on math ?

20 minutes

```
1 hr = 60 min
      20
   3)60
```

In a gym class, one of the girls makes 2 long jumps of 1.78 m and 2.19 m. How far does she jump altogether?

3.97 m

```
      1
    1.78
 + 2.19
   3.97
```

Poison Ivy has a vial of poison containing 40 ml. She uses $\frac{1}{4}$ of it. How much poison is left?

Batgirl runs 40 m in 8 seconds. At that speed, how far did she run in 1 second?

A large jar of coffee contains 2.25 kg. If 1.68 kg is left in the jar, how much has been used?

The Penguin has an umbrella factory. The factory can produce 25 umbrellas in 15 minutes. How many are produced in 1 hour?

In the Batcave, the computer is 41.63 cm wide and next to it is a printer which is 48.37 cm wide. How much space is left on the shelf for a scanner if the shelf is 1.5 m wide?

Problems involving time

Alfred spends 35 minutes cleaning the Batmobile each day. How many minutes does he spend cleaning it from Monday through Friday?

175 minutes

$$\begin{array}{r} \overset{2}{35} \\ \times\ 5 \\ \hline 175 \end{array}$$

The Joker spends 175 minutes eating breakfast from Monday through Friday. How long does he spend eating breakfast each day?

35 minutes

$$5\overline{)175} \quad = 35$$

The Penguin's factory is open from 9 A.M. to 5 P.M. It closes for lunch from noon until 1 P.M. How many hours is it open during a 5-day week?

Batman patrols the city for 15 minutes every morning and 10 minutes every evening. How many minutes does he patrol in a 7-day week?

I'M ON PATROL. BUT I NEED ANSWERS.

It takes 2 hours for one person to do a job. If the work is divided equally between four people, how long will it take?

Alfred spent 7 days welding new fencing around Wayne Manor. If he worked a total of 56 hours and he divided the work equally among the seven days, how long did he work each day?

It took Robin 45 hours to build a new computer circuit. If he spent 5 hours a day working on it:

How many days did it take?

How many hours a day would he have needed to finish it in 5 days?

Multiplying and dividing

Write the answer in the box.

26 x 100 = 2,600   400 ÷ 100 = 4

Write the answer in the box.

34 x 10 =   41 x 10 =   56 x 10 =

95 x 100 =   36 x 100 =   75 x 100 =

413 x 10 =   204 x 10 =   524 x 10 =

787 x 100 =   834 x 100 =   254 x 100 =

Write the quotient in the box.

120 ÷ 10 =   260 ÷ 10 =   480 ÷ 10 =

500 ÷ 100 =   800 ÷ 10 =   700 ÷ 100 =

20 ÷ 10 =   30 ÷ 10 =   60 ÷ 10 =

800 ÷ 100 =   100 ÷ 100 =   900 ÷ 100 =

Write the number that has been multiplied by 100.

[ ] x 100 = 4,600   [ ] x 100 = 72,300

[ ] x 100 = 32,500   [ ] x 100 = 25,000

[ ] x 100 = 1,200   [ ] x 100 = 45,600

[ ] x 100 = 8,400   [ ] x 100 = 62,300

Write the number that has been divided by 100.

[ ] ÷ 100 = 3   [ ] ÷ 100 = 7

[ ] ÷ 100 = 12   [ ] ÷ 100 = 18

[ ] ÷ 100 = 87   [ ] ÷ 100 = 23

[ ] ÷ 100 = 10   [ ] ÷ 100 = 64

THIS IS VERY PRODUCTIVE.

Identifying patterns

Continue each pattern.

Steps of 2: $\frac{1}{2}$ $2\frac{1}{2}$ $4\frac{1}{2}$ $\boxed{6\frac{1}{2}}$ $\boxed{8\frac{1}{2}}$ $\boxed{10\frac{1}{2}}$

Steps of 5:   3.5   8.5   13.5 $\boxed{18.5}$ $\boxed{23.5}$ $\boxed{28.5}$

Continue each pattern.

$5\frac{1}{2}$	$10\frac{1}{2}$	$15\frac{1}{2}$		
$2\frac{1}{4}$	$4\frac{1}{4}$	$6\frac{1}{4}$		
$8\frac{1}{3}$	$9\frac{1}{3}$	$10\frac{1}{3}$	$12\frac{1}{3}$	
$65\frac{3}{4}$	$55\frac{3}{4}$	$45\frac{3}{4}$		
$44\frac{1}{2}$	$40\frac{1}{2}$	$36\frac{1}{2}$		$24\frac{1}{2}$
$4\frac{2}{3}$	$7\frac{2}{3}$	$10\frac{2}{3}$		
7.5	6.5	5.5		
29.3	26.3	23.3	17.3	
82.6	73.6	64.6		
6.4	10.4	14.4		
14.2	16.2	18.2		24.2
21.8	28.8	35.8		
$13\frac{3}{4}$	$19\frac{3}{4}$	$25\frac{3}{4}$		
57.5	48.5	39.5	21.5	
$11\frac{1}{2}$	$10\frac{1}{2}$	$9\frac{1}{2}$		$6\frac{1}{2}$
8.4	11.4	14.4		

Products with odd and even numbers

Find the product of these numbers.

3 and 4   The product of 3 and 4 is 12

6 and 7   The product of 6 and 7 is 42

AGAINST ALL ODDS, I'LL MAKE THINGS EVEN.

Find the products of these odd and even numbers.

6 and 5   2 and 3

4 and 7   3 and 8

3 and 6   9 and 2

10 and 3   5 and 12

What do you notice about your answers? _____

_____

Find the products of these odd numbers.

7 and 5   1 and 9

11 and 5   5 and 7

9 and 5   9 and 3

3 and 7   3 and 13

What do you notice about your answers? _____

_____

Find the products of these even numbers.

4 and 2   2 and 8

6 and 8   4 and 6

10 and 2   6 and 10

8 and 4   2 and 4

What do you notice about your answers? _____

_____

Can you write a rule for the products with odd and even numbers?

_____

Factors of numbers from 66 to 100

The factors of 66 are: 1   2   3   6   11   22   33   66

Circle the factors of 94:   (1)   (2)   28   32   43   (47)   71   86   (94)

Write the factors of each number in the box.

The factors of 70 are

The factors of 83 are

The factors of 63 are

The factors of 85 are

The factors of 75 are

The factors of 99 are

The factors of 69 are

The factors of 72 are

The factors of 96 are

Circle the factors.

Which numbers are factors of 68?

1   2   3   4   5   6   7   8   9   11   12   17   34   35   62   68

Which numbers are factors of 95?

1   2   3   4   5   15   16   17   19   24   59   85   90   95   96

Which numbers are factors of 88?

1   2   3   4   5   6   8   10   11   15   22   33   38   44   87   88

Which numbers are factors of 73?

1   2   3   4   6   8   9   10   12   13   14   15   37   42   73

Some numbers have only factors of 1 and themselves. They are called prime numbers. Write all the prime numbers between 66 and 100 in the box.

Multiplying by two-digit numbers

Write the product for each problem.

```
  ¹¹
  56
× 32
─────
 112
1,680
─────
1,792
```

```
  ²¹
  45
× 43
─────
 135
1,800
─────
1,935
```

NO TIME TO WASTE – START MULTIPLYING!

Write the product for each problem.

| 84 | 47 | 23 | 56 |
| × 22 | × 25 | × 24 | × 23 |

| 75 | 64 | 51 | 45 |
| × 24 | × 33 | × 32 | × 34 |

Write the product for each problem.

| 65 | 72 | 84 | 85 |
| × 54 | × 68 | × 61 | × 79 |

| 94 | 58 | 37 | 75 |
| × 63 | × 57 | × 92 | × 26 |

Multiplying by two-digit numbers

Write the product for each problem.

```
    7          7
    6          6
   39         68
 × 87       × 98
  273        544
3,120      6,120
3,393      6,664
```

LAST PAGE! JUST FILL IN THE ANSWERS!

Write the product for each problem.

```
   86         76         94         99
 × 98       × 78       × 69       × 65
```

```
   74         67         94         87
 × 33       × 76       × 79       × 49
```

Write the product for each problem.

```
   46         84         87         58
 × 67       × 71       × 79       × 63
```

```
   73         79         96
 × 98       × 87       × 78
```

GREAT WORK! YOU'VE FIGURED OUT EVERYTHING NOW.

Answer Section with Parents' Notes

Grade 5
ages 10-11
Workbook

This section provides answers to all the activities in this book. These pages will enable you to mark your children's work, or they can be used by your children if they prefer to do their own marking.

The notes for each page help explain common errors and problems and, where appropriate, indicate the kind of practice needed to ensure that your children understand where and how they have made errors.

Multiplying by 10, 100, and 1,000

LET'S GO! WRITE THE ANSWERS IN THE BOXES.

$463 \times 10 = 4,630$ $234 \times 100 = 23,400$ $81 \times 1,000 = 81,000$

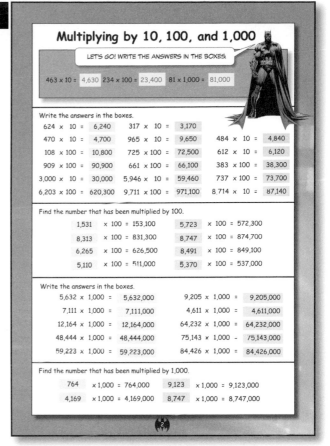

Write the answers in the boxes.

$624 \times 10 = 6,240$	$317 \times 10 = 3,170$
$470 \times 10 = 4,700$	$965 \times 10 = 9,650$ $484 \times 10 = 4,840$
$108 \times 100 = 10,800$	$725 \times 100 = 72,500$ $612 \times 10 = 6,120$
$909 \times 100 = 90,900$	$661 \times 100 = 66,100$ $383 \times 100 = 38,300$
$3,000 \times 10 = 30,000$	$5,946 \times 10 = 59,460$ $737 \times 100 = 73,700$
$6,203 \times 100 = 620,300$	$9,711 \times 100 = 971,100$ $8,714 \times 10 = 87,140$

Find the number that has been multiplied by 100.

$1,531 \times 100 = 153,100$	$5,723 \times 100 = 572,300$
$8,313 \times 100 = 831,300$	$8,747 \times 100 = 874,700$
$6,265 \times 100 = 626,500$	$8,491 \times 100 = 849,100$
$5,110 \times 100 = 511,000$	$5,370 \times 100 = 537,000$

Write the answers in the boxes.

$5,632 \times 1,000 = 5,632,000$	$9,205 \times 1,000 = 9,205,000$
$7,111 \times 1,000 = 7,111,000$	$4,611 \times 1,000 = 4,611,000$
$12,164 \times 1,000 = 12,164,000$	$64,232 \times 1,000 = 64,232,000$
$48,444 \times 1,000 = 48,444,000$	$75,143 \times 1,000 = 75,143,000$
$59,223 \times 1,000 = 59,223,000$	$84,426 \times 1,000 = 84,426,000$

Find the number that has been multiplied by 1,000.

$764 \times 1,000 = 764,000$	$9,123 \times 1,000 = 9,123,000$
$4,169 \times 1,000 = 4,169,000$	$8,747 \times 1,000 = 8,747,000$

Children should realize that multiplying by 10, 100, or 1,000 is the same as adding one, two, or three zeros. In the second and last sections, the child will need to divide the answer to find the number that has been multiplied.

3

The simplest form of fractions

Make these fractions equivalent by putting a number in each box. $\frac{60}{100} = \frac{6}{10}$ $\frac{3}{12} = \frac{1}{4}$

Make these fractions equivalent by putting a number in each box.

$\frac{30}{100} = \frac{3}{10}$	$\frac{80}{100} = \frac{20}{25}$	$\frac{80}{100} = \frac{8}{10}$	$\frac{15}{100} = \frac{3}{20}$
$\frac{5}{25} = \frac{1}{5}$	$\frac{25}{100} = \frac{1}{4}$	$\frac{12}{60} = \frac{1}{5}$	$\frac{8}{20} = \frac{2}{5}$
$\frac{10}{40} = \frac{2}{8}$	$\frac{2}{6} = \frac{1}{3}$	$\frac{10}{50} = \frac{1}{5}$	$\frac{2}{14} = \frac{1}{7}$
$\frac{4}{6} = \frac{2}{3}$	$\frac{10}{18} = \frac{5}{9}$	$\frac{4}{24} = \frac{1}{6}$	$\frac{7}{28} = \frac{1}{4}$
$\frac{9}{18} = \frac{1}{2}$	$\frac{6}{10} = \frac{3}{5}$	$\frac{12}{15} = \frac{4}{5}$	$\frac{8}{12} = \frac{2}{3}$
$\frac{9}{15} = \frac{3}{5}$	$\frac{21}{28} = \frac{3}{4}$	$\frac{6}{8} = \frac{3}{4}$	$\frac{4}{20} = \frac{1}{5}$
$\frac{20}{25} = \frac{4}{5}$	$\frac{12}{16} = \frac{3}{4}$	$\frac{2}{6} = \frac{1}{3}$	$\frac{15}{21} = \frac{5}{7}$
$\frac{6}{15} = \frac{2}{5}$	$\frac{3}{18} = \frac{1}{6}$	$\frac{4}{12} = \frac{1}{3}$	$\frac{8}{20} = \frac{4}{10}$

Write the answers in the boxes.

EQUALIZE THIS!

$\frac{1}{9} = \frac{2}{18} = \frac{3}{27} = \frac{4}{36} = \frac{5}{45} = \frac{6}{54}$

$\frac{1}{10} = \frac{2}{20} = \frac{3}{30} = \frac{4}{40} = \frac{5}{50} = \frac{6}{60}$

$\frac{3}{5} = \frac{12}{20} = \frac{15}{25} = \frac{18}{30} = \frac{21}{35} = \frac{24}{40}$

$\frac{5}{6} = \frac{10}{12} = \frac{15}{18} = \frac{20}{24} = \frac{25}{30} = \frac{30}{36}$

$\frac{3}{4} = \frac{6}{8} = \frac{12}{16} = \frac{15}{20} = \frac{18}{24} = \frac{21}{28}$

$\frac{1}{7} = \frac{2}{14} = \frac{3}{21} = \frac{4}{28} = \frac{5}{35} = \frac{6}{42}$

If children have problems with this page, explain to them that fractions remain the same as long as you multiply or divide the numerator and denominator by the same number.

Improper fractions and mixed numbers

THERE'S SOMETHING IMPROPER HERE!

Change this improper fraction to a mixed number. Don't forget you may need to reduce.

$\frac{27}{12} = 27 \div 12 = 2 \, r \, 0 = 2\frac{3}{12} = 2\frac{3 \div 3}{12 \div 4} = 2\frac{1}{4}$

Change these mixed numbers to improper fractions.

$1\frac{3}{4} = \frac{(1 \times 4) + 3}{4} = \frac{7}{4}$ $6\frac{1}{2} = \frac{(6 \times 2) + 1}{2} = \frac{13}{2}$

Change these improper fractions to mixed numbers.

$\frac{8}{3} = 2\frac{2}{3}$	$\frac{29}{12} = 2\frac{5}{12}$	$\frac{36}{7} = 5\frac{1}{7}$
$\frac{19}{6} = 3\frac{1}{6}$	$\frac{13}{9} = 1\frac{4}{9}$	$\frac{14}{5} = 2\frac{4}{5}$
$\frac{22}{5} = 4\frac{2}{5}$	$\frac{23}{3} = 7\frac{2}{3}$	$\frac{8}{5} = 1\frac{3}{5}$
$\frac{7}{2} = 3\frac{1}{2}$	$\frac{21}{2} = 10\frac{1}{2}$	$\frac{15}{4} = 3\frac{3}{4}$
$\frac{22}{4} = 5\frac{1}{2}$	$\frac{18}{8} = 2\frac{1}{4}$	$\frac{42}{9} = 4\frac{2}{3}$

Change these mixed numbers to improper fractions.

$3\frac{1}{4} = \frac{13}{4}$	$5\frac{1}{2} = \frac{11}{2}$	$2\frac{1}{4} = \frac{9}{4}$
$2\frac{1}{3} = \frac{7}{3}$	$6\frac{3}{4} = \frac{27}{4}$	$3\frac{3}{10} = \frac{33}{10}$
$5\frac{3}{8} = \frac{43}{8}$	$2\frac{2}{5} = \frac{12}{5}$	$3\frac{5}{6} = \frac{23}{6}$
$2\frac{3}{4} = \frac{11}{4}$	$2\frac{3}{8} = \frac{19}{8}$	$2\frac{7}{12} = \frac{31}{12}$
$2\frac{7}{10} = \frac{27}{10}$	$3\frac{9}{10} = \frac{39}{10}$	$4\frac{1}{8} = \frac{33}{8}$
$4\frac{1}{4} = \frac{17}{4}$	$8\frac{1}{2} = \frac{17}{2}$	$1\frac{5}{12} = \frac{17}{12}$

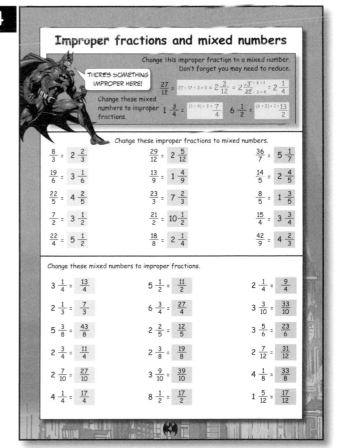

In the first part, children should see that you can divide the denominator by the numerator and place the remainder over the denominator. Use card circles cut into equal parts to reinforce the idea, e.g. how many whole circles can you make from 17 quarter circles?

Rounding decimals

Round these decimals to the nearest tenth.

6.23 is 6.2   6.27 is 6.3

5 OR MORE, RAISE THE SCORE, 4 OR LESS, LET IT REST!

Look at the digit to the right of the tenths. If it is 5 or more, increase the digit to the left by 1. If less than 5, just leave it out.   6.25 is 6.3

Round these decimals to the nearest tenth.

7.34 is 7.3	1.54 is 1.5	3.24 is 3.2
4.87 is 4.9	2.73 is 2.7	9.42 is 9.4
6.38 is 6.4	8.82 is 8.8	7.83 is 7.8
2.79 is 2.8	3.46 is 3.5	6.46 is 6.5

Round these decimals to the nearest tenth.

8.75 is 8.8	4.65 is 4.7	2.75 is 2.8
2.66 is 2.7	1.87 is 1.9	3.52 is 3.5
1.35 is 1.4	8.47 is 8.5	9.45 is 9.5
2.87 is 2.9	9.36 is 9.4	1.54 is 1.5

Round these decimals to the nearest tenth.

22.73 is 22.7	16.84 is 16.8	46.21 is 46.2
35.61 is 35.6	33.56 is 33.6	26.75 is 26.8
18.87 is 18.9	72.72 is 72.7	83.64 is 83.6
12.65 is 12.7	88.88 is 88.9	39.55 is 39.6
45.26 is 45.3	34.76 is 34.8	65.43 is 65.4

If children experience difficulties, point out that the significant digit to look at is in the second decimal place. The use of a number line may be helpful where the child is still unsure.

6

Adding with different numbers of digits

Work out the sum of each problem.

```
    432              176
  -  43            +  97
    475              273
```

Remember to regroup if you need to.

Work out the sum of each problem.

```
  256      283      207      576
+  31    +  15    +  83    +  12
  287      298      290      588

  317      542      271      324
+  72    +  29    +  18    +  45
  389      571      289      369
```

HURRY UP! GET ON THE CASE...

Write the answer in the box.

48 + 311 = 359   32 + 563 = 595

382 + 214 = 596   275 + 386 = 661

Write the missing numbers in the boxes.

```
  242      939      805      623
+  27    +  37    +  32    +  72
  269      976      837      695
```

Write the answer in the colored box. Use the space for working them out.

Robin has saved $276. For his birthday he is given another $32. How much does he have now?

```
  1
  276          $308
+  32
  308
```

$10 $10   25¢ 5¢ 25¢

The Joker sells 207 adult tickets for his show and 87 children's tickets. How many tickets are sold altogether?

```
  207          294
+  87
  294
```

This page and the next should be straightforward. Any errors will probably be due to a failure to carry or particularly in the second section, may occur where children have added digits with different place values.

7

Adding with different numbers of digits

Work out the sum of each problem.

```
       987           2,767
  + 423,123       + 12,844
    424,110         15,611
```

Remember to regroup if you need to.

Work out the sum of each problem.

```
    3,756      6,855,967          56
 + 27,594    + 153,462      + 2,738
   31,350      7,009,429       2,794

    5,783      205,836        5,776
 + 32,368    +   2,791    + 878,142
   38,151      208,627       883,918
```

Write the answer in the box.

6,783,201 + 914,875 = 7,698,076

YOU CAN'T BEAT ME...

415,739 + 24,683 = 440,422

Write in the missing numbers in these sums.

```
   5,387        321      6,752
 +   848    + 8,189    +   909
   6,235      8,510      7,661
```

Work out the answer to the problem. Use the space for working it out.

Harley Quinn has 1,253 playing cards in her collection. The Joker has 831. How many do they have altogether?

```
          1
          1,253
        +   831
  2,084    2,084
```

For problems in which the two numbers are not aligned vertically, ensure that children line up the digits in the ones place on the right side of the numbers. The most common error is not aligning the correct places.

Subtracting one number from another

Find the difference for each problem.

```
   834        431
 -  44      -  84
   790        347
```

Find the difference for each problem.

```
  834      580      437      175
-  12    -  60    -  56    -  54
  822      520      381      121

  579      364      289      280
-  42    -  62    -  68    -  30
  537      302      221      250

  483      756      253      841
-  26    -  17    -  16    -  28
  457      739      237      813
```

Write the answer in the box.

431 - 21 = 410   636 - 22 = 614

785 - 63 = 722   866 - 34 = 832

Find the difference for each problem.

There are 585 children in Gotham high school. If 38 children are on a field trip, how many children are still at school?

```
  7 15
  585          547
-  38
  547
```

There are 256 bats in the Batcave. If 37 fly away, how many are left?

```
  4 16
  256          219
-  37
  219
```

The most likely errors to occur in the first section will involve subtractions where a larger digit has to be taken away from a smaller digit. Children often take the small digit that is on the top away from the larger digit on the bottom.

Subtracting one number from another

SUBLIMINAL SUBTRACTION!

Work out the answer to each problem.

27,685	2,147,423
− 8,726	− 165,351
18,959	1,982,072

Work out the answer to each problem.

568,232	6,262,422	10,684	337,481
− 3,846	− 347,566	− 2,845	− 19,802
564,386	5,914,856	7,839	317,679

7,157,864	892,223	82,818	67,444
−3,633,976	− 746,489	− 7,465	− 28,647
3,523,888	145,734	75,353	38,797

3,732,522	872,813	4,794,872	116,387
− 3,176	− 52,284	− 355,257	− 2,799
3,729,346	820,529	4,439,615	113,588

Write the answer in the box.

4,635,652 − 1,754,871 = 2,880,781

975,830 − 7,642 = 968,188

Work out the answer to the problem. Use the space for working it out.

Batman was traveling in his Whirly-Bat at 2,635 feet above ground. He suddenly descended 142 feet. How high above ground was he now?

2,635 ft
− 142 ft
2,493 ft

2,493 ft

I HOPE ALFRED FIXED THE ENGINE...

See the notes for page 7.

10

Real-life problems

HA! HA! HA!

The Joker has $858.95 in the bank, and he spends $177.47 on a vacation. How much does he have left in the bank?

$681.48

$858.95
− $177.47
$681.48

In a wild chase, Robin drives 185 miles on the first day and 145 miles on the second day. How many miles has he traveled altogether?

330 miles

185 mi
+ 145 mi
330 mi

Batman spends $2,625 on a new computerized Crime Scene Kit, and $156 on special software. How much does he spend altogether?

$2,781

$2,625
+ $ 156
$2,781

Alfred is putting up shelves in an alcove in the Batcave. He has a board that is 3.56 m long, but the alcove is only 2.64 m long. How much must he cut off the board in order for it to fit?

0.92 m

3.56 m
− 2.64 m
0.92 m

Batman and Robin are going on vacation. If they travel 368 mi in the first week and 347 mi in the second week, how many miles have they traveled altogether?

715 mi

368 mi
+ 347 mi
715 mi

If the Batmobile had already gone 16,048 mi before the vacation, how many miles will it have gone by the end?

16,763 mi

16,048 mi
+ 715 mi
16,763 mi

In this page and the following two pages children can apply the skills of addition and subtraction to real-life problems, using various units of measurement. If the child is unsure which operation to use, discuss whether the answer will be larger or smaller.

11

Everyday problems

Alfred buys 415 ft of cable. If he uses 234 ft, how much does he have left?

181 ft

415 ft
− 234 ft
181 ft

Bruce Wayne travels by train for 120 mi, by bus for 48 mi, and then walks the final 3 mi to Wayne Manor. How far does he travel?

171 mi

120 mi
48 mi
+ 3 mi
171 mi

Commissioner Gordon works 185 hours a month. His wife works 72 hours a month. How many hours do they work altogether in a month?

257 hours

185 hrs
+ 72 hrs
257 hrs

Gotham high school collects money for the local children's home. If the pupils collect $275 in the first month, $210 in the second month, and $136 in the third month, how much do they collect altogether?

$621

$275
$210
− $136
$621

Batman and Robin are racing to a crime scene. Batman gets there in 12.75 seconds. Robin gets there in 14.83 seconds. Who got there first?

Batman got there first.

14.83 sec
− 12.75 sec
2.08 sec

How much faster was the crime buster who got there first?

He was 2.08 seconds faster than Robin.

Arkham Asylum orders 8,755 lb of potatoes. 6,916 lb are eaten. How many pounds of potatoes are left?

1,839 lb are left.

8,755 lb
− 6,916 lb
1,839 lb

See notes for page 10. Point out that an answer that will be larger will require addition, while one that will be smaller will require subtraction.

Everyday problems

The Riddler, Query, and Echo want to put their money together to buy a some new equipment. If the Riddler has $25.25, Query has $24.75, and Echo has $12.50, how much will they have to spend on the equipment?

They will have $62.50 to spend.

$25.25
$24.75
+ $12.50
$62.50

Gotham City candy store has 120 lb of taffy and sells 80 lb. How much does it have left?

It has 40 lb left.

120 lb
− 80 lb
40 lb

Gotham City bakery orders 148 lb of sugar, 564 lb of salt, and 984 lb of butter. What is the total weight of the order?

The total weight is 1,696 lb.

148 lb
564 lb
+ 984 lb
1,696 lb

Catwoman has to fill up with gas. After paying $42 for the gas, she has $145 left. How much did she have to start with??

$42
+ $145
$187

She had $187 to start with.

Robin is saving up to buy a guitar that costs $169.99. If he already has $73.47, how much more does he need?

He needs $96.52 more.

$169.99
− $ 73.47
$ 96.52

30 ft
30 ft
20 ft
+ 20 ft
100 ft

The exercise yard in Gotham City penitentiary is 30 ft long and 20 ft wide. How much fence is needed to surround all four sides?

100 ft of fence is needed.

See the notes for page 10 and 11.

Decimal addition

Write in the answers to these problems.

IT ALL ADDS UP! JUST FILL IN THE BOXES.

```
  47.15        43.99
+ 19.36      + 12.76
  66.51        56.75
```

Write the answer to each problem.

```
  63.72      85.17      28.46      24.76      73.49
+ 77.92    + 68.21    + 64.84    + 89.14    + 18.75
 141.64     153.38      93.30     113.90      92.24

  46.67      32.88      39.47      58.32      38.84
+ 12.99    + 43.02    + 81.70    + 14.95    + 22.65
  59.66      75.90     121.17      73.27      61.49
```

Write the answer to each problem.

```
  75.80      56.78      81.97      39.48      58.35
+ 22.98    + 73.47    + 23.59    + 75.43    + 28.67
  98.78     130.25     105.56     114.91      87.02

  85.78      65.37      53.75      85.74      73.76
+ 31.45    + 28.99    + 80.76    + 39.47    + 41.27
 117.23      94.36     134.51     125.21     115.03
```

Write in the answer to each problem.

33.97 + 24.62 = 58.59   63.84 + 29.81 = 93.65   37.19 + 28.24 = 65.43

76.39 + 43.78 = 120.17   34.43 + 25.64 = 60.07   32.44 + 21.88 = 54.32

52.38 + 38.43 = 90.81   68.67 + 29.82 = 98.49   37.89 + 82.15 = 120.04

84.77 + 39.12 = 123.89   21.99 + 79.32 = 101.31   52.45 + 34.58 = 87.03

On these two pages, children are dealing with two decimal places. The most likely mistakes will be errors involving carrying, or in the third section, where they are working horizontally. Remind children to line up the decimal points when working vertically.

14

Decimal addition

Write in the answer to each problem. Remember to line up the decimal points and write zeros for place holders.

WHAT'S THE POINT?

```
  296.48        73.00
+ 131.70    + 269.23
  428.18      342.23
```

Write in the answer to each problem.

```
  378.76      491.83      964.71       32.045
+  25.84    +  37.84    + 321.20    + 204.990
  404.60      529.67    1,285.91      237.035

  306.00      471.932     842.010     675.82
+ 844.24    + 755.260    +  11.842    + 105.00
1,150.24    1,227.192     853.852     780.82

   37.82       65.24      178.935     184.70
+ 399.71    + 605.27    + 599.410    + 372.81
  437.53      670.51      778.345     557.51

  443.27      563.00      703.95      825.360
+  75.00    + 413.98    +  85.22    + 249.857
  518.27      976.98      789.17    1,075.217
```

Write in the sum for each problem.

527 + 134.8 = 661.8   85.42 + 321.75 = 407.17

501.8 + 361.93 = 863.73   558.32 + 137.945 = 696.265

27 + 142.07 = 169.07   75.31 + 105.37 = 180.68

421 + 136.25 = 557.25   92.31 + 241.73 = 334.04

153.3 + 182.02 = 335.32   491.445 + 105.37 = 596.815

Watch out for misalignment when children work on horizontal subtractions.

15

Decimal subtraction

What's the difference?

```
  59.76        57.18
- 21.47      - 22.09
  38.29        35.09
```

TAKE IT AWAY!

Write the difference for each problem.

```
  62.95      81.42      48.52      61.55
- 33.37    - 25.04    - 14.49    - 13.26
  29.58      56.38      34.03      48.29

  45.76      73.52      98.98      53.58
- 16.18    - 39.27    - 39.19    - 14.39
  29.58      34.25      59.79      39.19

  92.63      73.71      64.21      64.92
- 67.14    - 19.24    - 16.02    - 26.35
  25.49      54.47      48.19      38.57

  81.94      62.35      21.74      94.87
- 28.15    - 13.16    - 12.10    - 65.28
  53.79      49.19       9.64      29.59
```

Write the difference for each problem.

46.75 - 12.17 = 34.58   56.84 - 24.72 = 32.12

72.41 - 23.18 = 49.23   51.52 - 12.13 = 39.39

53.84 - 19.65 = 34.19   64.65 - 37.26 = 27.39

41.82 - 18.13 = 23.69   91.91 - 22.22 = 69.69

77.31 - 28.15 = 49.16   51.61 - 23.14 = 28.47

On this page and the next two pages, the most likely errors will result from a failure to use decomposition where necessary (see notes for pages 8 and 9). Watch out for misalignment when children work on horizontal subtractions.

16

Decimal subtraction

Write the difference for each problem.

```
  68.17        39.20
- 11.40      - 13.15
  56.77        26.05
```

NO ONE MESSES WITH THE JOKER.

Work out the difference for each problem.

```
  64.77      35.612     66.37      63.20
- 35.3     - 26.19    - 21.9     - 15.36
  29.47       9.422     44.47      47.84

  63.14      35.612     99.235     55.492
- 32       - 13.207    - 33.70    - 27.66
  31.14      22.405     65.535     27.832

  63.20      62.1       68         63.14
- 15.36    - 29.34    - 31.5     - 32
  47.84      32.76      36.5       31.14

  55.492     85         53.64      95.15
- 27.66    - 26.32    - 23       - 31.356
  27.832     58.68      30.64      63.794
```

Write the difference for each problem.

63.4 - 24.51 = 38.89   72.6 - 53.71 = 18.89

92.197 - 63.28 = 28.917   61.16 - 24.4 = 36.76

91.3 - 33 = 58.3   81.815 - 55.9 = 25.915

41.24 - 14.306 = 26.934   52.251 - 22.42 = 29.831

92.84 - 23 = 69.84   94.31 - 27.406 = 66.904

On this page, the most common error will result from not writing the numbers to the same number of decimal places before subtracting. Adding zeros for placeholders helps avoid misalignment.

17

Multiplying larger numbers by ones

Write the product for each problem.

529	1,273
× 4	× 5
2,116	6,365

TIME AND TIME AGAIN, THAT'S HOW OFTEN I SAVE THE DAY!

Write the product for each problem.

455	126	831	724
× 2	× 3	× 3	× 4
910	378	2,493	2,896

105	253	282	349
× 4	× 5	× 5	× 6
420	1,265	1,410	2,094

465	328	562	161
× 6	× 6	× 4	× 4
2,790	1,968	2,248	644

Write the product for each problem.

4,327	1,352	3,764	1,578
× 3	× 3	× 4	× 4
12,981	4,056	15,056	6,312

1,263	5,907	1,203	1,456
× 5	× 5	× 6	× 6
6,315	29,535	7,218	8,736

1,467	1,599	8,436	6,521
× 6	× 6	× 6	× 6
8,802	9,594	50,616	39,126

4,851	6,538	3,914	8,124
× 4	× 5	× 6	× 6
19,404	32,690	23,484	48,744

Make sure that children understand the convention of multiplication problems, i.e. multiply the ones first, work left, and regroup when necessary. This page will generally highlight gaps in knowledge of the 2, 3, 4, 5, and 6 multiplication tables.

18

Multiplying larger numbers by ones

Write the answer to each problem.

417	2,185
× 7	× 9
2,919	19,665

TO THE BATCAVE! LET'S SPEED UP.

Write the answer to each problem.

604	413	682	327
× 7	× 8	× 8	× 7
4,228	2,891	5,456	2,289

436	171	715	254
× 8	× 9	× 8	× 8
3,488	1,539	5,720	2,032

235	319	581	999
× 8	× 9	× 9	× 9
1,880	2,871	5,229	8,991

Work out the answer to each problem.

2,816	4,331	2,617	1,439
× 7	× 7	× 8	× 8
19,712	30,317	20,936	11,512

4,022	3,104	2,591	4,361
× 8	× 8	× 9	× 9
32,176	24,832	23,319	39,249

4,361	3,002	2,567	1,514
× 9	× 8	× 7	× 8
39,249	24,016	17,969	12,112

4,624	3,894	2,993	1,710
× 7	× 8	× 8	× 9
32,368	31,152	23,944	15,390

Any problems encountered on this page will be similar to those of the previous page. Gaps in the child's knowledge of multiplication tables 7, 8, and 9 will be highlighted here.

19

Real-life multiplication problems

There are 157 apples in each box. How many will there be in three boxes?

| 1 2 |
| 157 |
| × 3 |
| 471 |

471 apples

Each of the Penguin's fish crates can hold 660 fish. How many fish will five crates hold?

| 3 |
| 660 |
| × 5 |
| 3,300 |

3,300

A train on Gotham City transport system can take 425 passengers. How many can it take in five trips?

| 1 2 |
| 425 |
| × 5 |
| 2,125 |

2,125 passengers

Officer Dan Foley puts $278 a month into the bank. How much will he have put in after 6 months?

| 4 4 |
| 278 |
| × 6 |
| 1,668 |

$1,668

Gotham City theater can seat 4,536 people. If a play runs for 7 days, what is the maximum number of people who will be able to see the play?

| 3 2 4 |
| 4,536 |
| × 7 |
| 31,752 |

31,752 people

A Bat-Cycle costs $35,956. How much will it cost Batman to buy a bike for four of his friends?

| 2 3 2 2 |
| 35,956 |
| × 4 |
| 143,824 |

$143,824

The Batplane flies at a steady speed of 550 mph. How far will it travel in 6 hours?

| 3 |
| 550 |
| × 6 |
| 3,300 |

3,300 miles

This page provides an opportunity for children to apply their multiplication to real-life problems. As with previous multiplication work, gaps in the child's knowledge of multiplication facts will be highlighted.

20

Comparing and ordering decimals

Compare the decimals. Which decimal is greater?

2.2 and 3.1   0.45 and 0.6

Line them up vertically. Add zeros for place holders.

2.2	0.45
3.1	0.60
3 > 2, so 3.1 > 2.2	6 > 4, so 0.6 > 0.45

IT'S YOUR CHOICE.

Compare the decimals. Which decimal is greater?

8.9 and 8.1	0.4 and 0.52	3.6 and 0.94	0.5 and 0.68
8.9	0.52	3.6	0.68

1.5 and 1.8	0.41 and 4.10	8.6 and 6.8	5.45 and 5.41
1.8	4.10	8.6	5.45

Find the greatest decimal.

2.8 and 2.75 and 2.5	0.98 and 1.09 and 1.3	5.9 and 4.87 and 5.75
2.8	1.3	5.9

Write the decimals in order from greatest to least.

0.44 4.1 0.4	34.95 33.9 34.5	7.5 6.95 7.59
4.1, 0.44, 0.4	34.95, 34.5, 33.9	7.59, 7.5, 6.95

Find the answer to each problem.

Gotham City Weather Bureau reported 5.27 inches of rain in March, 6.54 inches in April, and 5.23 inches in May. Which month had the least rainfall?

May

| 5.23   6 > 5 |
| 5.27 |
| 6.54 |

Alfred walked 4.4 miles on Wednesday, 3.86 miles on Thursday, and 4.34 miles on Friday. Which day did he walk the farthest?

Wednesday

| 3.86   4 > 3 |
| 4.34   4 > 3 |
| 4.40 |

Before making any comparisons, children should write out each of the numbers with the same number of decimal places, lining up the decimal points vertically.

21

Converting units of measure

Convert 25 centimeters to millimeters.   Convert 200¢ to dollars.

25 × 10 =   **250 mm**   200 ÷ 100 =   **$2**

HOW LONG? HOW MUCH?

Convert these centimeters to millimeters.

30 cm	**300 mm**	45 cm	**450 mmm**		
15 cm	**150 mm**	24 cm	**240 mm**		
53 cm	**530 mm**	86 cm	**860 mm**	106 cm	**1,060 mm**
93 cm	**930 mm**	40 cm	**400 mm**	376 cm	**3,760 mm**

Convert these millimeters to centimeters.

40 mm	**4 cm**	100 mm	**10 cm**	130 mm	**13 cm**
50 mm	**5 cm**	80 mm	**8 cm**	300 mm	**30 cm**
120 mm	**12 cm**	10 mm	**1 cm**	550 mm	**55 cm**

Convert these dollars to cents.

$45	**4,500¢**	$500	**50,000¢**	$25	**2,500¢**
$12	**1,200¢**	$46	**4,600¢**	$95	**9,500¢**
$82	**8,200¢**	$8	**800¢**	$250	**25,000¢**

Convert these cents to dollars.

| 350¢ | **$3.50** | 800¢ | **$8.00** | 5,000¢ | **$50.00** |
| 250¢ | **$2.50** | 300¢ | **$3.00** | 450¢ | **$4.50** |

This page highlights problems with the relationship between millimeters and centimeters, and dollars and cents. Use a ruler or money to explain. Look out for answers such as $3.5. Remind children that, with money, we use zero in the hundredths column ($3.50).

22

Converting units of measure

Convert 300 centimeters to meters.   Convert 4 kilometers to meters.

300 ÷ 100 =   **3 m**   4 × 1,000 =   **4,000 m**

IT'S ALL A MATTER OF HUNDREDS AND THOUSANDS!

Convert these centimeters to meters.

400 cm	**4 m**	800 cm	**8 m**
9,000 cm	**90 m**	5,000 cm	**50 m**
7,800 cm	**78 m**	6,400 cm	**64 m**
46,700 cm	**467 m**	85,200 cm	**852 m**

Convert these meters to centimeters.

74 m	**7,400 cm**	39 m	**3,900 cm**	85 m	**8,500 cm**
59 m	**5,900 cm**	24 m	**2,400 cm**	48 m	**4,800 cm**
156 m	**15,600 cm**	217 m	**21,700 cm**	821 m	**82,100 cm**

Convert these meters to kilometers.

4,000 m	**4 km**	8,000 m	**8 km**	9,000 m	**9 km**
25,000 m	**25 km**	37,000 m	**37 km**	71,000 m	**71 km**
45,000 m	**45 km**	76,000 m	**76 km**	99,000 m	**99 km**

Convert these kilometers to meters.

| 6 km | **6,000 m** | 9 km | **9,000 m** | 3 km | **3,000 m** |
| 23 km | **23,000 m** | 56 km | **56,000 m** | 84 km | **84,000 m** |

As with page 21, check that children understand the relationship between centimeters and millimeters, and meters and kilometers. If they are secure in this understanding, this should be a straightforward page of multiplying and dividing by 100 and 1,000.

Areas of rectangles and squares

Find the area of this blue rectangle.

To find the area of a rectangle or square, we multiply length (l) by width (w).

(w) 25 in.
(l)
32 in.

$$\begin{array}{r} \overset{1}{3}\overset{}{2} \\ \times\ 25 \\ \hline 160 \\ + 640 \\ \hline 800 \text{ in.}^2 \end{array}$$

Area = **800 in.²**

NOW WHO'S LAUGHING?

Find the area of these rectangles and squares. You may need to do your work on a separate sheet.

22 in.
15 in.
330 in.²

10.4 ft
10.4 ft
108.16 ft²

22 ft
46 ft
1,012 ft²

45 mm
29 mm
1,305 mm²

78 mm
84 mm
6,552 mm²

99 in.
99 in.
9,801 in.²

27 in.
64 in.
1,728 in.²

69 in.
72 in.
4,968 in.²

For the exercises on this page, children need to multiply the two sides together to arrive at the area. If any answers are wrong, check the long multiplication, and if necessary, revise the method. Children may confuse area and perimeter, and add the sides together.

Perimeter of shapes

Find the perimeter of this brown rectangle.

To find the perimeter of a rectangle or square, we add the two lengths and the two widths together.

13.3 in.
77.4 in.   25.4 in.

$$\begin{array}{r} \overset{1\ 1}{1}3.3 \\ 13.3 \\ 25.4 \\ + 25.4 \\ \hline 77.4 \text{ in.} \end{array}$$

NO SHORT CIRCUITS!

Find the perimeter of these rectangles. You may need to do your work on an extra sheet.

20.6 ft
20.6 ft
82.4 ft

28.9 ft
48.3 ft
154.4 ft

134 mm
134 mm
536 mm

25 mm
55 mm
160 mm

35.6 ft
18.2 ft
107.6 ft

50.5 ft
50.5 ft
202 ft

17 in.
35 in.
104 in.

35 mm
19 mm
108 mm

On this page and the next, the most likely problem will be confusion with the area work done previously. Remind children to add the four sides together to get the perimeter.

Decimal place value

Work out the answer to the problem.

2.385

What is the place value of the digit 8?

EVERY DIGIT COUNTS!

Ones	Tenths	Hundredths	Thousandths	Ten-thousandths
2	3	8	5	0

2.3850
8 is in the hundredths place,
so its value is 8 hundredths.

Name the place value of the digit 8 in each of the problems.

0.289	2.0548	1.108	5.86
hundredths	ten-thousandths	thousandths	tenths

Name the place value of the digit in **bold**.

5.3947	7.564	5.408	0.5124
9 hundredths	4 thousandths	4 tenths	1 hundredth

8.356   1.062   4.622

Which number has a digit with the place value 6 tenths?   4.622

Which number has a digit with the place value 6 hundredths?   1.062

Which number has a digit with the place value 6 thousandths?   8.356

How much greater is the second decimal than the first?

7.46 7.56	3.171 3.172	0.751 0.761
one tenth more	one thousandth more	one hundredth more

Be sure that children understand that the place value of a digit is the place that it is in, while the value of the digit is the amount that it is worth in that place.

26

Speed problems

How long will it take the Penguin to travel 36 mi on his pogo umbrella if he travels at a constant speed of 9 mi per hour?   4 hours

Time = Distance ÷ Speed

If a car traveled 150 mi at a constant speed in 5 hours, at what speed was it traveling?   30 mph

Speed = Distance ÷ Time

If a bus travels for 5 hours at 40 mph, how far does it travel?   200 mi

Distance = Speed x Time

The Batmobile cruises along a road at a steady speed of 60 mph. How far will it travel in 5 hours?   60 x 5 = 300   300 mi

A train covers a distance of 560 mi in 8 hours. If it travels at a constant speed, how fast is it traveling? $8\overline{)560}$ = 70   70 mph

Bruce Wayne walks at a steady speed of 3 mph. How long will it take him to travel 18 miles? $3\overline{)18}$ = 6   6 hours

The old Batmobile had a top speed of 95 mph. What was the farthest it could travel in 3 hours?   95 x 3 = 285   285 mi

Robin has just done a long-distance training run, at an average speed of 6 mph. If it took him 4 hours, how far did he run?   6 x 4 = 24   24 mi

The Penguin pogos 50 miles around Gotham City at a steady speed of 10 mph. If he started at 3:00 P.M., at what time did he finish his journey? $10\overline{)50}$ = 5   3 + 5 = 8   8:00 P.M.

If children experience difficulties on this page, ask them what they need to find, i.e. speed, distance, or time, and refer to the formula necessary to do this. Encourage children to develop simple examples that will help them remember the formulas.

27

Conversion table

This is part of a conversion table that shows how to change dollars to euros, when 10 euros (10€) equal $1. To convert euros to dollars, divide by 10. To convert dollars to euros, multiply by 10.

U.S. Dollars	Euros (€)
1	10
2	20

How many euros would you get for $3?   30€

How much is 15€ worth? $1.50

How many dollars would you get for 40€?	$4.00
How many dollars would you get for 75€?	$7.50
How much is 1€ worth?	10¢
Change $55 into euros.	550€
What is $4.50 in euros?	45€
Change 250€ into dollars.	$25

U.S. Dollars	Euros
1	10
2	20
3	30
4	40
5	50
6	60
7	70
8	80
9	90
10	100

The rate then changes to 8€ to the dollar. The conversion chart now looks like the one shown here.

How many euros are worth $5?	40€
How many dollars can you get for 64€?	$8
How many euros are worth $9.50?	76€
How many euros can you get for $30?	240€
How many dollars would you get for 120€?	$15
What is the value of 4€?	50¢

U.S. Dollars	Euros
1	8
2	16
3	24
4	32
5	40
6	48
7	56
8	64
9	72
10	80

$10   1¢ 5¢ 25¢ $10

Most of the questions require reading off from a conversion chart. Errors may occur if the chart is not read across accurately. Children may need extra help for questions that involve amounts not on the chart. Check that the right chart is used for the second part.

Interpreting circle graphs

48 children voted for their favorite ice cream flavor. How many children voted for strawberry?

48 ÷ 4 = 12   so $\frac{1}{4}$ of 48 is 12

12 children voted for strawberry.

How many children voted for chocolate?

48 ÷ 8 = 6   6 x 3 = 18   so $\frac{3}{8}$ of 48 = 18

18 children voted for chocolate.

(Pie chart labels: Chocolate $\frac{3}{8}$, Vanilla $\frac{1}{4}$, $\frac{1}{8}$ Fudge, $\frac{1}{4}$ Strawberry)

A class of 30 children voted for their favorite Batman character.

How many voted for Harley Quinn?   6

How many did not vote for Batman?   18

How many more children voted for Robin than for the Joker?   3

How many children altogether voted for Catwoman and Harley Quinn?   9

(Pie chart labels: Batman $\frac{2}{5}$, Catwoman $\frac{1}{10}$, Joker $\frac{1}{10}$, Robin $\frac{1}{5}$, Harley Quinn $\frac{1}{5}$)

60 citizens of Gotham City were asked where they went on vacation last year. The circle graph shows the results.

(Pie chart labels: Another state 18, Canada or Mexico 10, Europe 5, Stayed home 15, In my state 12)

What fraction of people vacationed in their own state? $\frac{1}{5}$

What fraction of people vacationed in Canada or Mexico, or in Europe? $\frac{1}{4}$

What fraction of people did not stay at home? $\frac{3}{4}$

This page introduces pie charts. In the first section children are required to find fractions of an amount. If unsure, remind the child to divide the total by the denominator and multiply by the numerator. The most likely errors will come from misreading the question.

Probability scale 0 to 1

Look at this probability line.
Impossible = 0
Poor chance = 0.25
Fair = 0.5
Good chance = 0.75
Certain = 1

Write each letter in the correct place on the probability line.
a. It will be daylight in New Orleans at midnight.
b. The sun will come up tomorrow.
c. If I toss a coin it will come down heads.

a		c		b
0	0.25	0.5	0.75	1

e	b	a	c	d
0	0.25	0.5	0.75	1

Write each letter in the correct place on the probability line.
a. If the Joker cuts a pack of cards he will get a red card.
b. If he cuts a pack of cards he will get a diamond.
c. If he cuts a pack of cards he will get a diamond, a spade, or a club.
d. If he cuts a pack of cards he will get a diamond, a spade, a club, or a heart.
e. If he cuts a pack of cards it will be a 15.

b	c	e	d	a
0	0.25	0.5	0.75	1

Write each letter in the correct place on the probability line.
a. Next week, Wednesday will be the day after Tuesday.
b. There will be 33 days in February next year.
c. It will snow in Miami in May.
d. It will snow in Chicago in January.
e. The next person to knock on the door will be female.

The first section assumes a knowledge of the suits of a pack of cards. If children are unfamiliar with cards, some discussion will be necessary. In the second section, the examples have been chosen to fall into the categories listed on the probability line.

30

Likely outcomes

Throw one coin 20 times.

Keep a tally.

| H |卌 |||| |
| T | 卌 卌 | |

Put your results on a bar graph

COIN THROWS

What do you notice?

Heads and tails come up roughly the same number of times because there are only two possible outcomes and they are equally likely.

REMEMBER, LIFE IS NOT A GAMBLE IF YOU FIGURE IT OUT!

Predict what you think the outcome will be if you tossed two coins 48 times.

2 heads varies times   2 tails varies times   1 of each varies times

Now actually throw two coins 48 times and record your results on this tally chart.

2 heads	varies
2 tails	varies
1 of each	varies

Draw a bar graph to show your results.

COIN THROWS

Which result comes up the most often?

one of each

Can you explain why some results are more probable than others?

The reason is that there are four possible outcomes because "1 of each" could be achieved in two ways. So "1 of each" is twice as likely as "2 heads" or "2 tails".

Childrens' predictions in the first question may be considerably different from the result. Once the work is done check that children use the experience to improve their understanding of likely outcomes. The tally chart may differ from the one shown here.

31

Naming quadrilaterals

FAIR AND SQUARE?

Name this shape.

rhombus

Name these shapes.

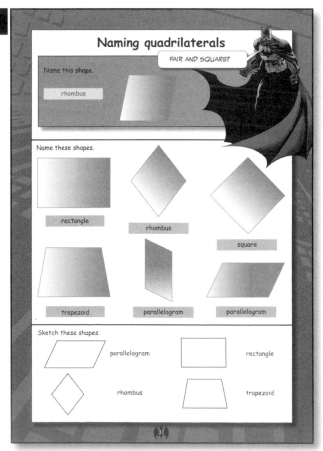

rectangle

rhombus

square

trapezoid

parallelogram

parallelogram

Sketch these shapes.

parallelogram

rectangle

rhombus

trapezoid

If children have problems identifying these shapes, it may be necessary to provide some more examples for identification practice.

Speed trials

HOW FAST ARE YOU?

Write the answers as fast as you can, but get them right!

4 x 10 = 40   8 x 2 = 16

Write the answers as fast as you can, but get them right!

3 x 2 =	6	1 x 5 =	5	4 x 10 =	40	1 x 3 =	3
2 x 2 =	4	10 x 5 =	50	8 x 10 =	80	2 x 3 =	6
5 x 2 =	10	0 x 5 =	0	6 x 10 =	60	10 x 3 =	30
1 x 2 =	2	3 x 5 =	15	1 x 10 =	10	8 x 3 =	24
6 x 2 =	12	4 x 5 =	20	5 x 10 =	50	6 x 3 =	18
4 x 2 =	8	8 x 5 =	40	3 x 10 =	30	4 x 3 =	12
7 x 2 =	14	6 x 5 =	30	7 x 10 =	70	7 x 3 =	21
9 x 2 =	18	7 x 5 =	35	0 x 10 =	0	0 x 3 =	0
10 x 2 =	20	9 x 5 =	45	2 x 10 =	20	5 x 3 =	15
8 x 2 =	16	5 x 5 =	25	9 x 10 =	90	3 x 3 =	9
0 x 2 =	0	3 x 5 =	15	10 x 10 =	100	8 x 4 =	32
2 x 7 =	14	5 x 3 =	15	10 x 1 =	10	7 x 4 =	28
2 x 1 =	2	5 x 8 =	40	10 x 7 =	70	6 x 4 =	24
2 x 4 =	8	5 x 9 =	45	10 x 4 =	40	3 x 4 =	12
3 x 7 =	21	5 x 7 =	35	10 x 3 =	30	10 x 4 =	40
2 x 5 =	10	5 x 4 =	20	10 x 5 =	50	0 x 4 =	0
2 x 9 =	18	5 x 1 =	5	10 x 8 =	80	3 x 4 =	12
2 x 6 =	12	4 x 7 =	28	10 x 6 =	60	9 x 4 =	36
2 x 8 =	16	5 x 10 =	50	10 x 2 =	20	5 x 4 =	20
2 x 3 =	6	5 x 2 =	10	10 x 9 =	90	2 x 4 =	8

All the 3s

You will need to know these:

1 × 3 = 3   2 × 3 = 6   3 × 3 = 9   4 × 3 = 12
5 × 3 = 15   10 × 3 = 30

GET SOME PRACTICE!

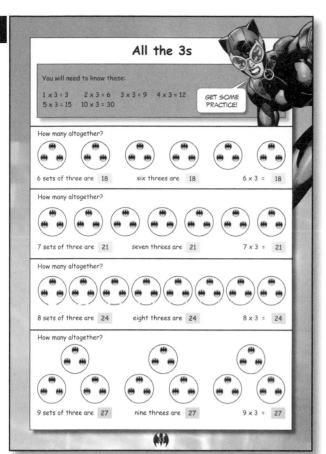

How many altogether?

6 sets of three are   18   six threes are   18   6 × 3 =   18

How many altogether?

7 sets of three are   21   seven threes are   21   7 × 3 =   21

How many altogether?

8 sets of three are   24   eight threes are   24   8 × 3 =   24

How many altogether?

9 sets of three are   27   nine threes are   27   9 × 3 =   27

34

All the 3s again

1, 2, 3... GO!!!

You should know all of the three times table.
1 × 3 = 3   2 × 3 = 6   3 × 3 = 9   4 × 3 = 12   5 × 3 = 15
6 × 3 = 18   7 × 3 = 21   8 × 3 = 24   9 × 3 = 27   10 × 3 = 30
Say these to yourself a few times.

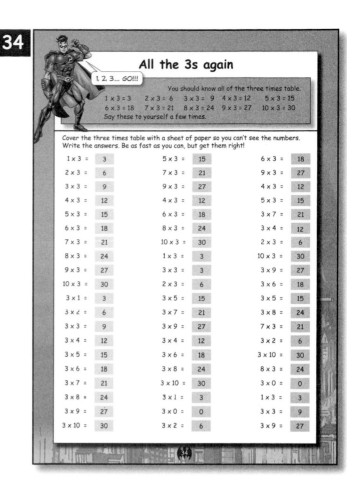

Cover the three times table with a sheet of paper so you can't see the numbers. Write the answers. Be as fast as you can, but get them right!

1 × 3 =	3	5 × 3 =	15	6 × 3 =	18
2 × 3 =	6	7 × 3 =	21	9 × 3 =	27
3 × 3 =	9	9 × 3 =	27	4 × 3 =	12
4 × 3 =	12	4 × 3 =	12	5 × 3 =	15
5 × 3 =	15	6 × 3 =	18	3 × 7 =	21
6 × 3 =	18	8 × 3 =	24	3 × 4 =	12
7 × 3 =	21	10 × 3 =	30	2 × 3 =	6
8 × 3 =	24	1 × 3 =	3	10 × 3 =	30
9 × 3 =	27	3 × 3 =	3	3 × 9 =	27
10 × 3 =	30	2 × 3 =	6	3 × 6 =	18
3 × 1 =	3	3 × 5 =	15	3 × 5 =	15
3 × 2 =	6	3 × 7 =	21	3 × 8 =	24
3 × 3 =	9	3 × 9 =	27	7 × 3 =	21
3 × 4 =	12	3 × 4 =	12	3 × 2 =	6
3 × 5 =	15	3 × 6 =	18	3 × 10 =	30
3 × 6 =	18	3 × 8 =	24	8 × 3 =	24
3 × 7 =	21	3 × 10 =	30	3 × 0 =	0
3 × 8 =	24	3 × 1 =	3	1 × 3 =	3
3 × 9 =	27	3 × 0 =	0	3 × 3 =	9
3 × 10 =	30	3 × 2 =	6	3 × 9 =	27

All the 4s

You should know these:

1 × 4 = 4   2 × 4 = 8   3 × 4 = 12   4 × 4 = 16   5 × 4 = 20   10 × 4 = 40

How many altogether?

6 sets of four are   24   six fours are   24   6 × 4 =   24

How many altogether?

7 sets of four are   28   seven fours are   28   7 × 4 =   28

How many altogether?

8 sets of four are   32   eight fours are   32   8 × 4 =   32

How many altogether?

9 sets of four are   36   nine fours are   36   9 × 4 =   36

36

All the 4s again

You should know all of the four times table by now.
1 × 4 = 4   2 × 4 = 8   3 × 4 = 12   4 × 4 = 16   5 × 4 = 20
6 × 4 = 24   7 × 4 = 28   8 × 4 = 32   9 × 4 = 36   10 × 4 = 40
Say these to yourself a few times.

OK, SO THAT'S ALL THE FOUR TIMES TABLE.

Cover the four times table with a sheet of paper so you can't see the numbers. Write the answers. Be as fast as you can, but get them right!

1 × 4 =	4	5 × 4 =	20	6 × 4 =	24
2 × 4 =	8	7 × 4 =	28	9 × 4 =	36
3 × 4 =	12	9 × 4 =	36	4 × 1 =	4
4 × 4 =	16	3 × 4 =	12	5 × 4 =	20
5 × 4 =	20	6 × 4 =	24	4 × 7 =	28
6 × 4 =	24	8 × 4 =	32	3 × 4 =	12
7 × 4 =	28	10 × 4 =	40	2 × 4 =	8
8 × 4 =	32	1 × 4 =	4	10 × 4 =	40
9 × 4 =	36	4 × 4 =	16	4 × 3 =	12
10 × 4 =	40	2 × 4 =	8	4 × 6 =	24
4 × 1 =	4	4 × 5 =	20	4 × 5 =	20
4 × 2 =	8	4 × 7 =	28	4 × 8 =	32
4 × 3 =	12	4 × 9 =	36	7 × 4 =	28
4 × 4 =	16	4 × 4 =	16	4 × 2 =	8
4 × 5 =	20	4 × 6 =	24	4 × 10 =	40
4 × 6 =	24	4 × 8 =	32	8 × 4 =	32
4 × 7 =	28	4 × 10 =	40	4 × 0 =	0
4 × 8 =	32	4 × 1 =	4	1 × 4 =	4
4 × 9 =	36	4 × 0 =	0	4 × 4 =	16
4 × 10 =	40	4 × 2 =	8	4 × 9 =	36

Speed trials

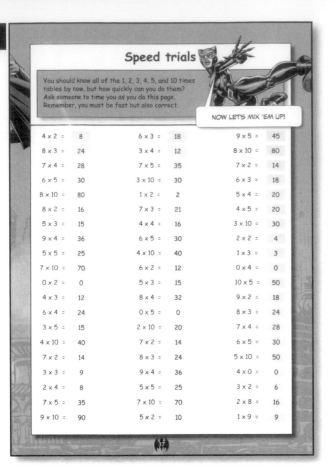

You should know all of the 1, 2, 3, 4, 5, and 10 times tables by now, but how quickly can you do them? Ask someone to time you as you do this page. Remember, you must be fast but also correct.

NOW LET'S MIX 'EM UP!

4 x 2 = 8	6 x 3 = 18	9 x 5 = 45
8 x 3 = 24	3 x 4 = 12	8 x 10 = 80
7 x 4 = 28	7 x 5 = 35	7 x 2 = 14
6 x 5 = 30	3 x 10 = 30	6 x 3 = 18
8 x 10 = 80	1 x 2 = 2	5 x 4 = 20
8 x 2 = 16	7 x 3 = 21	4 x 5 = 20
5 x 3 = 15	4 x 4 = 16	3 x 10 = 30
9 x 4 = 36	6 x 5 = 30	2 x 2 = 4
5 x 5 = 25	4 x 10 = 40	1 x 3 = 3
7 x 10 = 70	6 x 2 = 12	0 x 4 = 0
0 x 2 = 0	5 x 3 = 15	10 x 5 = 50
4 x 3 = 12	8 x 4 = 32	9 x 2 = 18
6 x 4 = 24	0 x 5 = 0	8 x 3 = 24
3 x 5 = 15	2 x 10 = 20	7 x 4 = 28
4 x 10 = 40	7 x 2 = 14	6 x 5 = 30
7 x 2 = 14	8 x 3 = 24	5 x 10 = 50
3 x 3 = 9	9 x 4 = 36	4 x 0 = 0
2 x 4 = 8	5 x 5 = 25	3 x 2 = 6
7 x 5 = 35	7 x 10 = 70	2 x 8 = 16
9 x 10 = 90	5 x 2 = 10	1 x 9 = 9

Some of the 6s

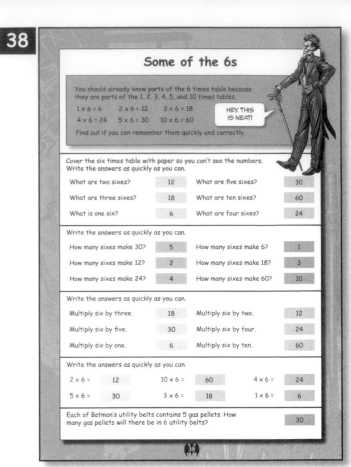

You should already know parts of the 6 times table because they are parts of the 1, 2, 3, 4, 5, and 10 times tables.

1 x 6 = 6   2 x 6 = 12   3 x 6 = 18
4 x 6 = 24   5 x 6 = 30   10 x 6 = 60

Find out if you can remember them quickly and correctly.

HEY THIS IS NEAT!

Cover the six times table with paper so you can't see the numbers. Write the answers as quickly as you can.

What are two sixes?	12	What are five sixes?	30
What are three sixes?	18	What are ten sixes?	60
What is one six?	6	What are four sixes?	24

Write the answers as quickly as you can.

How many sixes make 30?	5	How many sixes make 6?	1
How many sixes make 12?	2	How many sixes make 18?	3
How many sixes make 24?	4	How many sixes make 60?	10

Write the answers as quickly as you can.

Multiply six by three.	18	Multiply six by two.	12
Multiply six by five.	30	Multiply six by four.	24
Multiply six by one.	6	Multiply six by ten.	60

Write the answers as quickly as you can.

2 x 6 = 12	10 x 6 = 60	4 x 6 = 24
5 x 6 = 30	3 x 6 = 18	1 x 6 = 6

Each of Batman's utility belts contains 5 gas pellets. How many gas pellets will there be in 6 utility belts? — 30

The rest of the 6s

You need to learn these:

6 x 6 = 36   7 x 6 = 42
8 x 6 = 48   9 x 6 = 54

NO SHORT CUTS. YOU'VE GOTTA LEARN THEM.

This work will help you remember the 6 times table.

Complete these sequences.

6   12   18   24   30   36   42   48   54   60

5 x 6 = 30   so   6 x 6 = 30 plus another 6 = 36

18   24   30   36   42   48   54   60

6 x 6 = 36   so   7 x 6 = 36 plus another 6 = 42

6   12   18   24   30   36   42   48   54   60

7 x 6 = 42   so   8 x 6 = 42 plus another 6 = 48

6   12   18   24   30   36   42   48   54   60

8 x 6 = 48   so   9 x 6 = 48 plus another 6 = 54

6   12   18   24   30   36   42   48   54   60

Test yourself on the rest of the 6 times table.
Cover the above part of the page with a sheet of paper.

What are six sixes?	36	What are eight sixes?	48
What are seven sixes?	42	What are nine sixes?	54

8 x 6 = 48   7 x 6 = 42   6 x 6 = 36   9 x 6 = 54

Practice the 6s

You should know all of the 6 times table now, but how quickly can you remember it? Have someone time you as you do this page. Remember, you must be fast but also correct.

HA! REMEMBER, NO MISTAKES!

1 x 6 = 6	2 x 6 = 12	7 x 6 = 42
2 x 6 = 12	4 x 6 = 24	3 x 6 = 18
3 x 6 = 18	6 x 6 = 36	9 x 6 = 54
4 x 6 = 24	8 x 6 = 48	6 x 4 = 24
5 x 6 = 30	10 x 6 = 60	1 x 6 = 6
6 x 6 = 36	1 x 6 = 6	6 x 2 = 12
7 x 6 = 42	3 x 6 = 18	6 x 8 = 48
8 x 6 = 48	5 x 6 = 30	0 x 6 = 0
9 x 6 = 54	7 x 6 = 42	6 x 3 = 18
10 x 6 = 60	9 x 6 = 54	5 x 6 = 30
6 x 1 = 6	6 x 3 = 18	6 x 7 = 42
6 x 2 = 12	6 x 5 = 30	2 x 6 = 18
6 x 3 = 18	6 x 7 = 42	6 x 9 = 54
6 x 4 = 24	6 x 9 = 54	4 x 6 = 24
6 x 5 = 30	6 x 2 = 12	8 x 6 = 48
6 x 6 = 36	6 x 4 = 24	10 x 6 = 60
6 x 7 = 42	6 x 6 = 36	6 x 5 = 30
6 x 8 = 48	6 x 8 = 48	6 x 0 = 0
6 x 9 = 54	6 x 10 = 60	6 x 1 = 6
6 x 10 = 60	6 x 0 = 0	6 x 6 = 36

Speed trials

You should know all of the 1, 2, 3, 4, 5, 6, and 10 times tables by now, but how quickly can you remember them?
Ask someone to time you as you do this page.
Remember, you must be fast but also correct.

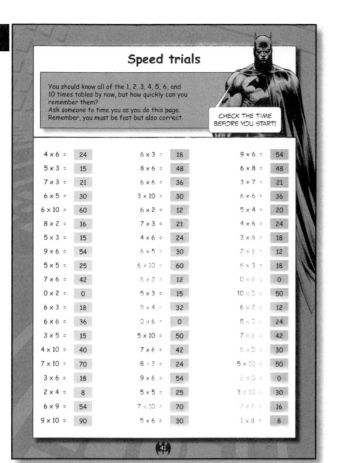

CHECK THE TIME BEFORE YOU START!

4 × 6 =	24	6 × 3 =	18	9 × 6 =	54
5 × 3 =	15	8 × 6 =	48	6 × 8 =	48
7 × 3 =	21	6 × 6 =	36	3 × 7 =	21
6 × 5 =	30	3 × 10 =	30	6 × 6 =	36
6 × 10 =	60	6 × 2 =	12	5 × 4 =	20
8 × 2 =	16	7 × 3 =	21	4 × 6 =	24
5 × 3 =	15	4 × 6 =	24	3 × 6 =	18
9 × 6 =	54	6 × 5 =	30	2 × 6 =	12
5 × 5 =	25	6 × 10 =	60	6 × 3 =	18
7 × 6 =	42	6 × 2 =	12	0 × 6 =	0
0 × 2 =	0	5 × 3 =	15	10 × 5 =	50
6 × 3 =	18	8 × 4 =	32	6 × 2 =	12
6 × 6 =	36	0 × 6 =	0	8 × 3 =	24
3 × 5 =	15	5 × 10 =	50	7 × 6 =	42
4 × 10 =	40	7 × 6 =	42	6 × 5 =	30
7 × 10 =	70	8 × 3 =	24	5 × 10 =	50
3 × 6 =	18	9 × 6 =	54	6 × 0 =	0
2 × 4 =	8	5 × 5 =	25	3 × 10 =	30
6 × 9 =	54	7 × 10 =	70	2 × 8 =	16
9 × 10 =	90	5 × 6 =	30	1 × 8 =	8

Some of the 7s

You should already know parts of the 7 times table because they are parts of the 1, 2, 3, 4, 5, 6, and 10 times tables.

1 × 7 = 7	2 × 7 = 14	3 × 7 = 21	4 × 7 = 28
5 × 7 = 35	6 × 7 = 42	10 × 7 = 70	

Find out if you can remember them quickly and correctly.

Cover the six times table with paper so you can't see the numbers.
Write the answers as quickly as you can.

What are three sevens?	21	What are four sevens?	28
What are two sevens?	14	What are six sevens?	42
What are five sevens?	35	What are ten sevens?	70

Write the answers as quickly as you can.

How many sevens make 14?	2	How many sevens make 28?	4
How many sevens make 35?	5	How many sevens make 21?	3
How many sevens make 70?	10	How many sevens make 42?	6

Write the answers as quickly as you can.

Multiply seven by three.	21	Multiply seven by six.	42
Multiply seven by five.	35	Multiply seven by two.	14
Multiply seven by four.	28	Multiply seven by ten.	70

Write the answers as quickly as you can.

10 × 7 =	70	4 × 7 =	28	5 × 7 =	35
3 × 7 =	21	6 × 7 =	42	2 × 7 =	14

Alfred spot-welds the rivets on six Bat gadgets. Each gadget needs seven welds. How many spot welds does Alfred make?   42

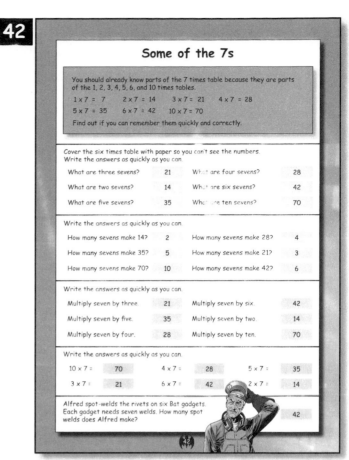

The rest of the 7s

You should now know all of the 1, 2, 3, 4, 5, 6, and 10 times tables. You need to learn only these parts of the seven times table.

7 × 7 = 49   7 × 8 = 56   7 × 9 = 63

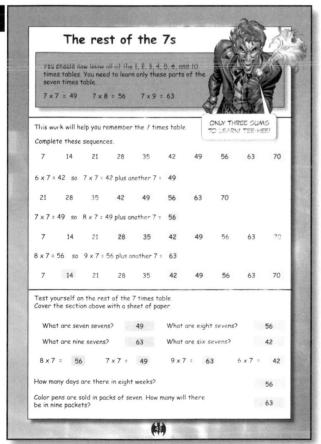

ONLY THREE SUMS TO LEARN! TEE-HEE!

This work will help you remember the 7 times table.

Complete these sequences.

7   14   21   28   35   42   49   56   63   70

6 × 7 = 42 so 7 × 7 = 42 plus another 7 = 49

21   28   35   42   49   56   63   70

7 × 7 = 49 so 8 × 7 = 49 plus another 7 = 56

7   14   21   28   35   42   49   56   63   70

8 × 7 = 56 so 9 × 7 = 56 plus another 7 = 63

7   14   21   28   35   42   49   56   63   70

Test yourself on the rest of the 7 times table.
Cover the section above with a sheet of paper.

What are seven sevens?	49	What are eight sevens?	56
What are nine sevens?	63	What are six sevens?	42

8 × 7 = 56   7 × 7 = 49   9 × 7 = 63   6 × 7 = 42

How many days are there in eight weeks?   56

Color pens are sold in packs of seven. How many will there be in nine packets?   63

Practice the 7s

You should know all of the 7 times table now, but how quickly can you remember it? Ask someone to time you as you do this page. Remember, you must be fast but correct.

FEELING SMART? HAVE SOMEONE TIME YOU!

1 × 7 =	7	2 × 7 =	14	7 × 6 =	42
2 × 7 =	14	4 × 7 =	28	3 × 7 =	21
3 × 7 =	21	6 × 7 =	42	9 × 7 =	63
4 × 7 =	28	8 × 7 =	56	7 × 4 =	28
5 × 7 =	35	10 × 7 =	70	1 × 7 =	7
6 × 7 =	42	1 × 7 =	7	7 × 2 =	14
7 × 7 =	49	3 × 7 =	21	7 × 8 =	56
8 × 7 =	56	5 × 7 =	35	0 × 7 =	0
9 × 7 =	63	7 × 7 =	49	7 × 3 =	21
10 × 7 =	70	9 × 7 =	63	5 × 7 =	35
7 × 1 =	7	7 × 3 =	21	7 × 7 =	49
7 × 2 =	14	7 × 5 =	35	2 × 7 =	14
7 × 3 =	21	7 × 7 =	49	7 × 9 =	63
7 × 4 =	28	7 × 9 =	63	4 × 7 =	28
7 × 5 =	35	7 × 2 =	14	8 × 7 =	56
7 × 6 =	42	7 × 4 =	28	10 × 7 =	70
7 × 7 =	49	7 × 6 =	42	7 × 5 =	35
7 × 8 =	56	7 × 8 =	56	7 × 0 =	0
7 × 9 =	63	7 × 10 =	70	7 × 1 =	7
7 × 10 =	70	7 × 0 =	0	6 × 7 =	42

Speed trials

You should know the 7 times table now, but how quickly can you remember it?
Ask someone to time you as you do this page.
Remember, you must be fast but also correct.

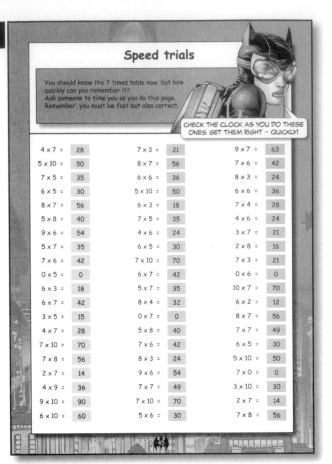

CHECK THE CLOCK AS YOU DO THESE ONES. GET THEM RIGHT – QUICKLY!

4 x 7 =	28	7 x 3 =	21	9 x 7 =	63
5 x 10 =	50	8 x 7 =	56	7 x 6 =	42
7 x 5 =	35	6 x 6 =	36	8 x 3 =	24
6 x 5 =	30	5 x 10 =	50	6 x 6 =	36
8 x 7 =	56	6 x 3 =	18	7 x 4 =	28
5 x 8 =	40	7 x 5 =	35	4 x 6 =	24
9 x 6 =	54	4 x 6 =	24	3 x 7 =	21
5 x 7 =	35	6 x 5 =	30	2 x 8 =	16
7 x 6 =	42	7 x 10 =	70	7 x 3 =	21
0 x 5 =	0	6 x 7 =	42	0 x 6 =	0
6 x 3 =	18	5 x 7 =	35	10 x 7 =	70
6 x 7 =	42	8 x 4 =	32	6 x 2 =	12
3 x 5 =	15	0 x 7 =	0	8 x 7 =	56
4 x 7 =	28	5 x 8 =	40	7 x 7 =	49
7 x 10 =	70	7 x 6 =	42	6 x 5 =	30
7 x 8 =	56	8 x 3 =	24	5 x 10 =	50
2 x 7 =	14	9 x 6 =	54	7 x 0 =	0
4 x 9 =	36	7 x 7 =	49	3 x 10 =	30
9 x 10 =	90	7 x 10 =	70	2 x 7 =	14
6 x 10 =	60	5 x 6 =	30	7 x 8 =	56

45

Some of the 8s

You should already know some of the 8 times table because it is part of the 1, 2, 3, 4, 5, 6, 7, and 10 times tables.

1 x 8 = 8   2 x 8 = 16   3 x 8 = 24   4 x 8 = 32
5 x 8 = 40   6 x 8 = 48   7 x 8 = 56   10 x 8 = 80

Find out if you can remember them.

Cover the eight times table with paper so you can't see the numbers.
Write the answers as quickly as you can.

What are three eights?	24	What are four eights?	32
What are two eights?	16	What are six eights?	48
What are five eights?	40	What are ten eights?	80

Write the answers as quickly as you can.

How many eights make 16?	2	How many eights make 24?	3
How many eights make 40?	5	How many eights make 56?	7
How many eights make 80?	10	How many eights make 48?	6

Write the answers as quickly as you can.

Multiply eight by three.	24	Multiply eight by six.	48
Multiply eight by five.	40	Multiply eight by two.	16
Multiply eight by four.	32	Multiply eight by ten.	80

Write the answers as quickly as you can.

6 x 8 =	48	2 x 8 =	16	7 x 8 =	56
4 x 8 =	32	5 x 8 =	40	3 x 8 =	24

The Penguin sells cans of soda in packs of eight. Robin buys seven packs. How many cans does he have?   56

46

The rest of the 8s

You need to learn only these parts of the eight times table.

8 x 8 = 64   9 x 8 = 72

This work will help you remember the 8 times table.

Complete these sequences.

8   16   24   32   40   48   56   64   72   80

7 x 8 = 56   so   8 x 8 = 56 plus another 8 =   64

24   32   40   48   56   64   72   80

8 x 8 = 64   so   9 x 8 = 64 plus another 8 =   72

8   16   24   32   40   48   56   64   72   80

8   16   24   32   40   48   56   64   72   80

Test yourself on the rest of the 8 times table.
Cover the section above with a sheet of paper.

What are seven eights?	56	What are eight eights?	64
What are nine eights?	72	What are six eights?	48

8 x 8 =   64   9 x 8 =   72   8 x 9 =   72   10 x 8 =   80

What number multiplied by 8 gives the answer 72?   9

A number multiplied by 8 gives the answer 64. What is the number?   8

A shopkeeper arranges Batman sweatshirts in piles of 8. How many sweatshirts will there be in 10 piles?   80

How many 8s make 56?   7

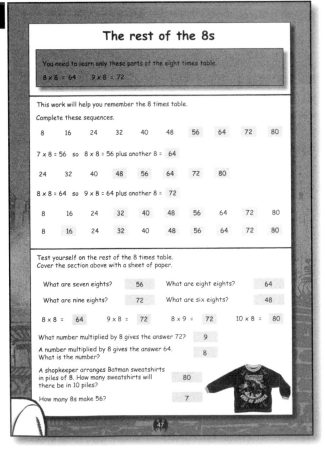

47

Practice the 8s

THIS IS A RACE AGAINST TIME. GET YOUR SPEED UP!

You should know all of the 8 times table now, but how quickly can you remember it?
Ask someone to time you as you do this page.
Be fast but also correct.

1 x 8 =	8	2 x 8 =	16	8 x 6 =	48
2 x 8 =	16	4 x 8 =	32	3 x 8 =	24
3 x 8 =	24	6 x 8 =	48	9 x 8 =	72
4 x 8 =	32	8 x 8 =	64	8 x 4 =	32
5 x 8 =	40	10 x 8 =	80	1 x 8 =	8
6 x 8 =	48	1 x 8 =	8	8 x 2 =	16
7 x 8 =	56	3 x 8 =	24	7 x 8 =	56
8 x 8 =	64	5 x 8 =	40	0 x 8 =	0
9 x 8 =	72	7 x 8 =	56	8 x 3 =	24
10 x 8 =	80	9 x 8 =	72	5 x 8 =	40
8 x 1 =	8	8 x 3 =	24	8 x 8 =	64
8 x 2 =	16	8 x 5 =	40	2 x 8 =	16
8 x 3 =	24	8 x 7 =	56	8 x 9 =	72
8 x 4 =	32	8 x 9 =	72	4 x 8 =	32
8 x 5 =	40	8 x 2 =	16	8 x 6 =	48
8 x 6 =	48	8 x 4 =	32	10 x 8 =	80
8 x 7 =	56	8 x 6 =	48	8 x 5 =	40
8 x 8 =	64	8 x 8 =	64	8 x 0 =	0
8 x 9 =	72	8 x 10 =	80	8 x 1 =	8
8 x 10 =	80	8 x 0 =	0	6 x 8 =	48

48

49

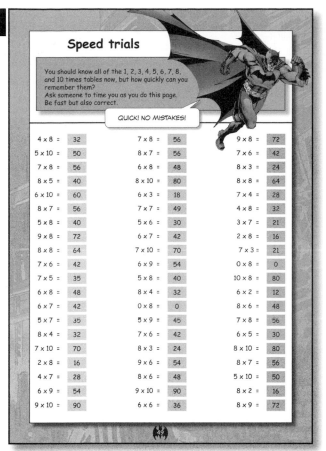

Speed trials

You should know all of the 1, 2, 3, 4, 5, 6, 7, 8, and 10 times tables now, but how quickly can you remember them?
Ask someone to time you as you do this page.
Be fast but also correct.

QUICK! NO MISTAKES!

4 x 8 = 32	7 x 8 = 56	9 x 8 = 72
5 x 10 = 50	8 x 7 = 56	7 x 6 = 42
7 x 8 = 56	6 x 8 = 48	8 x 3 = 24
8 x 5 = 40	8 x 10 = 80	8 x 8 = 64
6 x 10 = 60	6 x 3 = 18	7 x 4 = 28
8 x 7 = 56	7 x 7 = 49	4 x 8 = 32
5 x 8 = 40	5 x 6 = 30	3 x 7 = 21
9 x 8 = 72	6 x 7 = 42	2 x 8 = 16
8 x 8 = 64	7 x 10 = 70	7 x 3 = 21
7 x 6 = 42	6 x 9 = 54	0 x 8 = 0
7 x 5 = 35	5 x 8 = 40	10 x 8 = 80
6 x 8 = 48	8 x 4 = 32	6 x 2 = 12
6 x 7 = 42	0 x 8 = 0	8 x 6 = 48
5 x 7 = 35	5 x 9 = 45	7 x 8 = 56
8 x 4 = 32	7 x 6 = 42	6 x 5 = 30
7 x 10 = 70	8 x 3 = 24	8 x 10 = 80
2 x 8 = 16	9 x 6 = 54	8 x 7 = 56
4 x 7 = 28	8 x 6 = 48	5 x 10 = 50
6 x 9 = 54	9 x 10 = 90	8 x 2 = 16
9 x 10 = 90	6 x 6 = 36	8 x 9 = 72

49

50

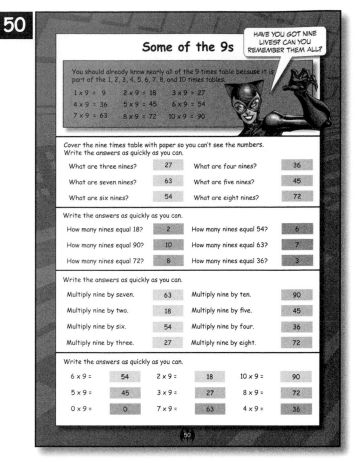

Some of the 9s

HAVE YOU GOT NINE LIVES? CAN YOU REMEMBER THEM ALL?

You should already know nearly all of the 9 times table because it is part of the 1, 2, 3, 4, 5, 6, 7, 8, and 10 times tables.

1 x 9 = 9	2 x 9 = 18	3 x 9 = 27
4 x 9 = 36	5 x 9 = 45	6 x 9 = 54
7 x 9 = 63	8 x 9 = 72	10 x 9 = 90

Cover the nine times table with paper so you can't see the numbers.
Write the answers as quickly as you can.

What are three nines?	27	What are four nines?	36
What are seven nines?	63	What are five nines?	45
What are six nines?	54	What are eight nines?	72

Write the answers as quickly as you can.

How many nines equal 18?	2	How many nines equal 54?	6
How many nines equal 90?	10	How many nines equal 63?	7
How many nines equal 72?	8	How many nines equal 36?	3

Write the answers as quickly as you can.

Multiply nine by seven.	63	Multiply nine by ten.	90
Multiply nine by two.	18	Multiply nine by five.	45
Multiply nine by six.	54	Multiply nine by four.	36
Multiply nine by three.	27	Multiply nine by eight.	72

Write the answers as quickly as you can.

6 x 9 = 54	2 x 9 = 18	10 x 9 = 90
5 x 9 = 45	3 x 9 = 27	8 x 9 = 72
0 x 9 = 0	7 x 9 = 63	4 x 9 = 36

50

51

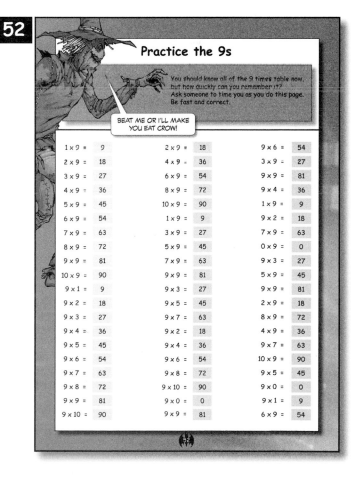

The rest of the 9s

You need to learn only this part of the nine times table.
9 x 9 = 81

YOU NEED ONLY LEARN ONE SUM. THAT'S SMART!

This work will help you remember the 9 times table.

Complete these sequences.

9   18   27   36   45   54   63   72   81   90

8 x 9 = 72   so   9 x 9 = 72 plus another 9 = 81

27   36   45   54   63   72   81   90

9   18   27   36   45   54   63   72   81   90

9   18   27   36   45   54   63   72   81   90

Look for a pattern in the nine times table.

1	x	9	=	09
2	x	9	=	18
3	x	9	=	27
4	x	9	=	36
5	x	9	=	45
6	x	9	=	54
7	x	9	=	63
8	x	9	=	72
9	x	9	=	81
10	x	9	=	90

Write down any patterns you can see. (There is more than one.)

The digits in every answer have a sum of 9.
If we take the first number of every answer, from top to bottom, we get
0, 1, 2, 3, 4, 5, 6, 7, 8, 9.
If we take the second number of every answer, from bottom to top, we get
0, 1, 2, 3, 4, 5, 6, 7, 8, 9.
The first and last answers are opposites (09 and 90), the second and the second
last answers are opposites (18 and 81), and so on.

51

52

Practice the 9s

You should know all of the 9 times table now, but how quickly can you remember it?
Ask someone to time you as you do this page.
Be fast and correct.

BEAT ME OR I'LL MAKE YOU EAT CROW!

1 x 9 = 9	2 x 9 = 18	9 x 6 = 54
2 x 9 = 18	4 x 9 = 36	3 x 9 = 27
3 x 9 = 27	6 x 9 = 54	9 x 9 = 81
4 x 9 = 36	8 x 9 = 72	9 x 4 = 36
5 x 9 = 45	10 x 9 = 90	1 x 9 = 9
6 x 9 = 54	1 x 9 = 9	9 x 2 = 18
7 x 9 = 63	3 x 9 = 27	7 x 9 = 63
8 x 9 = 72	5 x 9 = 45	0 x 9 = 0
9 x 9 = 81	7 x 9 = 63	9 x 3 = 27
10 x 9 = 90	9 x 9 = 81	5 x 9 = 45
9 x 1 = 9	9 x 3 = 27	9 x 9 = 81
9 x 2 = 18	9 x 5 = 45	2 x 9 = 18
9 x 3 = 27	9 x 7 = 63	8 x 9 = 72
9 x 4 = 36	9 x 2 = 18	4 x 9 = 36
9 x 5 = 45	9 x 4 = 36	9 x 7 = 63
9 x 6 = 54	9 x 6 = 54	10 x 9 = 90
9 x 7 = 63	9 x 8 = 72	9 x 5 = 45
9 x 8 = 72	9 x 10 = 90	9 x 0 = 0
9 x 9 = 81	9 x 0 = 0	9 x 1 = 9
9 x 10 = 90	9 x 9 = 81	6 x 9 = 54

52

Encourage children to notice patterns. It does not matter how they express these. One pattern is to deduct 1 from the number being multiplied. This gives the first digit of the answer. Then deduct this first digit from 9 to get the second digit of the answer.

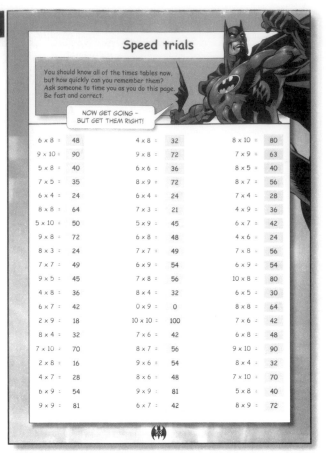

Speed trials

You should know all of the times tables now, but how quickly can you remember them? Ask someone to time you as you do this page. Be fast and correct.

> NOW GET GOING –
> BUT GET THEM RIGHT!

6 x 8 =	48	4 x 8 =	32	8 x 10 =	80
9 x 10 =	90	9 x 8 =	72	7 x 9 =	63
5 x 8 =	40	6 x 6 =	36	8 x 5 =	40
7 x 5 =	35	8 x 9 =	72	8 x 7 =	56
6 x 4 =	24	6 x 4 =	24	7 x 4 =	28
8 x 8 =	64	7 x 3 =	21	4 x 9 =	36
5 x 10 =	50	5 x 9 =	45	6 x 7 =	42
9 x 8 =	72	6 x 8 =	48	4 x 6 =	24
8 x 3 =	24	7 x 7 =	49	7 x 8 =	56
7 x 7 =	49	6 x 9 =	54	6 x 9 =	54
9 x 5 =	45	7 x 8 =	56	10 x 8 =	80
4 x 8 =	36	8 x 4 =	32	6 x 5 =	30
6 x 7 =	42	0 x 9 =	0	8 x 8 =	64
2 x 9 =	18	10 x 10 =	100	7 x 6 =	42
8 x 4 =	32	7 x 6 =	42	6 x 8 =	48
7 x 10 =	70	8 x 7 =	56	9 x 10 =	90
2 x 8 =	16	9 x 6 =	54	8 x 4 =	32
4 x 7 =	28	8 x 6 =	48	7 x 10 =	70
6 x 9 =	54	9 x 9 =	81	5 x 8 =	40
9 x 9 =	81	6 x 7 =	42	8 x 9 =	72

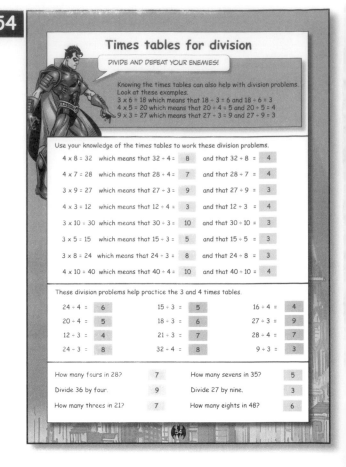

Times tables for division

> DIVIDE AND DEFEAT YOUR ENEMIES!

Knowing the times tables can also help with division problems. Look at these examples.
3 x 6 = 18 which means that 18 ÷ 3 = 6 and 18 ÷ 6 = 3
4 x 5 = 20 which means that 20 ÷ 4 = 5 and 20 ÷ 5 = 4
9 x 3 = 27 which means that 27 ÷ 3 = 9 and 27 ÷ 9 = 3

Use your knowledge of the times tables to work these division problems.

4 x 8 = 32	which means that 32 ÷ 4 = 8	and that 32 ÷ 8 = 4
4 x 7 = 28	which means that 28 ÷ 4 = 7	and that 28 ÷ 7 = 4
3 x 9 = 27	which means that 27 ÷ 3 = 9	and that 27 ÷ 9 = 3
4 x 3 = 12	which means that 12 ÷ 4 = 3	and that 12 ÷ 3 = 4
3 x 10 = 30	which means that 30 ÷ 3 = 10	and that 30 ÷ 10 = 3
3 x 5 = 15	which means that 15 ÷ 3 = 5	and that 15 ÷ 5 = 3
3 x 8 = 24	which means that 24 ÷ 3 = 8	and that 24 ÷ 8 = 3
4 x 10 = 40	which means that 40 ÷ 4 = 10	and that 40 ÷ 10 = 4

These division problems help practice the 3 and 4 times tables.

24 ÷ 4 =	6	15 ÷ 3 =	5	16 ÷ 4 =	4
20 ÷ 4 =	5	18 ÷ 3 =	6	27 ÷ 3 =	9
12 ÷ 3 =	4	21 ÷ 3 =	7	28 ÷ 4 =	7
24 ÷ 3 =	8	32 ÷ 4 =	8	9 ÷ 3 =	3

How many fours in 28?	7	How many sevens in 35?	5
Divide 36 by four.	9	Divide 27 by nine.	3
How many threes in 21?	7	How many eights in 48?	6

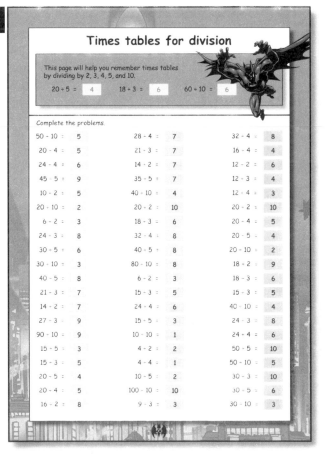

Times tables for division

This page will help you remember times tables by dividing by 2, 3, 4, 5, and 10.

20 ÷ 5 =	4	18 ÷ 3 =	6	60 ÷ 10 =	6

Complete the problems.

50 ÷ 10 =	5	28 ÷ 4 =	7	32 ÷ 4 =	8
20 ÷ 4 =	5	21 ÷ 3 =	7	16 ÷ 4 =	4
24 ÷ 4 =	6	14 ÷ 2 =	7	12 ÷ 2 =	6
45 ÷ 5 =	9	35 ÷ 5 =	7	12 ÷ 3 =	4
10 ÷ 2 =	5	40 ÷ 10 =	4	12 ÷ 4 =	3
20 ÷ 10 =	2	20 ÷ 2 =	10	20 ÷ 2 =	10
6 ÷ 2 =	3	18 ÷ 3 =	6	20 ÷ 4 =	5
24 ÷ 3 =	8	32 ÷ 4 =	8	20 ÷ 5 =	4
30 ÷ 5 =	6	40 ÷ 5 =	8	20 ÷ 10 =	2
30 ÷ 10 =	3	80 ÷ 10 =	8	18 ÷ 2 =	9
40 ÷ 5 =	8	6 ÷ 2 =	3	18 ÷ 3 =	6
21 ÷ 3 =	7	15 ÷ 3 =	5	15 ÷ 3 =	5
14 ÷ 2 =	7	24 ÷ 4 =	6	40 ÷ 10 =	4
27 ÷ 3 =	9	15 ÷ 5 =	3	24 ÷ 3 =	8
90 ÷ 10 =	9	10 ÷ 10 =	1	24 ÷ 4 =	6
15 ÷ 5 =	3	4 ÷ 2 =	2	50 ÷ 5 =	10
15 ÷ 3 =	5	4 ÷ 4 =	1	50 ÷ 10 =	5
20 ÷ 5 =	4	10 ÷ 5 =	2	30 ÷ 3 =	10
20 ÷ 4 =	5	100 ÷ 10 =	10	30 ÷ 5 =	6
16 ÷ 2 =	8	9 ÷ 3 =	3	30 ÷ 10 =	3

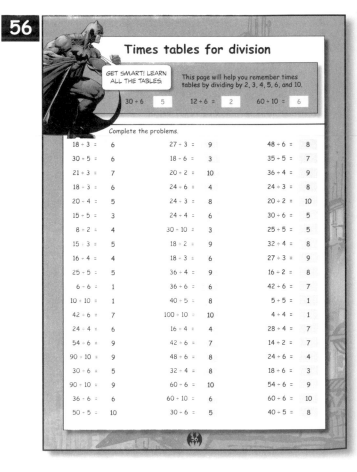

Times tables for division

> GET SMART! LEARN
> ALL THE TABLES.

This page will help you remember times tables by dividing by 2, 3, 4, 5, 6, and 10.

30 ÷ 6 =	5	12 ÷ 6 =	2	60 ÷ 10 =	6

Complete the problems.

18 ÷ 3 =	6	27 ÷ 3 =	9	48 ÷ 6 =	8
30 ÷ 5 =	6	18 ÷ 6 =	3	35 ÷ 5 =	7
21 ÷ 3 =	7	20 ÷ 2 =	10	36 ÷ 4 =	9
18 ÷ 3 =	6	24 ÷ 6 =	4	24 ÷ 3 =	8
20 ÷ 4 =	5	24 ÷ 3 =	8	20 ÷ 2 =	10
15 ÷ 5 =	3	24 ÷ 4 =	6	30 ÷ 6 =	5
8 ÷ 2 =	4	30 ÷ 10 =	3	25 ÷ 5 =	5
15 ÷ 3 =	5	18 ÷ 2 =	9	32 ÷ 4 =	8
16 ÷ 4 =	4	18 ÷ 3 =	6	27 ÷ 3 =	9
25 ÷ 5 =	5	36 ÷ 4 =	9	16 ÷ 2 =	8
6 ÷ 6 =	1	36 ÷ 6 =	6	42 ÷ 6 =	7
10 ÷ 10 =	1	40 ÷ 5 =	8	5 ÷ 5 =	1
42 ÷ 6 =	7	100 ÷ 10 =	10	4 ÷ 4 =	1
24 ÷ 4 =	6	16 ÷ 4 =	4	28 ÷ 4 =	7
54 ÷ 6 =	9	42 ÷ 6 =	7	14 ÷ 2 =	7
90 ÷ 10 =	9	48 ÷ 6 =	8	24 ÷ 6 =	4
30 ÷ 6 =	5	32 ÷ 4 =	8	18 ÷ 6 =	3
90 ÷ 10 =	9	60 ÷ 6 =	10	54 ÷ 6 =	9
36 ÷ 6 =	6	60 ÷ 10 =	6	60 ÷ 6 =	10
50 ÷ 5 =	10	30 ÷ 6 =	5	40 ÷ 5 =	8

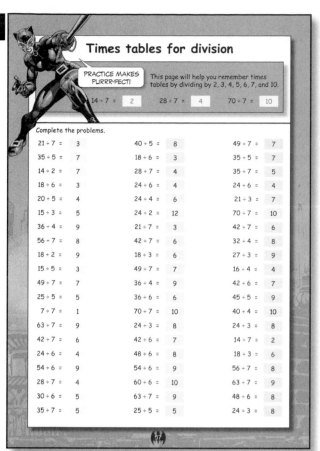

Times tables for division

PRACTICE MAKES PURRR-FECT!

This page will help you remember times tables by dividing by 2, 3, 4, 5, 6, 7, and 10.

$14 \div 7 =$ 2 $28 \div 7 =$ 4 $70 \div 7 =$ 10

Complete the problems.

$21 \div 7 =$ 3	$40 \div 5 =$ 8	$49 \div 7 =$ 7
$35 \div 5 =$ 7	$18 \div 6 =$ 3	$35 \div 5 =$ 7
$14 \div 2 =$ 7	$28 \div 7 =$ 4	$35 \div 7 =$ 5
$18 \div 6 =$ 3	$24 \div 6 =$ 4	$24 \div 6 =$ 4
$20 \div 5 =$ 4	$24 \div 4 =$ 6	$21 \div 3 =$ 7
$15 \div 3 =$ 5	$24 \div 2 =$ 12	$70 \div 7 =$ 10
$36 \div 4 =$ 9	$21 \div 7 =$ 3	$42 \div 7 =$ 6
$56 \div 7 =$ 8	$42 \div 7 =$ 6	$32 \div 4 =$ 8
$18 \div 2 =$ 9	$18 \div 3 =$ 6	$27 \div 3 =$ 9
$15 \div 5 =$ 3	$49 \div 7 =$ 7	$16 \div 4 =$ 4
$49 \div 7 =$ 7	$36 \div 4 =$ 9	$42 \div 6 =$ 7
$25 \div 5 =$ 5	$36 \div 6 =$ 6	$45 \div 5 =$ 9
$7 \div 7 =$ 1	$70 \div 7 =$ 10	$40 \div 4 =$ 10
$63 \div 7 =$ 9	$24 \div 3 =$ 8	$24 \div 3 =$ 8
$42 \div 7 =$ 6	$42 \div 6 =$ 7	$14 \div 7 =$ 2
$24 \div 6 =$ 4	$48 \div 6 =$ 8	$18 \div 3 =$ 6
$54 \div 6 =$ 9	$54 \div 6 =$ 9	$56 \div 7 =$ 8
$28 \div 7 =$ 4	$60 \div 6 =$ 10	$63 \div 7 =$ 9
$30 \div 6 =$ 5	$63 \div 7 =$ 9	$48 \div 6 =$ 8
$35 \div 7 =$ 5	$25 \div 5 =$ 5	$24 \div 3 =$ 8

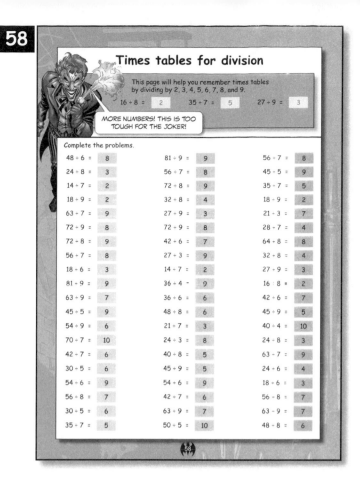

Times tables for division

This page will help you remember times tables by dividing by 2, 3, 4, 5, 6, 7, 8, and 9.

$16 \div 8 =$ 2 $35 \div 7 =$ 5 $27 \div 9 =$ 3

MORE NUMBERS! THIS IS TOO TOUGH FOR THE JOKER!

Complete the problems.

$48 \div 6 =$ 8	$81 \div 9 =$ 9	$56 \div 7 =$ 8
$24 \div 8 =$ 3	$56 \div 7 =$ 8	$45 \div 5 =$ 9
$14 \div 7 =$ 2	$72 \div 8 =$ 9	$35 \div 7 =$ 5
$18 \div 9 =$ 2	$32 \div 8 =$ 4	$18 \div 9 =$ 2
$63 \div 7 =$ 9	$27 \div 9 =$ 3	$21 \div 3 =$ 7
$72 \div 9 =$ 8	$72 \div 9 =$ 8	$28 \div 7 =$ 4
$72 \div 8 =$ 9	$42 \div 6 =$ 7	$64 \div 8 =$ 8
$56 \div 7 =$ 8	$27 \div 3 =$ 9	$32 \div 8 =$ 4
$18 \div 6 =$ 3	$14 \div 7 =$ 2	$27 \div 9 =$ 3
$81 \div 9 =$ 9	$36 \div 4 =$ 9	$16 \div 8 =$ 2
$63 \div 9 =$ 7	$36 \div 6 =$ 6	$42 \div 6 =$ 7
$45 \div 5 =$ 9	$48 \div 8 =$ 6	$45 \div 9 =$ 5
$54 \div 9 =$ 6	$21 \div 7 =$ 3	$40 \div 4 =$ 10
$70 \div 7 =$ 10	$24 \div 3 =$ 8	$24 \div 8 =$ 3
$42 \div 7 =$ 6	$40 \div 8 =$ 5	$63 \div 7 =$ 9
$30 \div 5 =$ 6	$45 \div 9 =$ 5	$24 \div 6 =$ 4
$54 \div 6 =$ 9	$54 \div 6 =$ 9	$18 \div 6 =$ 3
$56 \div 8 =$ 7	$42 \div 7 =$ 6	$56 \div 8 =$ 7
$30 \div 5 =$ 6	$63 \div 9 =$ 7	$63 \div 9 =$ 7
$35 \div 7 =$ 5	$50 \div 5 =$ 10	$48 \div 8 =$ 6

Times tables practice grids

This is a times tables grid.

X	3	4	5	6
7	21	28	35	42
8	24	32	40	48

CHECK OUT THE GRIDS IN THE BATCAVE.

Complete each times tables grid.

X	1	3	5	7	9
2	2	6	10	14	18
3	3	9	15	21	27

X	4	6
6	24	36
7	28	42
8	32	48

X	6	7	8	9	10
3	18	21	24	27	30
4	24	28	32	36	40
5	30	35	40	45	50

X	10	7	8	4	2
3	30	21	24	12	6
5	50	35	40	20	10
7	70	49	56	28	14

X	6	2	4	7
5	30	10	20	35
10	60	20	40	70

X	8	7	9	6
9	72	63	81	54
7	56	49	63	42

Times tables practice grids

Here are more times tables grids.

X	2	4	6
3	6	12	18
7	14	28	42

X	8	3	7	2
5	40	15	35	10
6	48	18	42	12
7	56	21	49	14

THESE BATS ARE TOO CLEVER FOR ME!

X	2	3	4	5
8	16	24	32	40
9	18	27	36	45

X	10	9	8	7
6	60	54	48	42
5	50	45	40	35
4	40	36	32	28

X	3	6
2	6	12
3	9	18
4	12	24
5	15	30
6	18	36
7	21	42

X	2	4	6	8
1	2	4	6	8
3	6	12	18	24
5	10	20	30	40
7	14	28	42	56
9	18	36	54	72
0	0	0	0	0

Times tables practice grids

Here are some other times tables grids.

DON'T GET GRID LOCK!

X	7	8	9	10
7	49	56	63	70
8	56	64	72	80

X	9	8	7	6	5	4
9	81	72	63	54	45	36
8	72	64	56	48	40	32
7	63	56	49	42	35	28

X	2	5	7	9
4	8	20	28	36
6	12	30	42	54
8	16	40	56	72

X	2	3	4	5	7
4	8	12	16	20	28
6	12	18	24	30	42
8	16	24	32	40	56

X	3	5	7
2	6	10	14
8	24	40	56
6	18	30	42
0	0	0	0
4	12	20	28
7	21	35	49

X	8	7	9	6
7	56	49	63	42
9	72	63	81	54
0	0	0	0	0
10	80	70	90	60
8	64	56	72	48
6	48	42	54	36

Speed trials

THESE ARE TRICKY – LIKE ME! WATCH OUT FOR THE SIGNS!

Try this final test.

42 ÷ 6 =	7	4 x 9 =	36	14 ÷ 2 =	7
7 x 4 =	28	18 ÷ 2 =	9	9 x 9 =	81
64 ÷ 8 =	8	6 x 8 =	48	15 ÷ 3 =	5
90 ÷ 10 =	9	21 ÷ 3 =	7	8 x 8 =	64
3 x 7 =	21	9 x 7 =	63	24 ÷ 4 =	6
6 x 8 =	48	36 ÷ 4 =	9	7 x 8 =	56
48 ÷ 6 =	8	4 x 6 =	24	30 ÷ 5 =	6
7 x 7 =	49	45 ÷ 5 =	9	6 x 6 =	36
9 x 5 =	45	8 x 5 =	40	27 ÷ 3 =	9
45 ÷ 9 =	5	42 ÷ 6 =	7	9 x 5 =	45
3 x 9 =	27	7 x 9 =	63	49 ÷ 7 =	7
56 ÷ 8 =	7	35 ÷ 7 =	5	8 x 6 =	48
36 ÷ 4 =	9	9 x 3 =	27	72 ÷ 8 =	9
24 ÷ 3 =	8	24 ÷ 8 =	3	9 x 7 =	63
36 ÷ 9 =	4	8 x 2 =	16	54 ÷ 9 =	6
6 x 7 =	42	36 ÷ 9 =	4	7 x 6 =	42
4 x 4 =	16	6 x 10 =	60	10 ÷ 10 =	1
32 ÷ 8 =	4	80 ÷ 10 =	8	7 x 7 =	49
49 ÷ 7 =	7	6 x 9 =	54	16 ÷ 8 =	2
25 ÷ 5 =	5	16 ÷ 2 =	8	7 x 9 =	63
56 ÷ 7 =	8	54 ÷ 9 =	6	63 ÷ 7 =	9

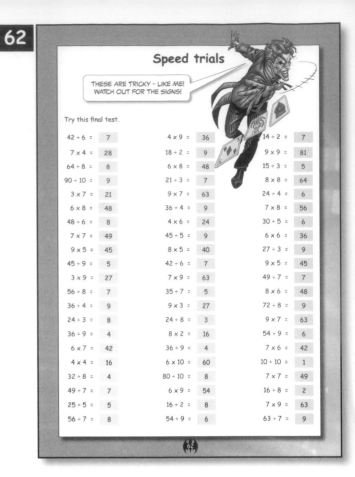

Line of symmetry

If a plane figure is divided into two congruent (matching) parts, the line that divides the two parts is called a line of symmetry.

Draw as many lines of symmetry as you can find on each of these shapes.

Draw a line of symmetry on each of these shapes.

Draw as many lines of symmetry as you can find on each of these shapes.

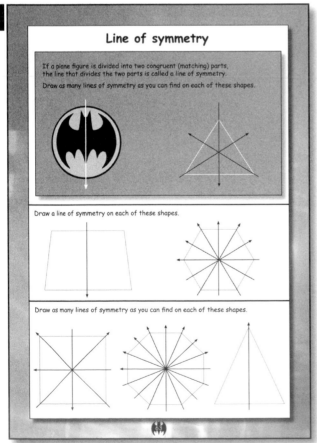

If children find it difficult to see where a line of symmetry falls, talk about where the shape could be folded so that both parts overlap exactly.

Ordering large numbers

Write these numbers in order, starting with the least.

256	9,644,327	39,214	9,631
256	9,613	39,214	9,644,327

YOU'RE OUT OF ORDER!

Write these numbers in order, starting with the least.

327,914	3,654,212	47,900	3,825	416
416	3,825	47,900	327,914	3,654,212
72,463	8,730,241	261	5,247	643,292
261	5,247	72,463	643,292	8,730,241
6,436	643	64,370	6,430	643,000
643	6,430	6,436	64,370	643,000
593,102	761	374,239	91,761	1,425
761	1,425	91,761	374,239	593,102
9,641,471	260,453	59,372	657,473	4,290
4,290	59,372	260,453	657,473	9,641,471
5,600,200	500,200	5,200	50,200	52,000
5,200	50,200	52,000	500,200	5,600,200
9,900	999	900,200	920,200	9,200,000
999	9,900	900,200	920,200	9,200,000

At the Gotham City elections
The Penguin got 900,540 votes,
The Joker got 830,580 votes,
Robin got 8,305,800 votes,
Batman got 9,764,201 votes,
and the Riddler got 849,999 votes.

Place the candidates in order.

1st	Batman
2nd	Robin
3rd	The Penguin
4th	The Riddler
5th	The Joker

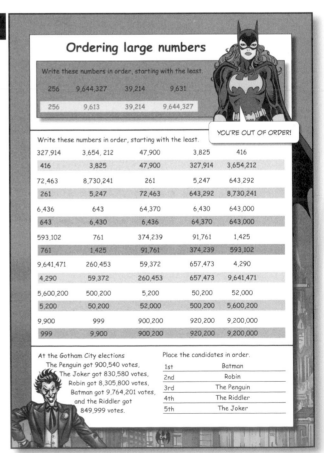

If children are weak on place value, help them identify the significant digits when sorting a group of numbers. Take care when the same digits are used but with different place values.

65

Rounding whole numbers

Round these numbers to the nearest hundred.

529 → 500   1,687 → 1,700

If the place to the right of the place you are rounding is 5 or more, round the previous number up.

652 → 700

ROUND 'EM ALL UP - OR DOWN!

Round to the nearest hundred.

687	700	234	200	8,467	8,500	3,561	3,600
16,543	16,500	4,855	4,900	769	800	1,300	1,300
22,751	22,800	227	200	792	800	354	400

Round to the nearest ten-thousand.

23,478	20,000	618,600	620,000	58,473	60,000	452,899	450,000
209,544	210,000	32,059	30,000	67,414	70,000	33,500	30,0000
89,388	90,000	801,821	800,000	134,800	130,000	45,010	50,000

Round to the nearest ten.

77	80	386	390	53	50	65	70
1,392	1,400	15	20	12,489	12,490	2,861	2,860
75	80	715	720	34	30	18,149	18,150

Round to the nearest thousand.

3,284	3,000	112,810	113,000	10,518	11,000	83,477	83,000
8,499	8,000	225,500	226,000	4,500	5,000	6,112	6,000
1,059	1,000	93,606	94,000	6,752	7,000	2,550	3,000

If children are confused about where to round, help them underline the rounding place and circle the digit to its right—that is the digit to compare to 5.

66

Choosing units of measure

Circle the units that are the closest estimate.
The amount of orange juice in a full glass.

(6 fluid ounces)   4 pints   2 gallons

USE YOUR BRAIN. MAKE A GOOD GUESS!

Circle the units that are the closest estimate.

The weight of a box of cereal	(15 ounces)	3 pounds	2 tons
The length of a football field	20 feet	(100 yards)	1 mile
The area of a rug	90 sq. inches	(108 sq. feet)	1 sq. mile
The amount of cough medicine in a bottle	(3 fluid ounces)	2 cups	1 quart
The distance from home plate to first base	120 inches	(90 feet)	6 yards
The weight of a package of sugar	7 ounces	(5 pounds)	$\frac{1}{2}$ ton
The length of an airport runway	(2 miles)	50 yards	500 feet
The amount of water in a full pail	8 fluid ounces	2 pints	(3 gallons)
The area of a place mat	(144 sq. inches)	6 sq. feet	1 sq. mile

Children need mental benchmarks for each of the units in order to choose the best unit to measure. Suggest examples, such as the weight of a few raisins for an ounce and the weight of a shoe for a pound.

67

Comparing fractions

Which is greater, $\frac{2}{3}$ or $\frac{3}{4}$? $\frac{3}{4}$

The common denominator of 3 and 4 is 12.

$\frac{2 \times 4 = 8}{3 \times 4 = 12}$ So $\frac{2}{3} = \frac{8}{12}$ $\frac{3 \times 3 = 9}{4 \times 3 = 12}$ So $\frac{3}{4} = \frac{9}{12}$

Since $\frac{9}{12}$ is greater than $\frac{8}{12}$, then $\frac{3}{4}$ must be greater than $\frac{2}{3}$.

Which is greater?

$\frac{1}{2}$ or $\frac{5}{8}$ $\frac{5}{8}$ $\frac{1}{4}$ or $\frac{1}{3}$ $\frac{1}{3}$ $\frac{5}{6}$ or $\frac{7}{9}$ $\frac{5}{6}$ $\frac{1}{3}$ or $\frac{4}{9}$ $\frac{4}{9}$

$\frac{7}{10}$ or $\frac{8}{9}$ $\frac{8}{9}$ $\frac{2}{5}$ or $\frac{3}{8}$ $\frac{2}{5}$ $\frac{7}{8}$ or $\frac{8}{10}$ $\frac{7}{8}$ $\frac{2}{3}$ or $\frac{7}{12}$ $\frac{2}{3}$

$\frac{5}{8}$ or $\frac{2}{3}$ $\frac{2}{3}$ $\frac{2}{5}$ or $\frac{2}{3}$ $\frac{2}{3}$ $\frac{4}{15}$ or $\frac{1}{3}$ $\frac{1}{3}$ $\frac{1}{4}$ or $\frac{3}{8}$ $\frac{3}{8}$

Which two fractions in each row are equal?

$\frac{5}{8}$	$\frac{1}{4}$	$\frac{7}{8}$	$\frac{3}{8}$	$\frac{3}{12}$	$\frac{4}{12}$

$\frac{1}{4}$ and $\frac{3}{12}$

$\frac{7}{10}$	$\frac{6}{9}$	$\frac{5}{8}$	$\frac{9}{12}$	$\frac{1}{2}$	$\frac{3}{4}$

$\frac{8}{12}$ and $\frac{3}{4}$

$\frac{9}{12}$	$\frac{4}{8}$	$\frac{3}{8}$	$\frac{7}{14}$	$\frac{6}{14}$	$\frac{7}{12}$

$\frac{4}{8}$ and $\frac{7}{14}$

$\frac{4}{7}$	$\frac{9}{10}$	$\frac{6}{7}$	$\frac{2}{6}$	$\frac{3}{9}$	$\frac{3}{8}$

$\frac{2}{6}$ and $\frac{3}{9}$

$\frac{3}{10}$	$\frac{5}{15}$	$\frac{2}{10}$	$\frac{3}{15}$	$\frac{4}{10}$	$\frac{7}{15}$

$\frac{2}{10}$ and $\frac{3}{15}$

LET'S GO! THERE'S MORE WORK TO BE DONE.

Put these fractions in order, starting with the least.

$\frac{1}{2}$ $\frac{5}{6}$ $\frac{2}{3}$ $\frac{1}{2}$ $\frac{2}{3}$ $\frac{5}{6}$

$\frac{2}{3}$ $\frac{8}{15}$ $\frac{3}{5}$ $\frac{8}{15}$ $\frac{3}{5}$ $\frac{2}{3}$

Difficulty in finding a common denominator indicates a weakness in times tables knowledge. Children need to convert all the fractions in the later questions into a common form before answering the question. Be careful that they do not try to guess the answer.

Converting fractions to decimals

Convert these fractions to decimals.

$\frac{3}{10} = 0.3$

(because the three goes in the tenths column)

DON'T GET FRACTIOUS ABOUT FRACTIONS.

$\frac{7}{100} = 0.07$

(because the seven goes in the hundredths column)

Convert these fractions to decimals.

$\frac{4}{100} = 0.04$	$\frac{6}{100} = 0.06$	$\frac{1}{10} = 0.1$	$\frac{3}{100} = 0.03$
$\frac{6}{10} = 0.6$	$\frac{2}{10} = 0.2$	$\frac{8}{10} = 0.8$	$\frac{9}{10} = 0.9$
$\frac{4}{10} = 0.4$	$\frac{5}{10} = 0.5$	$\frac{1}{100} = 0.01$	$\frac{3}{100} = 0.03$
$\frac{2}{100} = 0.02$	$\frac{8}{100} = 0.08$	$\frac{7}{10} = 0.7$	$\frac{5}{100} = 0.05$

Convert $\frac{1}{4}$ to a decimal.

To do this we have to divide the bottom number into the top.

When we run out of numbers we put in the decimal point and enough zeros to finish the sum. Be careful to keep the decimal point in your answer above the decimal point in the sum.

```
    0.25
4) 1.00
     8
     20
     20
      0
```

Convert these fractions to decimals.

$\frac{1}{4} = 0.25$	$\frac{1}{2} = 0.5$	$\frac{4}{5} = 0.8$	$\frac{1}{5} = 0.2$
$\frac{1}{8} = 0.125$	$\frac{3}{4} = 0.75$	$\frac{3}{8} = 0.375$	$\frac{3}{5} = 0.6$

Difficulty in the first section highlights weakness in understanding place value to the first two decimal places. It may be necessary to reinforce understanding of 10ths and 100ths in decimals.

Adding fractions

Find the sum of each problem.

$\frac{1}{5} + \frac{3}{5} = \frac{4}{5}$ $\frac{4}{9} + \frac{2}{9} = \frac{6}{9} = \frac{2}{3}$

Add the numerators but keep the denominators the same. Remember to reduce to simplest form if you need to.

I'M KEEPING AN EYE ON THE ANSWERS!

Find the sum of each problem.

$\frac{2}{9} + \frac{5}{9} = \frac{7}{9}$	$\frac{2}{7} + \frac{3}{7} = \frac{5}{7}$	$\frac{1}{3} + \frac{1}{3} = \frac{2}{3}$
$\frac{2}{9} + \frac{3}{9} = \frac{5}{9}$	$\frac{2}{8} + \frac{1}{8} = \frac{3}{8}$	$\frac{3}{10} + \frac{6}{10} = \frac{9}{10}$
$\frac{4}{20} + \frac{5}{20} = \frac{9}{20}$	$\frac{1}{100} + \frac{16}{100} = \frac{17}{100}$	$\frac{7}{10} + \frac{2}{10} = \frac{9}{10}$
$\frac{2}{5} + \frac{1}{5} = \frac{3}{5}$	$\frac{1}{7} + \frac{3}{7} = \frac{4}{7}$	$\frac{4}{9} + \frac{1}{9} = \frac{5}{9}$
$\frac{1}{6} + \frac{2}{6} = \frac{3}{6} = \frac{1}{2}$	$\frac{19}{100} + \frac{31}{100} = \frac{50}{100} = \frac{1}{2}$	$\frac{5}{20} + \frac{10}{20} = \frac{15}{20} = \frac{3}{4}$
$\frac{4}{10} + \frac{4}{10} = \frac{8}{10} = \frac{4}{5}$	$\frac{3}{12} + \frac{6}{12} = \frac{9}{12} = \frac{3}{4}$	$\frac{2}{6} + \frac{2}{6} = \frac{4}{6} = \frac{2}{3}$
$\frac{3}{8} + \frac{3}{8} = \frac{6}{8} = \frac{3}{4}$	$\frac{1}{8} + \frac{3}{8} = \frac{4}{8} = \frac{1}{2}$	$\frac{5}{12} + \frac{1}{12} = \frac{6}{12} = \frac{1}{2}$
$\frac{1}{4} + \frac{1}{4} = \frac{2}{4} = \frac{1}{2}$	$\frac{4}{20} + \frac{1}{20} = \frac{5}{20} = \frac{1}{4}$	$\frac{1}{6} + \frac{3}{6} = \frac{4}{6} = \frac{2}{3}$
$\frac{3}{7} + \frac{3}{7} = \frac{6}{7}$	$\frac{2}{9} + \frac{2}{9} = \frac{4}{9}$	$\frac{13}{20} + \frac{5}{20} = \frac{18}{20} = \frac{9}{10}$
$\frac{81}{100} + \frac{9}{100} = \frac{90}{100} = \frac{9}{10}$	$\frac{5}{20} + \frac{8}{20} = \frac{13}{20}$	$\frac{2}{8} + \frac{3}{8} = \frac{5}{8}$
$\frac{6}{10} + \frac{2}{10} = \frac{8}{10} = \frac{4}{5}$	$\frac{28}{100} + \frac{47}{100} = \frac{75}{100} = \frac{3}{4}$	$\frac{72}{100} + \frac{18}{100} = \frac{90}{100} = \frac{9}{10}$

Difficulty in reducing a sum to a simpler form points to a weakness in finding the greatest common factor of the numerator and denominator. Children can reduce the answer in stages, first looking at whether 2 is a common factor, then 3, and so on.

70

Subtracting fractions

Find the difference of each problem.

$\frac{4}{5} - \frac{2}{5} = \frac{2}{5}$ $\frac{8}{9} - \frac{5}{9} = \frac{3}{9} = \frac{1}{3}$

Add the numerators but keep the denominators the same. Remember to reduce to simplest form if you need to.

EVERYTHING'S A RIDDLE TO ME!

Find the difference of each problem.

$\frac{4}{5} - \frac{1}{5} = \frac{3}{5}$ $\frac{5}{7} - \frac{2}{7} = \frac{3}{7}$

$\frac{5}{10} - \frac{4}{10} = \frac{1}{10}$ $\frac{6}{9} - \frac{2}{9} = \frac{4}{9}$

$\frac{7}{8} - \frac{3}{8} = \frac{4}{8} = \frac{1}{2}$	$\frac{14}{20} - \frac{8}{20} = \frac{6}{20} = \frac{3}{10}$	$\frac{4}{6} - \frac{1}{6} = \frac{3}{6} = \frac{1}{2}$
$\frac{11}{12} - \frac{7}{12} = \frac{4}{12} = \frac{1}{4}$	$\frac{17}{20} - \frac{12}{20} = \frac{5}{20} = \frac{1}{4}$	$\frac{8}{12} - \frac{2}{12} = \frac{6}{12} = \frac{1}{2}$
$\frac{8}{9} - \frac{2}{9} = \frac{6}{9} = \frac{2}{3}$	$\frac{12}{12} - \frac{2}{12} = \frac{10}{12} = \frac{5}{6}$	$\frac{8}{10} - \frac{3}{10} = \frac{5}{10} = \frac{1}{2}$
$\frac{6}{10} - \frac{4}{10} = \frac{2}{10} = \frac{1}{5}$	$\frac{6}{8} - \frac{4}{8} = \frac{2}{8} = \frac{1}{4}$	$\frac{9}{12} - \frac{5}{12} = \frac{4}{12} = \frac{1}{3}$
$\frac{3}{4} - \frac{1}{4} = \frac{2}{4} = \frac{1}{2}$	$\frac{6}{8} - \frac{1}{8} = \frac{5}{8}$	$\frac{18}{20} - \frac{4}{20} = \frac{12}{20} = \frac{3}{5}$
$\frac{4}{6} - \frac{2}{6} = \frac{2}{6} = \frac{1}{3}$	$\frac{7}{12} - \frac{6}{12} = \frac{1}{12}$	$\frac{5}{8} - \frac{2}{8} = \frac{3}{8}$
$\frac{5}{7} - \frac{1}{7} = \frac{4}{7}$	$\frac{5}{16} - \frac{1}{16} = \frac{4}{16} = \frac{1}{4}$	$\frac{70}{100} - \frac{60}{100} = \frac{10}{100} = \frac{1}{10}$

See the notes on page 69.

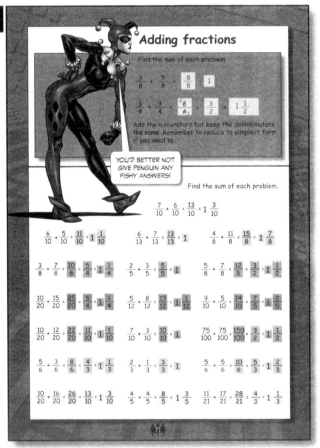

71

Adding fractions

Find the sum of each problem.

$\frac{3}{8} + \frac{5}{8} = \frac{8}{8} \mid 1$

$\frac{3}{4} + \frac{3}{4} = \frac{6}{4} = \frac{3}{2} = 1\frac{1}{2}$

Add the numerators but keep the denominators the same. Remember to reduce to simplest form if you need to.

YOU'D BETTER NOT GIVE PENGUIN ANY FISHY ANSWERS!

Find the sum of each problem.

$\frac{7}{10} + \frac{6}{10} = \frac{13}{10} = 1\frac{3}{10}$

$\frac{6}{10} + \frac{5}{10} = \frac{11}{10} = 1\frac{1}{10}$	$\frac{6}{13} + \frac{7}{13} = \frac{13}{13} = 1$	$\frac{4}{8} + \frac{11}{8} = \frac{15}{8} = 1\frac{7}{8}$
$\frac{3}{8} + \frac{7}{8} = \frac{10}{8} = \frac{5}{4} = 1\frac{1}{4}$	$\frac{2}{5} + \frac{3}{5} = \frac{5}{5} = 1$	$\frac{5}{8} + \frac{7}{8} = \frac{12}{8} = \frac{3}{2} = 1\frac{1}{2}$
$\frac{10}{20} + \frac{15}{20} = \frac{25}{20} = \frac{5}{4} = 1\frac{1}{4}$	$\frac{5}{12} + \frac{8}{12} = \frac{13}{12} = 1\frac{1}{12}$	$\frac{9}{10} + \frac{5}{10} = \frac{14}{10} = \frac{7}{5} = 1\frac{2}{5}$
$\frac{10}{20} + \frac{12}{20} = \frac{22}{20} = \frac{11}{10} = 1\frac{1}{10}$	$\frac{7}{10} + \frac{3}{10} = \frac{10}{10} = 1$	$\frac{75}{100} + \frac{75}{100} = \frac{150}{100} = \frac{3}{2} = 1\frac{1}{2}$
$\frac{5}{6} + \frac{3}{6} = \frac{8}{6} = \frac{4}{3} = 1\frac{1}{3}$	$\frac{2}{3} + \frac{1}{3} = \frac{3}{3} = 1$	$\frac{5}{6} + \frac{6}{6} = \frac{10}{6} = \frac{5}{3} = 1\frac{2}{3}$
$\frac{10}{20} + \frac{16}{20} = \frac{26}{20} = \frac{13}{10} = 1\frac{3}{10}$	$\frac{4}{5} + \frac{4}{5} = \frac{8}{5} = 1\frac{3}{5}$	$\frac{11}{21} + \frac{17}{21} = \frac{28}{21} = \frac{4}{3} = 1\frac{1}{3}$

If children leave the answer as a fraction or do not reduce it, they are completing only one of the two steps to finding the simplest form. Have them write the answer as a mixed number first, and then reduce the fracton part.

Adding fractions

Find the sum of each problem. Remember to find the common denominator and reduce if you need to.

$\frac{2}{3} + \frac{1}{6} = \frac{4}{6} + \frac{1}{6} = \frac{5}{6}$

$\frac{3}{4} + \frac{5}{6} = \frac{9}{12} + \frac{10}{12} = \frac{19}{12} = 1\frac{7}{12}$

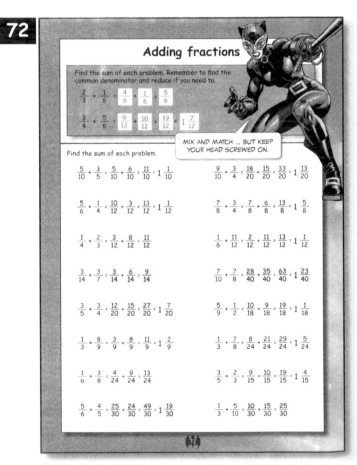

MIX AND MATCH ... BUT KEEP YOUR HEAD SCREWED ON.

Find the sum of each problem.

$\frac{5}{10} + \frac{3}{5} = \frac{5}{10} + \frac{6}{10} = \frac{11}{10} = 1\frac{1}{10}$	$\frac{9}{10} + \frac{3}{4} = \frac{18}{20} + \frac{15}{20} = \frac{33}{20} = 1\frac{13}{20}$
$\frac{5}{6} + \frac{1}{4} = \frac{10}{12} + \frac{3}{12} = \frac{13}{12} = 1\frac{1}{12}$	$\frac{7}{8} + \frac{3}{4} = \frac{7}{8} + \frac{6}{8} = \frac{13}{8} = 1\frac{5}{8}$
$\frac{1}{4} + \frac{2}{3} = \frac{3}{12} + \frac{8}{12} = \frac{11}{12}$	$\frac{1}{6} + \frac{11}{12} = \frac{2}{12} + \frac{11}{12} = \frac{13}{12} = 1\frac{1}{12}$
$\frac{3}{14} + \frac{3}{7} = \frac{3}{14} + \frac{6}{14} = \frac{9}{14}$	$\frac{7}{10} + \frac{7}{8} = \frac{28}{40} + \frac{35}{40} = \frac{63}{40} = 1\frac{23}{40}$
$\frac{3}{5} + \frac{3}{4} = \frac{12}{20} + \frac{15}{20} = \frac{27}{20} = 1\frac{7}{20}$	$\frac{5}{9} + \frac{1}{2} = \frac{10}{18} + \frac{9}{18} = \frac{19}{18} = 1\frac{1}{18}$
$\frac{1}{3} + \frac{8}{9} = \frac{3}{9} + \frac{8}{9} = \frac{11}{9} = 1\frac{2}{9}$	$\frac{1}{3} + \frac{7}{8} = \frac{8}{24} + \frac{21}{24} = \frac{29}{24} = 1\frac{5}{24}$
$\frac{1}{6} + \frac{3}{8} = \frac{4}{24} + \frac{9}{24} = \frac{13}{24}$	$\frac{3}{5} + \frac{2}{3} = \frac{9}{15} + \frac{10}{15} = \frac{19}{15} = 1\frac{4}{15}$
$\frac{5}{6} + \frac{4}{5} = \frac{25}{30} + \frac{24}{30} = \frac{49}{30} = 1\frac{19}{30}$	$\frac{1}{3} + \frac{5}{10} = \frac{10}{30} + \frac{15}{30} = \frac{25}{30}$

Difficulty in finding a common denonminator indicates a weakness in finding the least common multiple of two numbers. Children can always find a common denominator by multiplying the given denominators.

73

Subtracting fractions

Find the difference for each problem. Find the common denominator and reduce if you need to.

$$\frac{7}{9} - \frac{1}{3} = \frac{7}{9} - \frac{3}{9} = \frac{4}{9}$$

$$\frac{7}{10} - \frac{3}{8} = \frac{28}{40} - \frac{15}{40} = \frac{13}{40}$$

SUBLIME SUBTRACTION! CAN YOU FIGURE THEM ALL OUT?

Find the difference for each problem.

$$\frac{7}{8} - \frac{1}{2} = \frac{7}{8} - \frac{4}{8} = \frac{3}{8} \qquad \frac{5}{6} - \frac{1}{4} = \frac{10}{12} - \frac{3}{12} = \frac{7}{12}$$

$$\frac{7}{10} - \frac{1}{8} = \frac{28}{40} - \frac{5}{40} = \frac{23}{40} \qquad \frac{3}{7} - \frac{1}{5} = \frac{15}{35} - \frac{7}{35} = \frac{8}{35}$$

$$\frac{11}{12} - \frac{1}{6} = \frac{11}{12} - \frac{2}{12} = \frac{9}{12} = \frac{3}{4} \qquad \frac{9}{10} - \frac{3}{4} = \frac{36}{40} - \frac{30}{40} = \frac{6}{40} = \frac{3}{20}$$

$$\frac{7}{9} - \frac{1}{3} = \frac{7}{9} - \frac{3}{9} = \frac{2}{9} \qquad \frac{5}{9} - \frac{1}{4} = \frac{20}{36} - \frac{9}{36} = \frac{11}{36}$$

$$\frac{9}{16} - \frac{1}{8} = \frac{9}{16} - \frac{2}{16} = \frac{7}{16} \qquad \frac{7}{12} - \frac{1}{3} = \frac{7}{12} - \frac{4}{12} = \frac{3}{12} = \frac{1}{4}$$

$$\frac{6}{7} - \frac{2}{5} = \frac{30}{35} - \frac{14}{35} = \frac{16}{35} \qquad \frac{3}{10} - \frac{1}{7} = \frac{21}{70} - \frac{10}{70} = \frac{11}{70}$$

$$\frac{5}{8} - \frac{1}{6} = \frac{15}{24} - \frac{4}{24} = \frac{11}{24} \qquad \frac{4}{5} - \frac{1}{4} = \frac{16}{20} - \frac{5}{20} = \frac{11}{20}$$

$$\frac{2}{3} - \frac{1}{2} = \frac{4}{6} - \frac{3}{6} = \frac{1}{6} \qquad \frac{3}{5} - \frac{1}{4} = \frac{12}{20} - \frac{5}{20} = \frac{7}{20}$$

See the notes on page 72.

74

Adding mixed numbers

Find the sum of each problem.

$$8\frac{10}{30} + 1\frac{3}{30} = 9\frac{13}{30}$$

$$3\frac{1}{4} + 1\frac{1}{6} = 3\frac{3}{12} + 1\frac{2}{12} = 4\frac{5}{12}$$

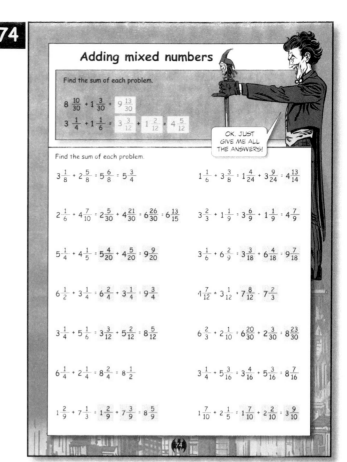

OK, JUST GIVE ME ALL THE ANSWERS!

Find the sum of each problem.

$$3\frac{1}{8} + 2\frac{5}{8} = 5\frac{6}{8} = 5\frac{3}{4} \qquad 1\frac{1}{6} + 3\frac{3}{8} = 1\frac{4}{24} + 3\frac{9}{24} = 4\frac{13}{24}$$

$$2\frac{1}{6} + 4\frac{7}{10} = 2\frac{5}{30} + 4\frac{21}{30} = 6\frac{26}{30} = 6\frac{13}{15} \qquad 3\frac{2}{3} + 1\frac{1}{9} = 3\frac{6}{9} + 1\frac{1}{9} = 4\frac{7}{9}$$

$$5\frac{1}{4} + 4\frac{1}{5} = 5\frac{4}{20} + 4\frac{5}{20} = 9\frac{9}{20} \qquad 3\frac{1}{6} + 6\frac{2}{9} = 3\frac{3}{18} + 6\frac{4}{18} = 9\frac{7}{18}$$

$$6\frac{1}{2} + 3\frac{1}{4} = 6\frac{2}{4} + 3\frac{1}{4} = 9\frac{3}{4} \qquad 4\frac{7}{12} + 3\frac{1}{12} = 7\frac{8}{12} = 7\frac{2}{3}$$

$$3\frac{1}{4} + 5\frac{1}{6} = 3\frac{3}{12} + 5\frac{2}{12} = 8\frac{5}{12} \qquad 6\frac{2}{3} + 2\frac{1}{10} = 6\frac{20}{30} + 2\frac{3}{30} = 8\frac{23}{30}$$

$$6\frac{1}{4} + 2\frac{1}{4} = 8\frac{2}{4} = 8\frac{1}{2} \qquad 3\frac{1}{4} + 5\frac{3}{16} = 3\frac{4}{16} + 5\frac{3}{16} = 8\frac{7}{16}$$

$$1\frac{2}{9} + 7\frac{1}{3} = 1\frac{2}{9} + 7\frac{3}{9} = 8\frac{5}{9} \qquad 1\frac{7}{10} + 2\frac{1}{5} = 1\frac{7}{10} + 2\frac{2}{10} = 3\frac{9}{10}$$

A common error is forgetting to recopy the whole number when renaming the mixed numbers. Children can recopy both the whole numbers first, then rename the two fractions.

75

Subtracting mixed numbers

Find the difference.

I CAN EASILY FIND THE DIFFERENCE FROM UP HERE.

$$2\frac{7}{8} - 1\frac{5}{8} = 1\frac{2}{8} = 1\frac{1}{4}$$

$$9\frac{9}{10} - 6\frac{5}{8} = 9\frac{36}{40} - 6\frac{25}{40} = 3\frac{11}{40}$$

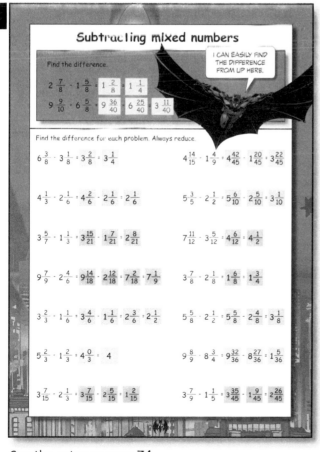

Find the difference for each problem. Always reduce.

$$6\frac{3}{8} - 3\frac{1}{8} = 3\frac{2}{8} = 3\frac{1}{4} \qquad 4\frac{14}{15} - 1\frac{4}{9} = 4\frac{42}{45} - 1\frac{20}{45} = 3\frac{22}{45}$$

$$4\frac{1}{3} - 2\frac{1}{6} = 4\frac{2}{6} - 2\frac{1}{6} = 2\frac{1}{6} \qquad 5\frac{3}{5} - 2\frac{1}{2} = 5\frac{6}{10} - 2\frac{5}{10} = 3\frac{1}{10}$$

$$3\frac{5}{7} - 1\frac{1}{3} = 3\frac{15}{21} - 1\frac{7}{21} = 2\frac{8}{21} \qquad 7\frac{11}{12} - 3\frac{5}{12} = 4\frac{6}{12} = 4\frac{1}{2}$$

$$9\frac{7}{9} - 2\frac{4}{6} = 9\frac{14}{18} - 2\frac{12}{18} = 7\frac{2}{18} = 7\frac{1}{9} \qquad 3\frac{7}{8} - 2\frac{1}{8} = 1\frac{6}{8} = 1\frac{3}{4}$$

$$3\frac{2}{3} - 1\frac{1}{6} = 3\frac{4}{6} - 1\frac{1}{6} = 2\frac{3}{6} = 2\frac{1}{2} \qquad 5\frac{5}{8} - 2\frac{1}{2} = 5\frac{5}{8} - 2\frac{4}{8} = 3\frac{1}{8}$$

$$5\frac{2}{3} - 1\frac{2}{3} = 4\frac{0}{3} = 4 \qquad 9\frac{8}{9} - 8\frac{3}{4} = 9\frac{32}{36} - 8\frac{27}{36} = 1\frac{5}{36}$$

$$3\frac{7}{15} - 2\frac{1}{3} = 3\frac{7}{15} - 2\frac{5}{15} = 1\frac{2}{15} \qquad 3\frac{7}{9} - 1\frac{1}{5} = 3\frac{35}{45} - 1\frac{9}{45} = 2\frac{26}{45}$$

See the notes on page 74.

Adding mixed numbers and fractions

Find the sum of each problem. Remember to find the common denominator and reduce if you need to.

$$4\frac{3}{4} + \frac{3}{4} = 4\frac{6}{4} = 5\frac{2}{4} = 5\frac{1}{2}$$

$$3\frac{1}{2} + \frac{2}{3} = 3\frac{3}{6} + \frac{4}{6} = 3\frac{7}{6} = 4\frac{1}{6}$$

IT'S GETTING TRICKY! FIGURE IT OUT!

Find the sum of each problem.

$$6\frac{3}{4} + \frac{3}{4} = 6\frac{6}{4} = 7\frac{2}{4} = 7\frac{1}{2} \qquad 3\frac{3}{4} + \frac{7}{8} = 3\frac{18}{24} + \frac{21}{24} = 3\frac{39}{24} = 4\frac{15}{24}$$

$$3\frac{3}{8} + \frac{7}{8} = 3\frac{10}{8} = 4\frac{1}{4} \qquad 7\frac{7}{10} + \frac{1}{2} = 7\frac{7}{10} + \frac{5}{10} = 7\frac{12}{10} = 8\frac{1}{5}$$

$$3\frac{3}{7} + \frac{6}{7} = 3\frac{9}{7} = 4\frac{2}{7} \qquad 4\frac{3}{4} + \frac{4}{5} = 4\frac{15}{20} + \frac{16}{20} = 4\frac{31}{20} = 5\frac{11}{20}$$

$$4\frac{5}{6} + \frac{2}{3} = 4\frac{5}{6} + \frac{4}{6} = 4\frac{9}{6} = 5\frac{1}{2} \qquad 2\frac{1}{2} + \frac{3}{4} = 2\frac{2}{4} + \frac{3}{4} = 2\frac{5}{4} = 3\frac{1}{4}$$

$$4\frac{7}{8} + \frac{1}{4} = 4\frac{7}{8} + \frac{2}{8} = 4\frac{9}{8} = 5\frac{1}{8} \qquad 4\frac{5}{7} + \frac{3}{4} = 4\frac{20}{28} + \frac{21}{28} = 4\frac{41}{28} = 5\frac{13}{28}$$

$$3\frac{7}{8} + \frac{1}{2} = 3\frac{7}{8} + \frac{4}{8} = 3\frac{11}{8} = 4\frac{3}{8} \qquad 4\frac{2}{3} + \frac{3}{8} = 4\frac{16}{24} + \frac{9}{24} = 4\frac{25}{24} = 5\frac{1}{24}$$

$$2\frac{9}{10} + \frac{2}{5} = 2\frac{9}{10} + \frac{4}{10} = 2\frac{13}{10} = 3\frac{3}{10} \qquad 3\frac{5}{6} + \frac{4}{5} = 3\frac{25}{30} + \frac{24}{30} = 3\frac{49}{30} = 5\frac{19}{30}$$

The most difficult step is renaming the answer as a proper mixed number. If children have trouble, get them to first rename the fractional part as a mixed number, and then add the 1 from this mixed number to the other whole number part.

Simple use of parentheses

Work out these problems.

$(4 + 6) - (2 + 1) =$ $\boxed{10 - 3 = 7}$

$(2 \times 5) + (10 - 4) =$ $\boxed{10 + 6 = 16}$

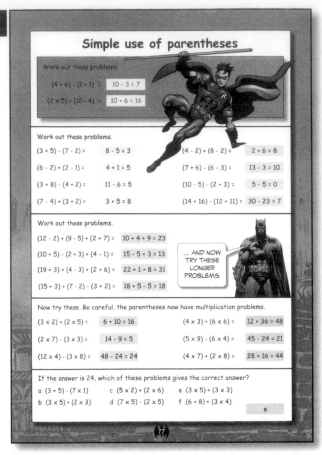

Work out these problems.

$(3 + 5) - (7 - 2) =$ $\boxed{8 - 5 = 3}$ $(4 - 2) + (8 - 2) =$ $\boxed{2 + 6 = 8}$

$(6 - 2) + (2 - 1) =$ $\boxed{4 + 1 = 5}$ $(7 + 6) - (6 - 3) =$ $\boxed{13 - 3 = 10}$

$(3 + 8) - (4 + 2) =$ $\boxed{11 - 6 = 5}$ $(10 - 5) - (2 + 3) =$ $\boxed{5 - 5 = 0}$

$(7 - 4) + (3 + 2) =$ $\boxed{3 + 5 = 8}$ $(14 + 16) - (12 + 11) =$ $\boxed{30 - 23 = 7}$

Work out these problems.

$(12 - 2) + (9 - 5) + (2 + 7) =$ $\boxed{10 + 4 + 9 = 23}$

$(10 + 5) - (2 + 3) + (4 - 1) =$ $\boxed{15 - 5 + 3 = 13}$

$(19 + 3) + (4 - 3) + (2 + 6) =$ $\boxed{22 + 1 + 8 = 31}$

$(15 + 3) + (7 - 2) - (3 + 2) =$ $\boxed{18 + 5 - 5 = 18}$

... AND NOW TRY THESE LONGER PROBLEMS.

Now try these. Be careful, the parentheses now have multiplication problems.

$(3 \times 2) + (2 \times 5) =$ $\boxed{6 + 10 = 16}$ $(4 \times 3) + (6 \times 6) =$ $\boxed{12 + 36 = 48}$

$(2 \times 7) - (3 \times 3) =$ $\boxed{14 - 9 = 5}$ $(5 \times 9) - (6 \times 4) =$ $\boxed{45 - 24 = 21}$

$(12 \times 4) - (3 \times 8) =$ $\boxed{48 - 24 = 24}$ $(4 \times 7) + (2 \times 8) =$ $\boxed{28 + 16 = 44}$

If the answer is 24, which of these problems gives the correct answer?

a $(3 + 5) - (7 \times 1)$ c $(5 \times 2) + (2 \times 6)$ e $(3 \times 5) + (3 \times 3)$

b $(3 \times 5) + (2 \times 3)$ d $(7 \times 5) - (2 \times 5)$ f $(6 + 8) + (3 \times 4)$ $\boxed{e}$

Errors on this page will most likely be the result of choosing the wrong order of operation. Remind children that they must work out the brackets first, before they add or subtract the results. Concentration and careful reading should prevent any problems.

78

Simple use of parentheses

Work out these problems.

$(3 + 2) \times (4 + 1) =$ $\boxed{5 \times 5 = 25}$

$(10 \times 5) \div (10 - 5) =$ $\boxed{50 \div 5 = 10}$

Remember to work out the problems inside the parentheses first.

NOW TRY THESE. NO JOKES!

Work out these problems.

$(5 - 2) \times (8 - 2) =$ $\boxed{18}$ $(11 - 5) \times (9 - 2) =$ $\boxed{42}$

$(9 + 5) \div (2 + 5) =$ $\boxed{2}$ $(8 + 20) \div (12 - 10) =$ $\boxed{14}$

$(7 + 3) \times (8 - 4) =$ $\boxed{40}$ $(9 + 21) \div (8 - 5) =$ $\boxed{10}$

$(14 - 6) \times (3 + 4) =$ $\boxed{56}$ $(14 - 3) \times (6 + 1) =$ $\boxed{77}$

$(14 + 4) \div (13 - 7) =$ $\boxed{3}$ $(9 + 3) \times (6 + 1) =$ $\boxed{84}$

$(10 + 10) \div (2 + 3) =$ $\boxed{4}$ $(6 + 9) - (8 - 3) =$ $\boxed{3}$

Work out these problems.

$(5 \times 4) \div (2 \times 2) =$ $\boxed{5}$ $(4 \times 3) \div (1 \times 2) =$ $\boxed{6}$

$(8 \times 5) \div (4 \times 1) =$ $\boxed{10}$ $(3 \times 5) \times (1 \times 2) =$ $\boxed{30}$

$(6 \times 4) \div (3 \times 4) =$ $\boxed{2}$ $(6 \times 4) \div (4 \times 2) =$ $\boxed{3}$

$(2 \times 4) \times (2 \times 3) =$ $\boxed{48}$ $(8 \times 4) \div (2 \times 2) =$ $\boxed{8}$

If the answer is 30, which of these problems gives the correct answer?

a $(3 \times 5) \times (2 \times 2)$ c $(12 \times 5) \div (8 + 4)$ e $(5 \times 12) - (2 \times 5)$

b $(4 \times 5) \times (5 \times 2)$ d $(20 \div 2) \times (12 \div 3)$ f $(9 \times 5) - (10 \div 2)$ $\boxed{c}$

If the answer is 8, which of these problems gives the correct answer?

a $(10 \div 2) \times (4 - 4)$ c $(12 \times 4) \div (6 \times 2)$ e $(8 + 4) \times (8 \div 1)$

b $(9 \div 3) \times (3 \times 2)$ d $(24 \div 6) \times (8 \div 4)$ f $(16 - 4) \times (20 \div 4)$ $\boxed{d}$

This page continues the work of the previous page, but the brackets are multiplied or divided. It may be necessary to remind children to read carefully, as several operations take place in each equation.

Simple use of parentheses

Work out these problems.

$(5 + 3) + (9 \times 2) =$ $\boxed{8 + 7 = 15}$

$(5 + 2) - (4 - 1) =$ $\boxed{7 - 3 = 4}$

$(4 + 2) \times (3 + 1) =$ $\boxed{6 \times 4 = 24}$

$(3 \times 5) \div (9 - 6) =$ $\boxed{15 \div 3 = 5}$

Remember to work out the parentheses first.

YOU'VE GOTTA FIND ALL THE LITTLE PIECES FIRST TO GET THE BIG PICTURE.

Work out these problems.

$(9 - 2) + (6 + 4) =$ $\boxed{17}$ $(7 + 3) - (9 - 2) =$ $\boxed{3}$

$(15 - 5) + (2 + 3) =$ $\boxed{15}$ $(11 \times 2) - (3 \times 2) =$ $\boxed{16}$

$(15 - 3) + (8 \times 2) =$ $\boxed{21}$ $(12 \times 2) - (3 \times 3) =$ $\boxed{15}$

$(15 - 5) + (3 \times 4) =$ $\boxed{15}$ $(9 \times 3) - (7 \times 3) =$ $\boxed{6}$

$(6 - 2) + (9 \times 2) =$ $\boxed{21}$ $(20 \div 5) - (8 \div 2) =$ $\boxed{0}$

$(5 \times 10) - (12 \times 4) =$ $\boxed{2}$ $(5 + 4) + (7 - 3) =$ $\boxed{13}$

Now try these.

$(4 + 8) \div (3 \times 2) =$ $\boxed{2}$ $(6 \times 4) \div (3 \times 2) =$ $\boxed{4}$

$(9 + 5) \div (2 \times 1) =$ $\boxed{7}$ $(7 \times 4) \div (3 + 4) =$ $\boxed{4}$

$(3 + 6) \times (3 \times 3) =$ $\boxed{81}$ $(5 \times 5) \div (10 \div 2) =$ $\boxed{5}$

$(24 \div 2) \times (3 \times 2) =$ $\boxed{72}$ $(8 \times 6) \div (2 \times 12) =$ $\boxed{2}$

Write down the letters of all the problems that make 25.

a $(2 \times 5) \times (3 \times 2)$ c $(40 \div 2) + (10 - 2)$ e $(6 \times 5) - (10 \div 2)$

b $(5 \times 5) + (7 - 2)$ d $(10 \times 5) - (5 \times 5)$ f $(10 \times 10) \div (10 - 6)$ $\boxed{c, d, e, f}$

Write down the letters of all the problems that make 20.

a $(10 \div 2) \times (4 \div 4)$ c $(8 \times 4) - (6 \times 2)$ e $(10 \div 2) + (20 \div 2)$

b $(7 \times 3) - (3 \div 3)$ d $(20 - 4) \times (8 \div 2)$ f $(14 \div 2) + (2 \times 7)$ $\boxed{b, c}$

This page reinforces all the elements of the previous two pages. Again, the most likely cause of error will be lack of concentration.

Multiplying decimals

Work out these problems.

4.6	3.9	8.4
× 3	× 5	× 8
13.8	19.5	67.2

I'VE GOT ALL THE ANSWERS! CAN YOU FIND THESE ONES?

Work out these problems.

7.4	3.6	6.5	4.2	3.8
× 2	× 4	× 4	× 2	× 2
14.8	14.4	26.0	8.4	7.6

4.7	9.1	5.6	1.7	5.1
× 3	× 3	× 3	× 2	× 2
14.1	27.3	16.8	3.4	10.2

4.2	4.7	1.8	3.4	3.7
× 4	× 4	× 5	× 5	× 5
16.8	18.8	9.0	17.0	18.5

2.5	2.3	5.3	7.3	5.1
× 5	× 6	× 7	× 8	× 9
12.5	13.8	37.1	58.4	45.9

7.9	8.4	8.7	7.5	9.9
× 9	× 9	× 8	× 8	× 6
71.1	75.6	69.6	60.0	59.4

6.8	5.6	6.8	7.4	8.3
× 7	× 6	× 7	× 9	× 9
47.6	33.6	47.6	66.6	74.7

7.4	2.9	3.8	7.7	9.4
× 8	× 7	× 8	× 7	× 9
59.2	20.3	30.4	53.9	84.6

Ensure that children work from right to left. Problems will highlight gaps in their knowledge of times tables. Remind them that the number they are multiplying has one decimal place, so their answer must have one decimal place also, and this can be put in at the end.

81

Multiplying decimals

Work out these problems.

37.5	26.2	65.3
× 2	× 5	× 9
75.0	131.0	587.7

I GIVE UP! CAN YOU FIGURE OUT THESE PROBLEMS?

Work out these problems.

54.3	93.1	34.6	55.3	35.4
× 2	× 2	× 2	× 3	× 3
108.6	186.2	69.2	165.9	106.2

46.7	25.6	16.5	51.4	37.3
× 4	× 4	× 3	× 5	× 5
186.8	102.4	49.5	257.0	186.5

12.3	46.3	17.6	36.5	73.4
× 5	× 5	× 6	× 6	× 7
61.5	231.5	105.6	219.0	513.8

37.5	20.3	73.5	92.4	47.9
× 7	× 7	× 7	× 6	× 6
262.5	142.1	514.5	554.4	287.4

53.9	75.7	28.2	79.4	99.9
× 8	× 8	× 8	× 8	× 9
431.2	605.6	225.6	635.2	899.1

37.8	14.8	36.5	46.7	27.3
× 9	× 9	× 9	× 8	× 7
340.2	133.2	328.5	373.6	191.1

39.6	84.3	68.5	73.5	57.6
× 6	× 9	× 8	× 9	× 6
237.6	758.7	548.0	661.5	345.6

This page further revises multiplication, using larger numbers.

82

Real-life problems

Robin earns $3.50 a day on his paper route. How much does he earn in a week?

$24.50

$$\begin{array}{r} \overset{3}{\$3.50} \\ \times\ 7 \\ \hline \$24.50 \end{array}$$

When Poison Ivy subtracts the width of her closet from the length of her bedroom wall she finds she has 3.65 m of wall space left. If the closet is 0.87 m wide, what is the length of her bedroom wall?

4.52 m

$$\begin{array}{r} \overset{1\ 1}{0.87} \\ +\ 3.65 \\ \hline 4.52 \end{array}$$

The Joker buys Harley Quinn a bunch of flowers for $15.95 and some candy for $3.76. If he has $5.84 left, how much did he start with?

$25.55

$$\begin{array}{r} \overset{1\ 1}{15.95} \\ +\ 3.76 \\ \hline \$19.71 \end{array} \qquad \begin{array}{r} \overset{1}{19.71} \\ +\ 5.84 \\ \hline \$25.55 \end{array}$$

Alfred is making some shelves for the Batcave. Each shelf has to be 75.5 cm long. If the wood he is using is 160 cm long, how many pieces will he need to make six shelves?

3 pieces

75.5 × 2 = 151
Alfred can make 2 shelves per piece of wood.
6 ÷ 2 = 3

Gotham City transit station uses 78.5 barrels of oil a day. If they have a weekly delivery of 480 barrels, how much will they have left after six days?

9 barrels

$$\begin{array}{r} \overset{5\ 3}{78.5} \\ \times\ 6 \\ \hline 471.0 \end{array} \qquad \begin{array}{r} 480 \\ -\ 471 \\ \hline 9 \end{array}$$

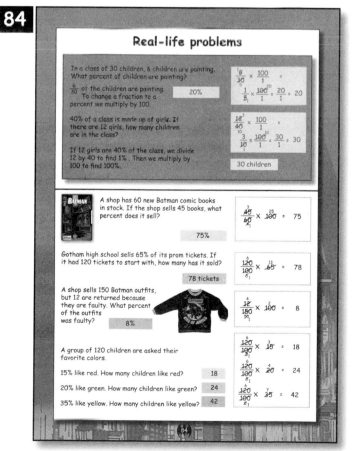

Alfred is preparing food for a banquet at Wayne Manor. He needs 20.5 lbs of flour to make pastry, 13.6 lbs of flour to make cakes, and 2.4 lbs for sauces. How much flour does Alfred need altogether?

36.5 lbs

$$\begin{array}{r} \overset{1}{20.5} \\ 13.6 \\ +\ 2.4 \\ \hline 36.5 \end{array}$$

This page provides an opportunity to apply math skills to real-life problems. Children will need to choose the operations carefully. Some questions require more than one operation.

83

Real-life problems

A comic-book writer writes 8.5 pages of his book a day. How many pages will he write in nine days?

76.5 pages

$$\begin{array}{r} \overset{4}{8.5} \\ \times\ 9 \\ \hline 76.5 \end{array}$$

After driving 147.7 mi Batman stops at a service station. If he has another 115.4 mi to go, how long will his trip be?

263.1 mi

$$\begin{array}{r} \overset{1\ 1}{147.7} \\ +\ 115.4 \\ \hline 263.1 \end{array}$$

The Penguin divides his money equally among four separate banks. If he has $78.55 in each bank, what is the total of his savings?

$314.20

$$\begin{array}{r} \overset{3\ 2\ 2}{\$78.55} \\ \times\ 4 \\ \hline \$314.20 \end{array}$$

Batgirl buys two bottles of perfume; one contains 48.5 ml and the other contains 125.5 ml. How much more perfume is in the larger of the two bottles?

77 ml

$$\begin{array}{r} \overset{1\ 1\ 15}{125.5} \\ -\ 48.5 \\ \hline 77.0 \end{array}$$

In Bruce Wayne's bathroom, seven tiles, each 15.75 cm wide, fit exactly across the width of the shower. How wide is the shower?

110.25 cm

$$\begin{array}{r} \overset{4\ 5\ 3}{15.75} \\ \times\ 7 \\ \hline 110.25 \end{array}$$

The Joker spends 6.25 minutes telling a joke. How long would it take to tell eight jokes?

50 minutes

$$\begin{array}{r} \overset{2\ 4}{6.25} \\ \times\ 8 \\ \hline 50.00 \end{array}$$

This page also revises various operations applied to real-life situations.

84

Real-life problems

In a class of 30 children, 6 children are painting. What percent of children are painting?

20%

$\frac{6}{30}$ of the children are painting. To change a fraction to a percent we multiply by 100.

$$\frac{\overset{1}{6}}{\underset{1}{30}} \times \frac{100}{1} = \frac{1}{\underset{1}{5}} \times \frac{\overset{20}{100}}{1} = \frac{20}{1} = 20$$

40% of a class is made up of girls. If there are 12 girls, how many children are in the class?

30 children

If 12 girls are 40% of the class, we divide 12 by 40 to find 1%. Then we multiply by 100 to find 100%.

$$\frac{\overset{3}{12}}{\underset{10}{40}} \times \frac{100}{1} = \frac{3}{\underset{10}{10}} \times \frac{\overset{30}{100}}{1} = \frac{30}{1} = 30$$

A shop has 60 new Batman comic books in stock. If the shop sells 45 books, what percent does it sell?

75%

$$\frac{\overset{3}{45}}{\underset{4}{60}} \times \overset{25}{100} = 75$$

Gotham high school sells 65% of its prom tickets. If it had 120 tickets to start with, how many has it sold?

78 tickets

$$\frac{\overset{6}{120}}{\underset{1}{100}} \times \overset{13}{65} = 78$$

A shop sells 150 Batman outfits, but 12 are returned because they are faulty. What percent of the outfits was faulty?

8%

$$\frac{\overset{2}{12}}{\underset{50}{150}} \times \overset{2}{100} = 8$$

A group of 120 children are asked their favorite colors.

15% like red. How many children like red? — 18

20% like green. How many children like green? — 24

35% like yellow. How many children like yellow? — 42

$$\frac{\overset{6}{120}}{\underset{1}{100}} \times \overset{3}{15} = 18$$

$$\frac{\overset{6}{120}}{\underset{1}{100}} \times \overset{4}{20} = 24$$

$$\frac{\overset{6}{120}}{\underset{1}{100}} \times \overset{7}{35} = 42$$

In question 1, children should see that the answer can be expressed as a fraction, which can then be converted to a percentage by multiplying by 100.

85

Conversions: length

Units of length	
12 inches	1 foot
3 feet	1 yard
5,280 feet	1 mile
1,760 yards	1 mile

This conversion table shows how to convert inches, feet, yards, and miles.

Batman's jumpline is 3 yards long. How many feet is it?

$3 \times 3 = 9$
$9 \times 12 = 108$ 9 feet long

Robin's jumpline is 120 inches long. How many feet is it?

$120 \div 12 = 10$ 10 feet long

IT'S EASY ONCE YOU KNOW HOW!

Convert each measurement to feet.

36 inches $36 \div 12 = 3$ **3 feet**	12 inches $12 \div 12 = 1$ **1 foot**	48 inches $48 \div 12 = 4$ **4 feet**

Convert each measurement to yards.

6 feet $6 \div 3 = 2$ **2 yards**	12 feet $12 \div 3 = 4$ **4 yards**	27 feet $27 \div 3 = 9$ **9 yards**	36 feet $36 \div 3 = 12$ **12 yards**

Convert each measurement to inches.

4 feet $4 \times 12 = 48$ **48 inches**	12 feet $12 \times 12 = 144$ **144 inches**	8 feet $8 \times 12 = 96$ **96 inches**	5 feet $5 \times 12 = 60$ **60 inches**

Convert each measurement.

4 yards $(4 \times 3) \times 12 = 144$ **144 inches**	5 yards $(5 \times 3) \times 12 = 180$ **180 inches**	4 miles $4 \times 5,280 =$ **20,120 feet**	1 mile $5,280 \times 12 =$ **63,360 inches**
15,840 feet $15,840 \div 5,280$ **3 miles**	31,680 feet $31,680 \div 5,280$ **6 miles**	1,760 yards $1,760 \div 1,760$ **1 mile**	3,520 yards $3,520 \div 1,760$ **2 miles**

If children are confused whether to mulitply or divide, have them think about whether the new unit is a longer or a shorter unit. If the unit is longer, there will be fewer of them, so division will be the appropriate operation to use.

86

Conversions: capacity

Units of length	
8 fluid ounces	1 cup
2 cups	1 pint
2 pints	1 quart
4 quarts	1 gallon

This conversion table shows how to convert ounces, cups, pints, quarts, and gallons.

Robin's pitcher holds 6 cups. How many pints does it hold?

$6 \div 2 = 3$ 3 pints

Alfred's pitcher holds 8 pints. How many cups does it hold?

$8 \times 2 = 16$ 16 cups

DON'T CONFUSE CUPS AND QUARTS OR YOU'LL GET IN A MESS!

Convert each measurement to cups.

32 fluid ounces $32 \div 8 = 4$ **4 cups**	16 fluid ounces $16 \div 8 = 2$ **2 cups**	96 fluid ounces $96 \div 8 = 12$ **12 cups**

Convert each measurement to pints.

6 cups $6 \div 2 = 3$ **3 pints**	12 cups $12 \div 2 = 6$ **6 pints**	30 quarts $30 \div 2 = 15$ **15 pints**	6 quarts $6 \div 2 = 3$ **3 pints**

Convert each measurement to gallons.

16 quarts $16 \div 4 = 4$ **4 gallons**	32 quarts $32 \div 4 = 3$ **8 gallons**	100 quarts $100 \div 4 = 25$ **25 gallons**	20 quarts $20 \div 4 = 5$ **5 gallons**

Convert each measurement.

3 gallons $3 \times 4 \times 2 = 24$ **24 pints**	5 quarts $5 \times 2 \times 2 = 20$ **20 cups**	36 cups $36 \div 4 = 9$ **9 quarts**	72 pints $72 \div 8 = 9$ **9 gallons**
1 quart $1 \times 2 \times 2 \times 8 = 32$ **32 fluid ounces**	240 fluid ounces $240 \div 8 = 30$ cups **15 pints**	7 quarts $7 \times 4 = 28$ **28 cups**	11 pints $11 \times 8 = 88$ **88 pints**

See the notes for page 85.

87

Fraction of a number

Work out to find the fraction of the number. Write the answer in the box.

$\frac{1}{6}$ of 42

$\frac{1}{6} \times 42 = \frac{42}{6} = 7$

$1 \times 7 = 7$

so $\frac{1}{6}$ of 42 = 7

$\frac{1}{4}$ of 100 = $\frac{100}{4}$ = **25**

$\frac{3}{5}$ of 35

$\frac{1}{5} \times 35 = \frac{35}{5} = 7$

$3 \times 7 = 21$

so $\frac{3}{5}$ of 35 = 21

$\frac{1}{3}$ of 69 = $\frac{69}{3}$ = **23**

WE'RE BACK TO FRACTIONS AGAIN NOW. MOTOR ON!

Work out to find the fraction of the number. Write the answer in the box.

$\frac{1}{8}$ of 72	9	$\frac{1}{5}$ of 250	50	$\frac{1}{2}$ of 38	19
$\frac{1}{9}$ of 54	6	$\frac{1}{2}$ of 84	42	$\frac{1}{6}$ of 72	12
$\frac{1}{4}$ of 52	13	$\frac{1}{7}$ of 140	20	$\frac{1}{3}$ of 36	12
$\frac{1}{5}$ of 175	35	$\frac{1}{8}$ of 64	8	$\frac{1}{4}$ of 100	25
$\frac{1}{6}$ of 300	50	$\frac{1}{9}$ of 81	9	$\frac{1}{2}$ of 114	57
$\frac{1}{10}$ of 100	10	$\frac{1}{5}$ of 55	11	$\frac{1}{7}$ of 140	20
$\frac{3}{4}$ of 100	75	$\frac{2}{3}$ of 75	50	$\frac{4}{7}$ of 42	24
$\frac{2}{5}$ of 25	10	$\frac{5}{8}$ of 40	25	$\frac{2}{3}$ of 27	18
$\frac{5}{9}$ of 36	20	$\frac{2}{3}$ of 225	150	$\frac{5}{6}$ of 120	100
$\frac{3}{4}$ of 56	42	$\frac{5}{7}$ of 133	95	$\frac{2}{3}$ of 180	120
$\frac{4}{5}$ of 100	80	$\frac{2}{10}$ of 100	20	$\frac{3}{8}$ of 64	24
$\frac{2}{3}$ of 210	140	$\frac{4}{9}$ of 90	40	$\frac{7}{8}$ of 72	63

If children have difficulty with the first step, have them use long division to find the quotient.

Showing decimals

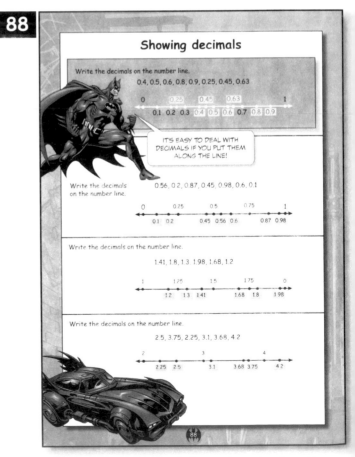

Write the decimals on the number line.
0.4, 0.5, 0.6, 0.8, 0.9, 0.25, 0.45, 0.63

IT'S EASY TO DEAL WITH DECIMALS IF YOU PUT THEM ALONG THE LINE!

Write the decimals on the number line.   0.56, 0.2, 0.87, 0.45, 0.98, 0.6, 0.1

Write the decimals on the number line.
1.41, 1.8, 1.3, 1.98, 1.68, 1.2

Write the decimals on the number line.
2.5, 3.75, 2.25, 3.1, 3.68, 4.2

If children are confused about where to place the decimals to hundredths, have them first fill in all of the tenths on the number line. Then ask which of those tenths the decimals to hundredths fall between.

Area of right-angled triangles

Find the area of this right-angled triangle.

Because the area of this triangle is half the area of the rectangle shown, we can find the area of the rectangle and then divide it by two to find the area of the triangle.

So the area = (8 cm x 4 cm) ÷ 2
= 32 cm² ÷ 2 = 16cm²

Area = 16 cm²

4 cm

8 cm

Find the area of these right-angled triangles.

IT'S EASY TO FIND THE AREA
IF THE ANGLE IS RIGHT!

5 cm
3 cm
12 cm
30 cm²

10 cm
2 cm
15 cm²

9 cm
9 cm²

4 cm
14 cm
28 cm²

6 cm
5 cm
15 cm²

6 cm
8 cm
24 cm²

6 cm
12 cm
36 cm²

3 cm
20 cm
4 cm
30 cm²

7 cm
14 cm²

The operation of multiplying the sides together and dividing by two should offer no serious difficulty to children, but make sure they are really clear about why they are doing this.

90

Speed problems

How long would it take to travel 120 mi at 8 mph?
(Time = Distance ÷ Speed)
15 hours

$\begin{array}{r} 15 \\ 8\overline{)120} \end{array}$

If a bus takes 3 hours to travel 150 mi, how fast is it going?
(Speed = Distance ÷ Time)
50 mph

$\begin{array}{r} 50 \\ 3\overline{)150} \end{array}$

If a car travels at 60 mph for 2 hours, how far has it gone?
(Distance = Speed x Time)
120 mi

$\begin{array}{r} 60 \\ \times\ 2 \\ \hline 120 \end{array}$

If the Penguin walks for 6 miles at a steady speed of 3 mph, how long will it take him?
2 hours

$\frac{6}{3} = 2$

Batman travels 120 mi in 3 hours. If he went at a steady speed, how fast was he going.
40 mph

$\begin{array}{r} 40 \\ 3\overline{)120} \end{array}$

Robin drives at a steady speed of 40 mph. How far will he travel in 4 hours?
160 mi

$\begin{array}{r} 40 \\ \times\ 4 \\ \hline 160 \end{array}$

Catwoman walks 10 mi at 4 mph. Robin walks 12 mi at 5 mph. Which of them will take the longest?
Catwoman

$\begin{array}{cc} 2\ 1/2 & 2\ 2/5 \\ 4\overline{)10} & 5\overline{)12} \end{array}$

A bat flies for 30 minutes at 10 mph and for 1 hour at 15 mph. How far has it traveled altogether?
20 mi

$\begin{array}{l} 5 \ (30 \text{ mins} = \frac{1}{2} \text{ hour}) \\ 2\overline{)10} \quad 5 + 15 = 20 \end{array}$

Catwoman rides her bike 340 mi in 120 minutes. What speed is she traveling at?
2 hours 50 minutes

$\begin{array}{l} 120 \text{ min} = 2 \text{ h} \\ 170 \\ 2\overline{)340} \end{array}$

If children experience difficulty on this page, ask them what they need to find—speed, distance, or time—and refer them to the necessary formula. Encourage them to develop simple examples that will help them remember the formulas.

91

Conversion tables

Draw a table to convert dollars to cents.

$	cents
1	100
2	200
3	300

Complete the conversion table.
Hint: look for a pattern.

CONVERTING IS EASY FOR ME... JUST LIKE TOSSING A COIN!

Weeks	Days
1	7
2	14
3	21
4	28
5	35
6	42
7	49
8	56
9	63
10	70

If there are 60 minutes in 1 hour, make a conversion chart for up to 10 hours.

TIME'S TICKING AWAY!

Hours	Minutes
1	60
2	120
3	180
4	240
5	300
6	360
7	420
8	480
9	540
10	600

Children will grasp that they are dealing with multiples of 7 and later, 60. Any problems will be due to weaknesses in tables or from missing out numbers as they work down the chart. Encourage care and concentration.

Reading bar graphs

ROBIN'S SAVING DEPOSITS

Amount in dollars / Months

Look at this graph of Robin's savings deposits.

In which month did Robin save $25?
May

How much more money did Robin save in July than in June?
$15

TREES IN GOTHAM CITY PARK

Kind of tree: Ash, Oak, Maple, Pine / Number of trees

How many maple trees were planted?
7

The same number of ash trees were planted as what other kind of tree?
Pine

How many more oak trees were planted than maple trees?
2

ATTENDANCE AT GAMES

Amount in dollars / Years

In which year did 5,000 people attend the games?
2004

How many people attended the games in 2001?
4,000

The biggest increase in attendance was between which years?
2003-04

If children have difficulties with computation problems, have them write down each of the numbers they read off the graph before computing with them.

Expanded form

POSITION MEANS VALUE!

What is the value of 3 in 2,308?	300
Write 32,804 in expanded form.	30,000 + 2,000 + 800 + 4

What is the value of 7 in these numbers?

37	7	872	70	56,870	70
13,704	700	62,740	700	467,834	7,000
3,576	70	12,907	7	16,792	700

What is the value of 5 in these numbers?

14,532	500	853	50	8,657	50
22,458	50	256,784	50,000	75,783	5,000
6,045	5	86,548	500	875	5

Circle the numbers that have a 7 with the value of seventy thousand.

457,682   67,924   (870,234)   (372,987)

(171,345)   767,707   (79,835)   16,757

Write the numbers in expanded form.

42,573	40,000 + 2,000 + 500 + 70 + 3
208,967	200,000 + 8,000 + 900 + 60 + 7
8,794	8,000 + 700 + 90 + 4
50,735	50,000 + 700 + 30 + 5

Some children are confused about how to represent the zeros in a number. Be sure they know to skip those terms when they write the expanded form.

94

Cubes of small numbers

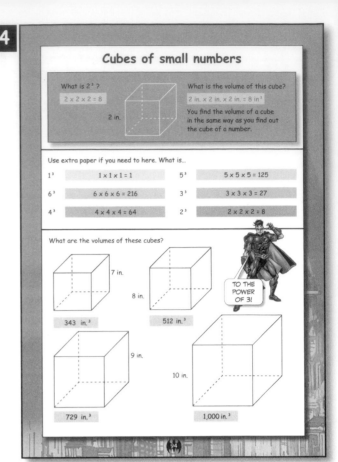

What is 2^3 ?	What is the volume of this cube?
$2 \times 2 \times 2 = 8$	2 in. $\times$ 2 in. $\times$ 2 in. = 8 in^3
	You find the volume of a cube in the same way as you find out the cube of a number.

2 in.

Use extra paper if you need to here. What is...

1^3	$1 \times 1 \times 1 = 1$	5^3	$5 \times 5 \times 5 = 125$
6^3	$6 \times 6 \times 6 = 216$	3^3	$3 \times 3 \times 3 = 27$
4^3	$4 \times 4 \times 4 = 64$	2^3	$2 \times 2 \times 2 = 8$

What are the volumes of these cubes?

TO THE POWER OF 3!

7 in.   343 in.^{3}

8 in.   512 in.^{3}

9 in.   729 in.^{3}

10 in.   1,000 in.^{3}

The most common mistake children make is confusing three cubed with three times three, especially when they are working quickly through the examples. It is necessary to reinforce the concept of cubing a number. Children may need some paper for their working out.

95

Multiplying fractions

To find the product, multiply the numerators, multiply the denominators, then reduce answer to the simplest form.

$$\frac{3}{8} \times \frac{4}{7} = \frac{12}{56} = \frac{3}{14}$$

DON'T GIVE UP... YOU CAN DO IT!

Write the product.

$\frac{1}{2} \times \frac{1}{2} = \frac{1}{4}$ $\frac{4}{10} \times \frac{3}{8} = \frac{3}{20}$ $6 \times \frac{3}{4} = \frac{9}{2} = 4\frac{1}{2}$

$6 \times \frac{1}{3} = 2$ $\frac{3}{5} \times \frac{5}{7} = \frac{3}{7}$ $\frac{3}{5} \times \frac{5}{6} = \frac{1}{2}$

$\frac{2}{3} \times \frac{2}{5} = \frac{4}{15}$ $4 \times \frac{1}{16} = \frac{1}{4}$ $10 \times \frac{5}{8} = \frac{25}{4} = 6\frac{1}{4}$

$\frac{1}{4} \times 16 = 4$ $\frac{4}{9} \times \frac{1}{4} = \frac{1}{9}$ $\frac{3}{4} \times \frac{4}{9} = \frac{1}{3}$

$\frac{1}{3} \times \frac{9}{10} = \frac{3}{10}$ $\frac{3}{4} \times \frac{2}{9} = \frac{1}{6}$ $12 \times \frac{7}{10} = \frac{42}{5} = 8\frac{2}{5}$

$\frac{1}{3} \times \frac{2}{3} = \frac{2}{9}$ $\frac{1}{8} \times 7 = \frac{7}{8}$ $\frac{1}{4} \times \frac{3}{4} = \frac{3}{16}$

$8 \times \frac{5}{6} = \frac{20}{3} = 6\frac{2}{3}$ $\frac{1}{8} \times \frac{4}{9} = \frac{1}{18}$ $\frac{1}{6} \times \frac{5}{6} = \frac{5}{36}$

$25 \times \frac{1}{2} = \frac{25}{2} = 12\frac{1}{2}$ $\frac{5}{9} \times \frac{9}{10} = \frac{1}{2}$ $\frac{3}{4} \times \frac{4}{5} = \frac{3}{5}$

Remind children that any whole number is also a fraction with 1 as the denominator. If children do not want to reduce ahead of time, they can multiply numerators and denominators separately, then reduce.

More complex fraction problems

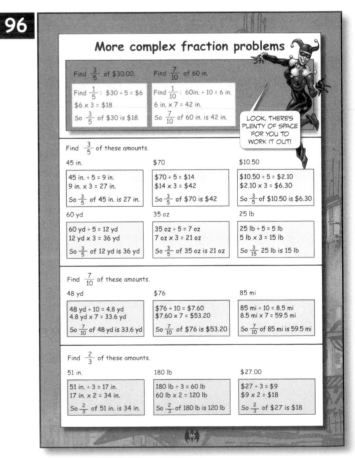

Find $\frac{3}{5}$ of $30.00.	Find $\frac{7}{10}$ of 60 in.
Find $\frac{1}{5}$: $30 ÷ 5 = $6	Find $\frac{1}{10}$: 60in. ÷ 10 = 6 in.
$6 × 3 = $18	6 in. × 7 = 42 in.
So $\frac{3}{5}$ of $30 is $18	So $\frac{7}{10}$ of 60 in. is 42 in.

LOOK, THERE'S PLENTY OF SPACE FOR YOU TO WORK IT OUT!

Find $\frac{3}{5}$ of these amounts.

45 in.	$70	$10.50
45 in. ÷ 5 = 9 in. 9 in. x 3 = 27 in. So $\frac{3}{5}$ of 45 in. is 27 in.	$70 ÷ 5 = $14 $14 x 3 = $42 So $\frac{3}{5}$ of $70 is $42	$10.50 ÷ 5 = $2.10 $2.10 x 3 = $6.30 So $\frac{3}{5}$ of $10.50 is $6.30
60 yd	35 oz	25 lb
60 yd ÷ 5 = 12 yd 12 yd x 3 = 36 yd So $\frac{3}{5}$ of 12 yd is 36 yd	35 oz ÷ 5 = 7 oz 7 oz x 3 = 21 oz So $\frac{3}{5}$ of 35 oz is 21 oz	25 lb ÷ 5 = 5 lb 5 lb x 3 = 15 lb So $\frac{3}{15}$ 25 lb is 15 lb

Find $\frac{7}{10}$ of these amounts.

48 yd	$76	85 mi
48 yd ÷ 10 = 4.8 yd 4.8 yd x 7 = 33.6 yd So $\frac{7}{10}$ of 48 yd is 33.6 yd	$76 ÷ 10 = $7.60 $7.60 x 7 = $53.20 So $\frac{7}{10}$ of $76 is $53.20	85 mi ÷ 10 = 8.5 mi 8.5 mi x 7 = 59.5 mi So $\frac{7}{10}$ of 85 mi is 59.5 mi

Find $\frac{2}{3}$ of these amounts.

51 in.	180 lb	$27.00
51 in. ÷ 3 = 17 in. 17 in. x 2 = 34 in. So $\frac{2}{3}$ of 51 in. is 34 in.	180 lb ÷ 3 = 60 lb 60 lb x 2 = 120 lb So $\frac{2}{3}$ of 180 lb is 120 lb	$27 ÷ 3 = $9 $9 x 2 = $18 So $\frac{2}{3}$ of $27 is $18

Ensure that children are dividing the amount by the denominator and multiplying the result by the numerator. You could explain that we divide by the bottom to find one part and multiply by the top to find the number of parts we want.

Finding percentages

Find 30% of 140. $\frac{140}{100} \times 30 = 42$ (Divide by 100 to find 1% and then multiply by 30 to find 30%.)

Find 12% of 75. $\frac{75}{100}^{3} \times 12^{3} = 9$ (Divide by 100 to find 1% and then multiply by 12 to find 12%.)

Find 30% of these numbers.

420 $\frac{420}{100} \times 30 = 126$ 260 $\frac{260}{100} \times 30 = 78$

30 $\frac{30}{100} \times 30 = 9$ 160 $\frac{160}{100} \times 30 = 48$

Find 60% of these numbers.

50 $\frac{50}{100} \times 60 = 30$ 270 $\frac{270}{100} \times 60 = 162$

120 $\frac{120}{100} \times 60 = 72$ 540 $\frac{540}{100} \times 60 = 324$

Find 45% of these numbers.

60 oz $\frac{60}{100} \times 45 = 27$ oz 600 mi $\frac{600}{100} \times 45 = 270$ mi

80 yd $\frac{80}{100} \times 45 = 36$ yd 220 yd $\frac{220}{100} \times 45 = 99$ yd

Find 12% of these numbers.

$125 $\frac{125}{100} \times 12 = 15 600 ft $\frac{600}{100} \times 12 = 72$ ft

$775 $\frac{775}{100} \times 12 = 93 150 yd $\frac{150}{100} \times 12 = 18$ yd

FRACTIONS? PERCENTAGES? WHO NEEDS THEM? YOU!

The most common error when finding percentages is to reverse the operation, i.e. to divide by the percentage required and multiply by 100. Explain again that if the whole is 100% we divide the number by 100 to find 1% and then multiply by the percentage we want.

Addition

Work out the answer to each problem.

```
  645        1,472
4,823          96
+ 1,433     8,391
 6,901      + 564
           10,523
```

Remember to regroup if you need to.

THESE SUMS ARE GETTING LONGER.

Find each sum.

```
 6,931     7,694      486        532
 8,174     3,722    8,560      8,420
+  219     + 612    + 7,924    +  348
15,324    12,028    16,970     9,300
```

```
 2,560      382      7,154     6,492
 6,548    6,582        532       378
+  499    + 3,291    + 287    + 2,436
 9,607    10,255     7,973     9,306
```

Find each sum.

```
 8,562     6,329      324      5,268
   629       845    8,265         93
 9,432     4,328       27      2,076
+  312     +  27    + 4,620    +  398
18,935    11,529    13,236     7,835
```

```
 8,794     6,526      459         84
   659     5,209    1,560        146
 3,212        38    7,643      2,362
+  961     + 124    + 154     + 9,268
13,626    11,897     9,816     11,860
```

This page should be fairly straightforward, but errors may creep in as the lists get longer toward the end. Errors will most likely be mistakes in adding the longer lists, adding across place value, or a failure to regroup.

More addition

Work out the answer to each problem.

```
23,714     11,541
 9,024        861
+  348     29,652
33,086     +    5
           42,059
```

Remember to regroup if you need to.

I THINK WE ALL NEED TO REGROUP!

Find each sum.

```
18,342     49,568       978
   133      2,425    23,476
+ 4,609    +   32    + 4,385
23,084     52,025    28,839
```

```
   371     84,119       200        274
42,747         27    72,654      8,542
+   42     + 2,643    + 9,220    + 9,762
43,160     86,789    82,074     18,578
```

Find each sum.

```
24,679        78     67,592     61,320
 4,308     2,001      4,374        314
    65    62,472         22         62
+  217     + 123    + 8,465    + 5,732
29,269     64,674    80,453     67,428
```

```
63,473     2,785          6     34,629
   267        29        205      4,572
35,306       812     32,428        843
+   43     + 5,228    + 4,620    +    4
99,089      8,854    37,259     40,048
```

Any problems on this page will be similar to those encountered on the previous page. As the numbers get larger, errors are more likely to occur.

Dividing by ones

$477 \div 2$ can be written in two ways:

$238 \frac{1}{2}$ or $238 \text{ r } 1$

$2)\overline{477}$ $2)\overline{477}$

NOW TRY THESE.

Work out the answers to these problems. Use fraction remainders.

$294\frac{1}{2}$ $282\frac{1}{3}$ $127\frac{3}{5}$ $124\frac{2}{7}$

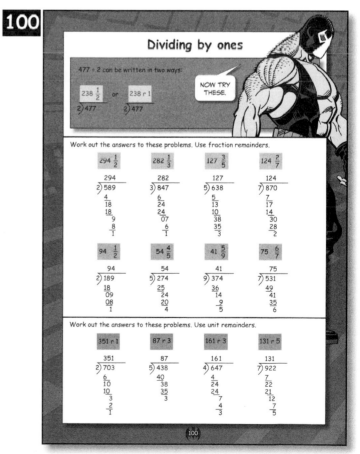

Work out the answers to these problems. Use unit remainders.

$351 \text{ r } 1$ $87 \text{ r } 3$ $161 \text{ r } 3$ $131 \text{ r } 5$

```
  351        87       161       131
2)703     5)438     4)647     7)922
  6         40        4         7
  10        38        24        22
  10        35        24        21
   3         3         7        12
   2                   4         7
   1                   3         5
```

Children may think that the two types of division represent different procedures. Point out that the only difference is in how to write the remainder.

101

Dividing by tens

361 ÷ 20 can be written in two ways:

$18\frac{1}{20}$ or $18\ r\ 1$

$20)\overline{361}$

YOU CAN DO IT!

Work out the answers to these problems. Use fraction remainders.

```
    9            6           4 27/80      6 8/90
    9            6             4            6
40)360       70)420       80)347       90)548
   360          420          320          540
     0            0           27            8

   50 6/10     22 17/20     95 3/10      11 21/30
   50           22           95           11
10)506       20)457       10)953       30)351
   50           40           90           30
    6           57           53           51
                40           50           30
                17            3           21
```

Work out the answers to these problems. Use unit remainders.

```
   8 r 27        8         10 r 23      9 r 7
   8             8           10           9
50)427       90)720       30)323       40)367
   400          720          300          360
    27            0           23            7

   47 r 13     10 r 43      12 r 17      35 r 7
   47           10           12           35
20)953       70)743       60)737       10)357
   80           70           60           30
  153           43          137           57
  140           00          120           50
   13           43           17            7
```

Children may have trouble deciding where to place digits in the quotient. Have them place the digit directly above the number being subtracted in that step.

102

Dividing by larger numbers

589 ÷ 15 can be written in two ways:

$39\frac{4}{15}$ or $39\ r\ 4$

$15)\overline{589}$

DIVIDE AND RULE!

Work out the answers to these problems. Use fraction remainders.

```
   8 1/46      7 3/70      6 5/22       8 7/57
   8            7            6            8
46)369       70)493       22)139       57)463
   368          490          132          456
     1            3            5            7

  29 9/28     12 19/65     15 4/17      7 22/51
  29           12           15            7
32)937       65)799       17)259       51)379
   64           65           17           357
  297          149           89           22
  288          130           85
    9           19            4
```

Work out the answers to these problems. Use unit remainders.

```
   8 r 29       4 r 17      4 r 39       9 r 23
   8            4            4            9
96)797       24)113       85)379       26)257
   768           96          340          234
    29           17           39           23

  31 r 7       12 r 39     28 r 13      14 r 43
  31           12           28           14
12)379       80)999       17)489       45)673
   36           80           34           45
   19          199          149          223
   12          160          136          180
    7           39           13           43
```

See the notes for page 101.

103

Everyday problems

Alfred has 6 m of copper tubing. If he uses 2.36 m, how much will he have left?

3.64 m

```
  6.00
- 2.36
  3.64
```

If he buys another 4.5 m of copper tubing, how much will he now have?

8.14 m

```
  3.64
+ 4.50
  8.14
```

The Penguin spends $36.65, $103.43, $68.99 and $35.60 in four different stores. How much money did he spend altogether?

$224.67

```
   36.65
  103.43
   68.99
+  35.60
  224.67
```

Batman has the following amounts of gasoline delivered to the Batcave in each year: 10,400 gallons in 2001; 13,350 gal in 2002; 14,755 gal in 2003; 9,656 gal in 2004 and 15,975 gal in 2005. How much did he have delivered over the five years?

64,136 gallons

```
  10,400
  13,350
  14,755
   9,656
+ 15,975
  64,136
```

If he had used 59,248 gallons in that time, how much gasoline did he have left at the end of 2005?

4,888 gallons

```
  64,136
- 59,248
   4,888
```

Batgirl runs 22.56 km to get away from the Joker. The Joker gives up - he runs 8,420 m less. How far did the Joker run?

14.14 km

```
  22.56
-  8.42
  14.14
```

What is the combined distance run by Batgirl and the Joker?

36.7 km

```
  22.56
+ 14.14
  36.70
```

Robin is 4ft 10 in. tall. Catwoman is 5 ft 1 in. tall. How much taller is Catwoman?

3 in.

```
  4 ft 13 in.
- 4 ft 10 in.
       3 in.
```

Children will apply subtraction and addition skills to real-life problems. if they are unsure about which operation to use, discuss whether the answer will be larger (addition) or smaller (subtraction). Take care when units of measurement need to be converted.

104

Real-life problems

A man walks 18.34 km on Saturday and 16.57 km on Sunday. How far did he walk that weekend?

34.91 km

```
  18.34
+ 16.57
  34.91
```

How much farther did he walk on Sunday?

1.77 km

```
  18.34
- 16.57
   1.77
```

Lockhaven Penitentiary exercise yard is rectangular. It measures 102.7 m by 95.6 m. What is the perimeter of the yard?

396.6 m

```
  102.7    95.6    205.4
x   2    x   2   + 191.2
  205.4   191.2    396.6
```

When Batman and Robin stand on a scale it reads $236\frac{1}{2}$ lb. When Batman steps off it reads $68\frac{1}{4}$ lb. How much does Batman weigh?

$168\frac{1}{4}$ lb

```
  236 1/2 = 236 2/4
            236
       -  68 1/4
          168 1/4
```

A rectangular room in the Batcave has an area of 32.58 m². When a carpet is put down, there is still 6.99 m² of floor showing. What is the area of the carpet?

25.59 m²

```
  32.58
-  6.99
  25.59
```

Echo and Query's combined height is $124\frac{3}{4}$ in. If Echo is $66\frac{1}{2}$ in, how tall is Query?

$58\frac{1}{4}$ in.

```
  66 1/2 = 66 2/4
           124 3/4
        -   66 2/4
            58 1/4
```

Four highways radiate from Gotham City. Route 1 is 1,246 mi long; Rte 2 is 399 mi long; Rte 3 is 1,327 mi long, and Rte 4 is 56 mi long. What is the total length of the four highways?

3,028 miles

```
  1,246
    399
  1,327
+    56
  3,028
```

The reserve gas tank in the Batmobile holds $25\frac{1}{2}$ quarts of gasoline. Alfred replaces it with a new one that holds 35 quarts. How much extra emergency gas is there?

$9\frac{1}{2}$ quarts

```
  35 = 34 2/4
       34 2/4
    - 25 1/2
       9 1/2
```

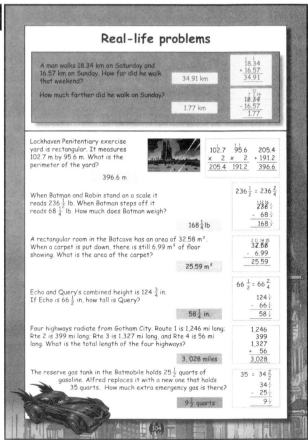

This page once again tests the skills of children in real-life problems. In the first question, make sure that they are finding the perimeter and not the area.

Real-life problems

Echo's weekend bag weighs $22\frac{1}{2}$ lb.
Query's weighs $24\frac{1}{2}$ lb.
How much more does Query's weigh than Echo's?

2 lb

$$24\frac{1}{2}$$
$$-22\frac{1}{2}$$
$$\overline{2}$$

What is the total weight of the two bags?

47 lb

$$24\frac{1}{2}$$
$$+22\frac{1}{2}$$
$$\overline{47}$$

Alfred is renovating Wayne Manor. He needs to put weather stripping around four sides of the front door. The door is 100 in. high and 60 in. wide. How many inches of weather stripping does he need?

320 in.

$$\begin{array}{r}100\\60\\100\\+\ 60\\\hline 320\end{array}$$

In a series of crime capers, the Joker steals $24,632, Catwoman steals $34,321, and Harley Quinn steals $22,971. How much do they steal altogether?

$81,924

$$\begin{array}{r}1\ 1\ 1\\24,632\\34,321\\+\ 22,971\\\hline 81,924\end{array}$$

How much more than the Joker does Catwoman steal?

$9,689

$$\begin{array}{r}2,13\ 12\ 11\ 11\\34,321\\-\ 24,632\\\hline 9,689\end{array}$$

How much more than Harley Quinn does the Joker steal?

$1,661

$$\begin{array}{r}3\ 15\ 13\\24,632\\-\ 22,971\\\hline 1,661\end{array}$$

An elevator says "Maximum weight 1,400 lb." If four people get in, weighing 198 lb, 132 lb, 254 lb, and 172 lb, how much more weight will the elevator hold?

644 lb

$$\begin{array}{r}2\ 1\\198\\132\\254\\+\ 172\\\hline 756\end{array}\qquad\begin{array}{r}0\ 13\ 9\ 10\\1,400\\-\ 756\\\hline 644\end{array}$$

See notes for page 104.

Multiplication by 2-digit numbers

Work out the answer to each problem.

$$\begin{array}{r}527\\\times\ 76\\\hline 3,162\\+\ 36,890\\\hline 40,052\end{array}\qquad\begin{array}{r}834\\\times\ 58\\\hline 6,672\\+\ 41,700\\\hline 48,372\end{array}$$

THIS SENDS ME INTO A SPIN! YOU'VE GOTTA WORK IT OUT!

Work out the answer to each problem.

$$\begin{array}{r}573\\\times\ 74\\\hline 2,292\\+\ 40,110\\\hline 42,402\end{array}\quad\begin{array}{r}795\\\times\ 68\\\hline 6,360\\+\ 47,700\\\hline 54,060\end{array}\quad\begin{array}{r}582\\\times\ 29\\\hline 5,238\\+\ 11,640\\\hline 16,878\end{array}\quad\begin{array}{r}788\\\times\ 38\\\hline 6,304\\+\ 23,640\\\hline 29,944\end{array}$$

$$\begin{array}{r}587\\\times\ 42\\\hline 1,174\\+\ 23,480\\\hline 24,654\end{array}\quad\begin{array}{r}995\\\times\ 37\\\hline 7,965\\+\ 29,850\\\hline 36,815\end{array}\quad\begin{array}{r}653\\\times\ 84\\\hline 2,612\\+\ 52,240\\\hline 54,852\end{array}\quad\begin{array}{r}757\\\times\ 85\\\hline 3,785\\+\ 60,560\\\hline 64,345\end{array}$$

$$\begin{array}{r}489\\\times\ 96\\\hline 2,934\\+\ 44,010\\\hline 46,944\end{array}\quad\begin{array}{r}158\\\times\ 61\\\hline 158\\+\ 9,480\\\hline 9,638\end{array}\quad\begin{array}{r}257\\\times\ 88\\\hline 2,056\\+\ 20,560\\\hline 22,616\end{array}\quad\begin{array}{r}175\\\times\ 43\\\hline 525\\+\ 7,000\\\hline 7,525\end{array}$$

$$\begin{array}{r}386\\\times\ 85\\\hline 1,930\\+\ 30,880\\\hline 32,810\end{array}\quad\begin{array}{r}539\\\times\ 73\\\hline 1,617\\+\ 37,730\\\hline 39,347\end{array}\quad\begin{array}{r}492\\\times\ 29\\\hline 4,428\\+\ 9,840\\\hline 14,268\end{array}\quad\begin{array}{r}783\\\times\ 63\\\hline 2,349\\+\ 46,980\\\hline 49,329\end{array}$$

Explain that multiplying by 84 means multiplying by 80, then by 4, and then adding the answers together. Multiplying by 10 (or 80) means adding a zero and multiplying by 1 (or 8). Multiplying by the tens digit first saves having to remember to put the zero later.

Division by ones

$47 \div 2$ can be written in two ways:

$23\frac{1}{2}$ $23 \text{ r } 1$

HMM! QUANTITIES OF QUOTIENTS...

Write the quotients for these problems with fraction remainders.

$$9\tfrac{1}{2}\quad\begin{array}{r}9\\2\overline{)19}\\18\\\hline 1\end{array}\qquad 4\tfrac{1}{4}\quad\begin{array}{r}4\\4\overline{)17}\\16\\\hline 1\end{array}\qquad 5\tfrac{2}{3}\quad\begin{array}{r}5\\3\overline{)17}\\15\\\hline 2\end{array}\qquad 8\tfrac{3}{4}\quad\begin{array}{r}8\\4\overline{)35}\\32\\\hline 3\end{array}$$

$$9\tfrac{1}{3}\quad\begin{array}{r}9\\3\overline{)28}\\27\\\hline 1\end{array}\qquad 23\tfrac{1}{2}\quad\begin{array}{r}23\\2\overline{)47}\\4\\\hline 7\\6\\\hline 1\end{array}\qquad 17\tfrac{2}{5}\quad\begin{array}{r}17\\5\overline{)87}\\5\\\hline 37\\35\\\hline 2\end{array}\qquad 10\tfrac{3}{5}\quad\begin{array}{r}10\\5\overline{)53}\\50\\\hline 3\end{array}$$

Write the quotients for these problems with unit remainders.

$$47 \text{ r } 1\quad\begin{array}{r}47\\2\overline{)95}\\8\\\hline 15\\14\\\hline 1\end{array}\qquad 41 \text{ r } 1\quad\begin{array}{r}41\\2\overline{)83}\\8\\\hline 3\\2\\\hline 1\end{array}\qquad 24 \text{ r } 1\quad\begin{array}{r}24\\2\overline{)49}\\4\\\hline 9\\8\\\hline 1\end{array}\qquad 16 \text{ r } 3\quad\begin{array}{r}16\\4\overline{)67}\\4\\\hline 27\\24\\\hline 3\end{array}$$

$$18 \text{ r } 1\quad\begin{array}{r}18\\4\overline{)73}\\4\\\hline 33\\32\\\hline 1\end{array}\qquad 20 \text{ r } 1\quad\begin{array}{r}20\\4\overline{)81}\\8\\\hline 1\end{array}\qquad 14 \text{ r } 2\quad\begin{array}{r}14\\5\overline{)72}\\5\\\hline 22\\20\\\hline 2\end{array}\qquad 19 \text{ r } 4\quad\begin{array}{r}19\\5\overline{)99}\\5\\\hline 49\\45\\\hline 4\end{array}$$

By now children will be comfortable with remainders. In the second section, they have to place a decimal point after the number being divided and add one or two zeros. Encourage them to use the last section as practice for the operation they found most difficult.

Dividing larger numbers

$645 \div 13$ can be written in two ways:

$49\frac{8}{13}$ or $49 \text{ r } 8$

$13\overline{)645}$

THIS DIVISION IS AS DEVILISH AS ME!

Work out the answer to each problem. Use fraction remainders.

$$8\tfrac{7}{45}\quad\begin{array}{r}8\\45\overline{)367}\\360\\\hline 7\end{array}\qquad 8\tfrac{17}{21}\quad\begin{array}{r}8\\21\overline{)179}\\168\\\hline 17\end{array}\qquad 8\tfrac{11}{16}\quad\begin{array}{r}8\\16\overline{)139}\\128\\\hline 11\end{array}\qquad 8\tfrac{34}{43}\quad\begin{array}{r}8\\43\overline{)378}\\344\\\hline 34\end{array}$$

$$3\tfrac{43}{50}\quad\begin{array}{r}3\\50\overline{)193}\\150\\\hline 43\end{array}\qquad 6\tfrac{25}{93}\quad\begin{array}{r}6\\93\overline{)583}\\558\\\hline 25\end{array}\qquad 27\tfrac{3}{13}\quad\begin{array}{r}27\\13\overline{)354}\\26\\\hline 94\\91\\\hline 3\end{array}\qquad 51\tfrac{4}{15}\quad\begin{array}{r}51\\15\overline{)769}\\75\\\hline 19\\15\\\hline 4\end{array}$$

Work out the answer to each problem. Use unit remainders.

$$4 \text{ r } 47\quad\begin{array}{r}6\\70\overline{)467}\\42\\\hline 47\end{array}\qquad 8 \text{ r } 61\quad\begin{array}{r}8\\84\overline{)733}\\672\\\hline 61\end{array}\qquad 8 \text{ r } 15\quad\begin{array}{r}8\\44\overline{)367}\\352\\\hline 15\end{array}\qquad 7 \text{ r } 25\quad\begin{array}{r}7\\62\overline{)459}\\434\\\hline 25\end{array}$$

$$18 \text{ r } 47\quad\begin{array}{r}18\\52\overline{)983}\\52\\\hline 463\\416\\\hline 47\end{array}\qquad 21 \text{ r } 16\quad\begin{array}{r}21\\35\overline{)751}\\70\\\hline 51\\35\\\hline 16\end{array}\qquad 22 \text{ r } 2\quad\begin{array}{r}22\\43\overline{)948}\\86\\\hline 88\\86\\\hline 2\end{array}\qquad 27 \text{ r } 6\quad\begin{array}{r}27\\31\overline{)843}\\62\\\hline 223\\217\\\hline 6\end{array}$$

See the notes on page 101.

109

Division of 3-digit decimal numbers

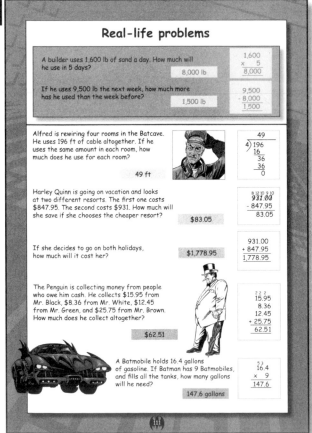

Work out these division sums.

0.89	0.74

```
    0.89        0.74
3)2.67       4)2.96
  24           28
   27           16
   27           16
    0            0
```

2.86	2.16	1.83	4.89

```
    2.86        2.16        1.83        4.89
2)5.72      4)8.64      4)7.32      2)9.78
  4           8           4           8
  17          6           33          17
  16          4           32          16
   12          24          12          18
   12          24          12          18
    0           0           0           0
```

1.56	1.34	1.75	0.82

NOW DO YOU GET THE POINT?

```
    1.56        1.34        1.75        0.82
3)4.68      4)5.36      5)8.75      4)3.28
  3           4           5           3.2
  16          13          37           8
  15          12          35           8
   18          16          25           0
   18          16          25
    0           0           0
```

1.47	3.12	2.81

```
    1.47        3.12        2.81
4)5.88      3)9.36      3)8.43
  4           9           6
  18          3           24
  16          3           24
   28          6           3
   28          6           3
    0           0           0
```

On this page, the decimal point has been incorporated into the middle of the number being divided. After the previous two pages, carrying across the decimal point should be familiar to children. No additional zeros need to be added on in this section.

110

Division of 3-digit decimals

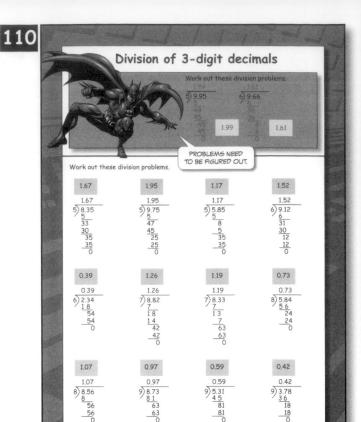

Work out these division problems.

```
    1.99        1.61
5)9.95      6)9.66
  5           6
  49          36
  45          36
   45          6
   45          6
    0          0
```

1.99	1.61

PROBLEMS NEED TO BE FIGURED OUT.

Work out these division problems.

1.67	1.95	1.17	1.52

```
    1.67        1.95        1.17        1.52
5)8.35      5)9.75      5)5.85      6)9.12
  5           5           5           6
  33          47          8           31
  30          45          5           30
   35          25          35          12
   35          25          35          12
    0           0           0           0
```

0.39	1.26	1.19	0.73

```
    0.39        1.26        1.19        0.73
6)2.34      7)8.82      7)8.33      8)5.84
  18          7           7           56
  54          18          13          24
  54          14          7           24
   0          42          63          0
              42          63
               0           0
```

1.07	0.97	0.59	0.42

```
    1.07        0.97        0.59        0.42
8)8.56      9)8.73      9)5.31      9)3.78
  8           81          45          36
  56          63          81          18
  56          63          81          18
   0           0           0           0
```

The comments on the previous page also apply to this one, but as the dividing numbers are larger any weakness in multiplication facts for 6, 7, 8, and 9 times table will show up.

111

Real-life problems

A builder uses 1,600 lb of sand a day. How much will he use in 5 days?

8,000 lb

```
 1,600
×     5
 8,000
```

If he uses 9,500 lb the next week, how much more has he used than the week before?

1,500 lb

```
 9,500
− 8,000
 1,500
```

Alfred is rewiring four rooms in the Batcave. He uses 196 ft of cable altogether. If he uses the same amount in each room, how much does he use for each room?

49 ft

```
    49
4)196
  16
  36
  36
   0
```

Harley Quinn is going on vacation and looks at two different resorts. The first one costs $847.95. The second costs $931. How much will she save if she chooses the cheaper resort?

$83.05

```
  8 12 10 9 10
  931.00
− 847.95
  83.05
```

If she decides to go on both holidays, how much will it cost her?

$1,778.95

```
  931.00
+ 847.95
1,778.95
```

The Penguin is collecting money from people who owe him cash. He collects $15.95 from Mr. Black, $8.36 from Mr. White, $12.45 from Mr. Green, and $25.75 from Mr. Brown. How much does he collect altogether?

$62.51

```
  2 2 2
  15.95
   8.36
  12.45
+ 25.75
  62.51
```

A Batmobile holds 16.4 gallons of gasoline. If Batman has 9 Batmobiles, and fills all the tanks, how many gallons will he need?

147.6 gallons

```
  5 3
  16.4
×    9
 147.6
```

This page provides an opportunity to apply the skills practiced. Children will need to select the operations necessary. If they are unsure about which operation to use, discuss whether the answer will be larger or smaller, which narrows down the options.

112

Rounding money

Underline the digit you want to round to, then look at the digit to the right.

Round to the nearest dollar.

$3.95 rounds to $4

$2.25 rounds to $2

Round to the nearest ten dollars.

$15.50 rounds to $20

$14.40 rounds to $10

ROUND UP THE CENTS TO TAKE CARE OF THE DOLLARS.

Round to the nearest dollar.

$2.70 rounds to $3 $1.75 rounds to $2

$9.65 rounds to $10 $6.95 rounds to $7

$4.15 rounds to $4 $3.39 rounds to $3 $7.14 rounds to $7

$7.75 rounds to $8 $4.30 rounds to $4 $2.53 rounds to $3

Round to the nearest ten dollars.

$38.35 rounds to $40 $32.75 rounds to $30 $85.05 rounds to $90

$22.75 rounds to $20 $66.70 rounds to $70 $24.55 rounds to $20

$56.85 rounds to $60 $14.95 rounds to $10 $15.00 rounds to $20

Round to the nearest hundred dollars.

$407.25 rounds to $400 $357.85 rounds to $400 $115.99 rounds to $100

$870.45 rounds to $900 $524.45 rounds to $500 $650.15 rounds to $700

$849.75 rounds to $800 $728.55 rounds to $700 $467.25 rounds to $500

If children have difficulty, have them decide which are the two nearest dollars, tens of dollars, or hundreds of dollars, and which of the two is closest to the number.

Estimating sums of money

Round to the leading digit. Estimate the sum.

$3.26 → $3
+ $4.82 → + $5
is about $8

$68.53 → $70
+ $34.60 → + $30
is about $100

IT'S HELPFUL TO THINK ABOUT IT…

Round to the leading digit. Estimate the sum.

$53.64 → $50
+ $28.40 → + $30
is about $80

$18.45 → $20
+ $23.05 → + $20
is about $40

$28.95 → $30
+ $34.22 → + $30
is about $60

$35.95 → $40
+ $12.70 → + $10
is about $50

$63.40 → $60
+ $47.80 → + $50
is about $110

$25.75 → $30
+ $32.20 → + $30
is about $60

$47.30 → $50
+ $23.85 → + $20
is about $70

$28.73 → $30
+ $32.60 → + $30
is about $60

$72.30 → $70
+ $10.40 → + $10
is about $80

$560.70 → $600
+ $332.40 → + $300
is about $900

$382.60 → $400
+ $238.50 → + $200
is about $600

$780.75 → $800
+ $98.75 → + $100
is about $900

Round to the leading digit. Estimate the sum.

$17.95 + $75.95 → $100

$20.35 + $32.87 → $50

$51.19 + $39.50 → $90

$875.90 + $103.20 → $1,000

$517.75 + $291.50 → $800

$48.87 + $90.34 → $140

$83.40 + $12.30 → $90

$90.34 + $16.20 → $110

In section 2, children need to estimate by rounding mentally. If they have trouble, have them write the rounded numbers above the originals first, and then add them.

Estimating differences of money

Round the numbers to the leading digit. Estimate the differences.

$8.75 → $9
- $4.83 → - $5
is about $4

$63.20 → $60
- $48.35 → - $50
is about $10

KEEP COUNTING THE CASH!

Round to the leading digit. Estimate the difference.

$27.80 → $30
- $11.90 → - $10
is about $20

$48.35 → $50
- $32.25 → - $30
is about $20

$89.20 → $90
- $22.40 → - $20
is about $70

$37.40 → $40
- $31.20 → - $30
is about $10

$58.20 → $60
- $17.30 → - $20
is about $40

$326.30 → $300
- $178.90 → - $200
is about $100

$54.10 → $50
- $33.80 → - $30
is about $20

$87.40 → $90
- $8.75 → - $10
is about $80

$783.90 → $800
- $417.60 → - $400
is about $400

Round to the leading digit. Estimate the difference.

$8.12 - $3.78
→ $8 - $4   = $4

$49.60 - $21.80
→ $50 - $20   = $30

$7.70 - $3.20
→ $8 - $3   = $5

$84.20 - $39.80
→ $80 - $40   = $40

$5.95 - $4.60
→ $6 - $5   = $1

$675.80 - $267.50
→ $700 - $300   = $400

$32.85 - $21.90
→ $30 - $20   = $10

$829.90 - $516.20
→ $800 - $500   = $300

$56.78 - $38.90
→ $60 - $40   = $20

$679.20 - $211.10
→ $700 - $200   = $500

See the comments on page 113.

Estimating sums and differences

Round to the leading digit. Estimate the sum or difference.

3,762 → 4,000
+ 1,204 → + 1,000
is about   5,000

287,257 → 300,000
- 98,592 → - 100,000
is about   200,000

Round to the leading digit. Estimate the sum or difference.

587 → 600
+ 496 → + 500
is about   1,100

22,945 → 20,000
- 12,356 → - 10,000
is about   10,000

8,265 → 8,000
+ 2,156 → + 2,000
is about   10,000

685,271 → 700,000
+ 213,876 → + 200,000
is about   900,000

57,998 → 60,000
- 22,135 → - 20,000
is about   40,000

492,076 → 500,000
+ 237,631 → + 200,000
is about   700,000

23,957 → 20,000
+ 14,702 → + 10,000
is about   30,000

8,752 → 9,000
- 2,398 → - 2,000
is about   7,000

62,973 → 60,000
+ 21,482 → + 20,000
is about   80,000

5,294 → 5,000
+ 3,813 → + 4,000
is about   9,000

736 → 700
+ 829 → + 800
is about   1,500

33,729 → 30,000
- 19,372 → - 20,000
is about   10,000

Write > or < for each problem.

IM GREATER THAN ALL OF THESE!

567 + 295   >   800

467 - 307   >   100

11,987 - 5,424   >   6,000

41,925 - 12,354   <   40,000

8,183 - 6,875   >   1,000

19,885 + 12,681   >   30,000

645,900 + 183,650   >   800,000

753 - 347   >   300

913,312 - 432,667   <   500,000

In section 2, children need to think about their estimates more carefully if the estimate is very close to the number on the right side of the equation. Have them look at the numbers in the next place to the right to adjust their estimates up or down.

Estimating products

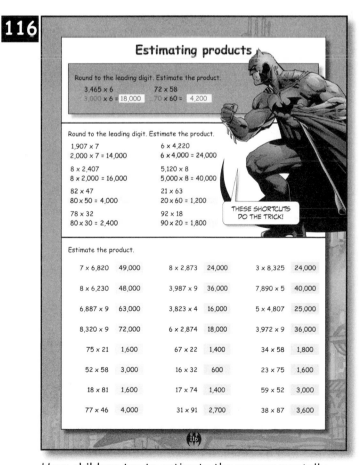

Round to the leading digit. Estimate the product.

3,465 × 6
3,000 × 6 = 18,000

72 × 58
70 × 60 = 4,200

Round to the leading digit. Estimate the product.

1,907 × 7
2,000 × 7 = 14,000

6 × 4,220
6 × 4,000 = 24,000

8 × 2,407
8 × 2,000 = 16,000

5,120 × 8
5,000 × 8 = 40,000

82 × 47
80 × 50 = 4,000

21 × 63
20 × 60 = 1,200

78 × 32
80 × 30 = 2,400

92 × 18
90 × 20 = 1,800

THESE SHORTCUTS DO THE TRICK!

Estimate the product.

7 × 6,820	49,000	8 × 2,873	24,000	3 × 8,325	24,000
8 × 6,230	48,000	3,987 × 9	36,000	7,890 × 5	40,000
6,887 × 9	63,000	3,823 × 4	16,000	5 × 4,807	25,000
8,320 × 9	72,000	6 × 2,874	18,000	3,972 × 9	36,000
75 × 21	1,600	67 × 22	1,400	34 × 58	1,800
52 × 58	3,000	16 × 32	600	23 × 75	1,600
18 × 81	1,600	17 × 74	1,400	59 × 52	3,000
77 × 46	4,000	31 × 91	2,700	38 × 87	3,600

Have children try to estimate the answer mentally. If they have trouble, have them write the rounded numbers first.

Estimating quotients

Round to the leading digit. Estimate the product.

2,934 · 6   2,356 · 5
3,000 · 6 = 500   2,500 · 5 = 500

DO YOU THINK I'M A COMPATIBLE NUMBER?

Round to compatible numbers. Estimate the quotient.

1,895 ÷ 8
1,600 ÷ 8 = 200

2,120 ÷ 4
2,000 ÷ 4 = 500

4,998 ÷ 6
4,800 ÷ 6 = 800

1,689 ÷ 3
1,800 ÷ 3 = 600

4,166 ÷ 5
4,000 ÷ 5 = 800

5,555 ÷ 9
5,400 ÷ 9 = 600

5,587 ÷ 7
5,600 ÷ 7 = 800

1,580 ÷ 2
1,600 ÷ 2 = 800

Estimate the quotient.

4,942 ÷ 7	700	8,208 ÷ 9	900	5,124 ÷ 5	1,000
3,712 ÷ 4	900	5,602 ÷ 6	900	2,275 ÷ 8	300
1,651 ÷ 3	500	4,143 ÷ 4	1,000	4,867 ÷ 9	500
7,153 ÷ 8	900	1,775 ÷ 2	900	3,294 ÷ 7	500
3,572 ÷ 6	600	2,896 ÷ 5	600	3,175 ÷ 4	800
1,472 ÷ 3	500	4,379 ÷ 6	700	2,987 ÷ 8	400
1,972 ÷ 4	500	3,672 ÷ 7	500	4,486 ÷ 9	500
2,687 ÷ 5	500	6,500 ÷ 8	800	2,895 ÷ 3	900

Children should round the dividend to a nearby number that can easily be divided by the divisor. Compatible numbers are ones that are just multiples of the divisor. Knowledge of basic division facts should allow these estimates to be done mentally.

Rounding mixed numbers

Round to the closest whole number

$2\frac{5}{6}$ $3\frac{2}{5}$

$\frac{5}{6}$ is more than $\frac{1}{2}$ $\frac{2}{5}$ is less than $\frac{1}{2}$

$2\frac{5}{6}$ rounds up to 3 $3\frac{2}{5}$ rounds down to 3

DON'T FIDDLE WITH FRACTIONS!

Circle the fractions that are more than $\frac{1}{2}$.

$\frac{1}{7}$ $\frac{3}{8}$ ⬭$\frac{5}{9}$ ⬭$\frac{7}{10}$ $\frac{2}{9}$ $\frac{3}{8}$ ⬭$\frac{6}{7}$ ⬭$\frac{2}{3}$

⬭$\frac{5}{6}$ $\frac{1}{3}$ $\frac{2}{5}$ ⬭$\frac{4}{7}$ ⬭$\frac{5}{8}$ $\frac{1}{7}$ ⬭$\frac{5}{6}$ $\frac{3}{5}$

Circle the fractions that are less than $\frac{1}{2}$.

⬭$\frac{2}{5}$ ⬭$\frac{2}{7}$ $\frac{3}{4}$ ⬭$\frac{3}{10}$ $\frac{6}{7}$ ⬭$\frac{2}{5}$ $\frac{5}{8}$ ⬭$\frac{1}{8}$

$\frac{2}{3}$ ⬭$\frac{4}{9}$ ⬭$\frac{1}{5}$ ⬭$\frac{1}{4}$ $\frac{6}{10}$ ⬭$\frac{3}{7}$ ⬭$\frac{3}{8}$ $\frac{6}{9}$

Round to the closest whole number

$6\frac{3}{4}$	7	$1\frac{1}{3}$	1	$5\frac{3}{8}$	5	$3\frac{2}{9}$	3
$2\frac{4}{5}$	3	$4\frac{7}{8}$	5	$4\frac{1}{4}$	4	$5\frac{1}{7}$	5
$5\frac{2}{5}$	5	$3\frac{2}{7}$	3	$7\frac{1}{3}$	7	$6\frac{9}{13}$	7
$7\frac{3}{9}$	7	$1\frac{1}{4}$	1	$3\frac{3}{5}$	4	$5\frac{7}{12}$	6
$4\frac{3}{5}$	5	$2\frac{2}{3}$	3	$1\frac{3}{8}$	1	$6\frac{5}{7}$	7

If children have trouble rounding, explain that if the numerator is less then half as big as the denominator, the fraction is less than one-half.

Calculate the mean

What is the mean of 6 and 10?   (6 + 10) ÷ 2 = 8

Tim, Tom, and Joe are Batman fans. Tim is 9, Tom is 10, and Joe is 5. What is their mean age?   (9 + 10 + 5) ÷ 3 = 8

Calculate the mean of these amounts.

8 and 4	6
9 and 3	6
6 and 12	9
17 and 21	19

CALCULATE THE MEAN? WHO'S MEAN AROUND HERE?

13 and 15	14
20 and 60	40

Calculate the mean of these amounts.

3, 5, and 7	5	5, 9, and 13	9
4, 8, and 12	8	4, 10, and 16	10
20, 35, and 65	40	$1, $1.50, $2.50, and $3	$2
3¢, 9¢, 12¢, and 16¢	10¢	5 g, 7 g, 8 g, and 8 g	7 g

The mean of two numbers is 9. If one of the numbers is 8, what is the other number?	10
The mean of three numbers is 4. If two of the numbers are 3 and 4, what is the other number?	5
The mean of three numbers is 5. If two of the numbers are 5 and 7, what is the other number?	3
The mean of four numbers is 7. If three of the numbers are 6, 5, and 12, what is the other number?	5

The average of a number list is known as the "mean." Children should add the list and divide by the number of numbers. In part 3, explain that if the mean is 9, the total must have been 18, so if they take away the number given they will find the number required.

Mean, median, and mode

Harley Quinn thows a dice 7 times. Here are her results: 4, 2, 1, 2, 4, 2, 6.

What is the mean?   (4 + 2 + 1 + 2 + 4 + 2 + 6) ÷ 7 = 3

What is the median? Put the numbers in order of size and find the middle number, example: 1, 2, 2, 2, 4, 4, 6.

The median is 2.

What is the mode?   The most common result, which is 2.

In 11 spelling tests, Robin scored the following: 15, 12, 15, 17, 11, 16, 19, 11, 3, 11, 13

What is his mean score?	13
What is his median score?	13
Write down the mode for his scores.	11

Gotham City soccer team scores the following number of goals in their first 9 matches: 2, 2, 1, 3, 2, 1, 2, 4, 1

What is the mean score?	2
What is the median score?	2
Write down the mode for their scores.	2

The Joker sets out cards in 11 piles. The numbers of cards in each piles is: 17, 15, 19, 17, 18, 19, 21, 17, 16, 22, 17

What is the mean number?   What is the median number in a pile?
18   17

What is the mode number of cards?
17

The work on this page leads on from previous work on the mean, but also expands it to the median and the mode. The biggest problem children may have is remembering which is which. Encourage them to develop a system that works for them.

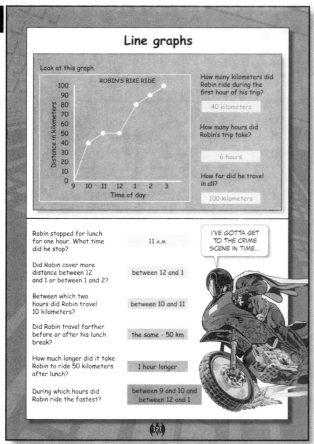

Children may have trouble deciding how far Robin traveled between two times. Have them find the distance at the starting and ending times, and then subtract to get the answer.

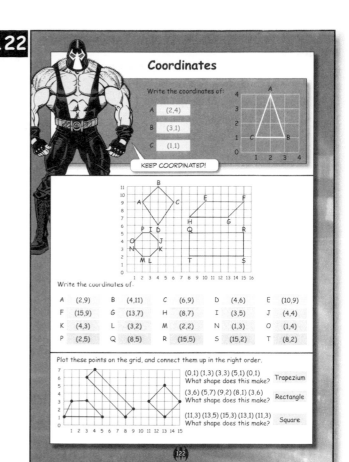

Children should remember to read off the horizontal coordinate first. In the second section, it is important that they join the coordinates in the order in which they are written to produce the intended shape.

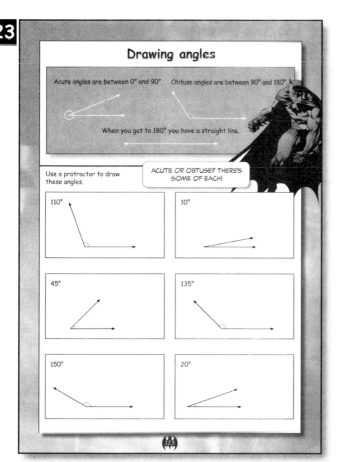

To do the work on this page and the next, children require a 360° protractor. Check that they read the protractor from the right direction. Remind children to mark the angles. This is important to avoid confusion when drawing reflex angles.

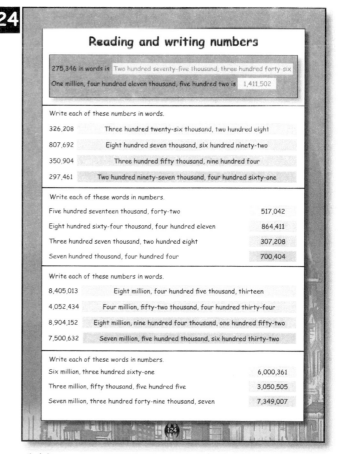

Children may use zeros incorrectly in numbers. In word form, zeros are omitted, but children should take care to include them when writing numbers in standard form.

Multiplying and dividing by 10

Write the answer in the box.

27 x 10 = 270

40 ÷ 10 = 4

PRACTICE MAKES PERFECT!

Write the product in the box.

84 x 10 = 840   35 x 10 = 350   72 x 10 = 720

77 x 10 = 770   18 x 10 = 180   56 x 10 = 560

156 x 10 = 1,560   274 x 10 = 2,740   372 x 10 = 3,720

387 x 10 = 3,870   928 x 10 = 9,280   495 x 10 = 4,950

Write the quotient in the box.

30 ÷ 10 = 3   60 ÷ 10 = 6   40 ÷ 10 = 4

70 ÷ 10 = 7   100 ÷ 10 = 10   360 ÷ 10 = 36

420 ÷ 10 = 42   930 ÷ 10 = 93   750 ÷ 10 = 75

840 ÷ 10 = 84   270 ÷ 10 = 27   470 ÷ 10 = 47

Write the product in the box.

72 x 10 = 720   12 x 10 = 120   37 x 10 = 370

65 x 10 = 650   83 x 10 = 830   29 x 10 = 290

372 x 10 = 3,720   165 x 10 = 1,650   814 x 10 = 8,140

846 x 10 = 8,460   932 x 10 = 9,320   635 x 10 = 6,350

Write the quotient in the box.

60 ÷ 10 = 6   10 ÷ 10 = 1   200 ÷ 10 = 20

490 ÷ 10 = 49   940 ÷ 10 = 94   780 ÷ 10 = 78

Children should realize that mutiplying a whole number by 10 means writing a zero at the end. To divide a multiple of ten by 10, simply take the final zero off the number. In the two final sections, the inverse operation is used for solving the problems.

Identifying patterns

Continue each pattern.

| Steps of 9: | 5 | 14 | 23 | 32 | 41 | 50 |
| Steps of 14: | 20 | 34 | 48 | 62 | 76 | 90 |

Continue each pattern.

4	34	64	94	124	154	184	214
10	61	112	163	214	265	316	367
48	100	152	204	256	308	360	412
20	37	54	71	88	105	122	139
25	100	175	250	325	400	475	550
25	45	65	85	105	125	145	165
8	107	206	305	404	503	602	701
7	25	43	61	79	97	115	133
22	72	122	172	222	272	322	372
60	165	270	375	480	585	690	795
13	37	61	85	109	133	157	181
11	30	49	68	87	106	125	144
32	48	64	80	96	112	128	144
36	126	216	306	396	486	576	666
32	54	76	98	120	142	164	186
26	127	228	329	430	531	632	733
12	72	132	192	252	312	372	432
32	50	68	86	104	122	140	158

Children should determine what number to add to the first number to make the second number, and check to make sure that adding the same number turns the second number into the third. They can then continue the pattern.

Recognizing multiples of 6, 7, and 8

Multiples are found by multiplying one number by another.
Circle all the multiples of 6.

8   (12)   15   (18)   20   (24)

Circle all the multiples of 6.

20	32	62	(6)	(42)	34
(24)	10	38	(72)	16	(60)
14	22	44	8	(30)	(18)
(66)	64	52	25	(54)	28

Circle all the multiples of 7.

27	34	(49)	36	47	(35)
(21)	60	58	19	(56)	26
(28)	73	40	46	23	(63)
18	25	(14)	37	69	27

Circle all the multiples of 8.

50	(32)	62	12	(16)	25
(56)	18	38	28	60	(24)
34	(72)	(48)	44	82	14
22	54	70	(40)	(64)	(80)

Circle the number that is a multiple of 6 and 7.

24   35   (42)   62   70   72

Circle all the numbers that are multiples of both 6 and 8.

16   (24)   28   (48)   54   60

THE MULTIPLES KEEP MULTIPLYING!

Success on this page will basically depend on a knowledge of multiplication tables. Where children experience difficulties, multiplication table practice should be encouraged.

Factors of numbers from 1 to 30

The factors of 10 are the numbers that divide evenly into 10:

| 1 | 2 | 5 | 10 |

Circle the factors of 4:   (1)   (2)   3   (4)

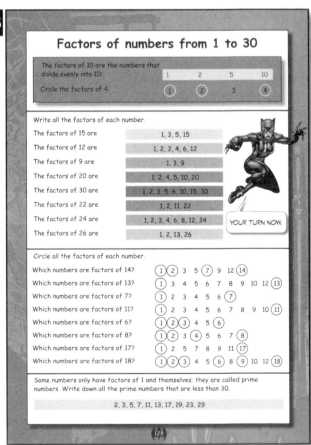

Write all the factors of each number.

The factors of 15 are   1, 3, 5, 15

The factors of 12 are   1, 2, 3, 4, 6, 12

The factors of 9 are   1, 3, 9

The factors of 20 are   1, 2, 4, 5, 10, 20

The factors of 30 are   1, 2, 3, 5, 6, 10, 15, 30

The factors of 22 are   1, 2, 11, 22

The factors of 24 are   1, 2, 3, 4, 6, 8, 12, 24

The factors of 26 are   1, 2, 13, 26

YOUR TURN NOW.

Circle all the factors of each number.

Which numbers are factors of 14?   (1) (2) 3 5 (7) 9 12 (14)

Which numbers are factors of 13?   (1) 3 4 5 6 7 8 9 10 12 (13)

Which numbers are factors of 7?   (1) 2 3 4 5 6 (7)

Which numbers are factors of 11?   (1) 2 3 4 5 6 7 8 9 10 (11)

Which numbers are factors of 6?   (1)(2)(3) 4 5 (6)

Which numbers are factors of 8?   (1)(2) 3 (4) 5 6 7 (8)

Which numbers are factors of 17?   (1) 2 5 7 8 9 11 (17)

Which numbers are factors of 18?   (1)(2)(3) 4 5 (6) 8 (9) 10 12 (18)

Some numbers only have factors of 1 and themselves; they are called prime numbers. Write down all the prime numbers that are less than 30.

2, 3, 5, 7, 11, 13, 17, 19, 23, 29

Encourage a systematic approach, such as starting at 1 and working forward to the number that is half of the number in question. Children often forget that 1 and the number itself are factors of a given number. You may need to point out that 1 is not a prime number.

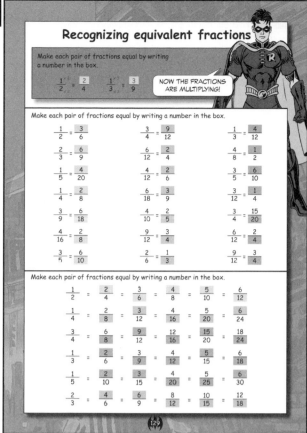

129

Recognizing equivalent fractions

Make each pair of fractions equal by writing a number in the box.

$\frac{1}{2} = \frac{2}{4}$ $\frac{1}{3} = \frac{3}{9}$

NOW THE FRACTIONS ARE MULTIPLYING!

Make each pair of fractions equal by writing a number in the box.

$\frac{1}{2} = \frac{3}{6}$ $\frac{3}{4} = \frac{9}{12}$ $\frac{1}{3} = \frac{4}{12}$

$\frac{2}{3} = \frac{6}{9}$ $\frac{6}{12} = \frac{2}{4}$ $\frac{4}{8} = \frac{1}{2}$

$\frac{1}{5} = \frac{4}{20}$ $\frac{4}{12} = \frac{2}{6}$ $\frac{3}{5} = \frac{6}{10}$

$\frac{1}{4} = \frac{2}{8}$ $\frac{6}{18} = \frac{3}{9}$ $\frac{3}{12} = \frac{1}{4}$

$\frac{3}{9} = \frac{6}{18}$ $\frac{4}{10} = \frac{2}{5}$ $\frac{3}{4} = \frac{15}{20}$

$\frac{4}{16} = \frac{2}{8}$ $\frac{9}{12} = \frac{3}{4}$ $\frac{6}{12} = \frac{2}{4}$

$\frac{3}{5} = \frac{6}{10}$ $\frac{2}{6} = \frac{1}{3}$ $\frac{9}{12} = \frac{3}{4}$

Make each pair of fractions equal by writing a number in the box.

$\frac{1}{2} = \frac{2}{4} = \frac{3}{6} = \frac{4}{8} = \frac{5}{10} = \frac{6}{12}$

$\frac{1}{4} = \frac{2}{8} = \frac{3}{12} = \frac{4}{16} = \frac{5}{20} = \frac{6}{24}$

$\frac{3}{4} = \frac{6}{8} = \frac{9}{12} = \frac{12}{16} = \frac{15}{20} = \frac{18}{24}$

$\frac{1}{3} = \frac{2}{6} = \frac{3}{9} = \frac{4}{12} = \frac{5}{15} = \frac{6}{18}$

$\frac{1}{5} = \frac{2}{10} = \frac{3}{15} = \frac{4}{20} = \frac{5}{25} = \frac{6}{30}$

$\frac{2}{3} = \frac{4}{6} = \frac{6}{9} = \frac{8}{12} = \frac{10}{15} = \frac{12}{18}$

If children have problems with this page, point out that fractions remain the same as long as you multiply both the numerator and denominator by the same number, or divide the numerator and denominator by the same number.

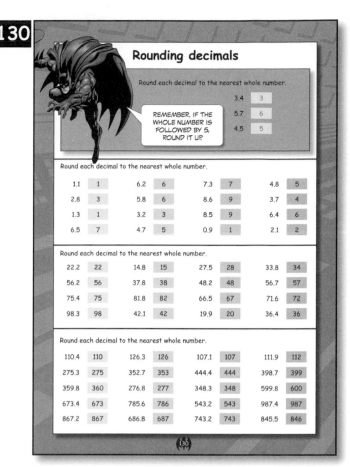

130

Rounding decimals

Round each decimal to the nearest whole number.

3.4 → 3
5.7 → 6
4.5 → 5

REMEMBER, IF THE WHOLE NUMBER IS FOLLOWED BY 5, ROUND IT UP!

Round each decimal to the nearest whole number.

1.1 → 1	6.2 → 6	7.3 → 7	4.8 → 5
2.8 → 3	5.8 → 6	8.6 → 9	3.7 → 4
1.3 → 1	3.2 → 3	8.5 → 9	6.4 → 6
6.5 → 7	4.7 → 5	0.9 → 1	2.1 → 2

Round each decimal to the nearest whole number.

22.2 → 22	14.8 → 15	27.5 → 28	33.8 → 34
56.2 → 56	37.8 → 38	48.2 → 48	56.7 → 57
75.4 → 75	81.8 → 82	66.5 → 67	71.6 → 72
98.3 → 98	42.1 → 42	19.9 → 20	36.4 → 36

Round each decimal to the nearest whole number.

110.4 → 110	126.3 → 126	107.1 → 107	111.9 → 112
275.3 → 275	352.7 → 353	444.4 → 444	398.7 → 399
359.8 → 360	276.8 → 277	348.3 → 348	599.8 → 600
673.4 → 673	785.6 → 786	543.2 → 543	987.4 → 987
867.2 → 867	686.8 → 687	743.2 → 743	845.5 → 846

If children experience difficulties you might want to use a number line showing tenths. Errors often occur when a number with 9 in the ones column is rounded up. Children also often neglect to alter the tens digit in a number such as 19.9.

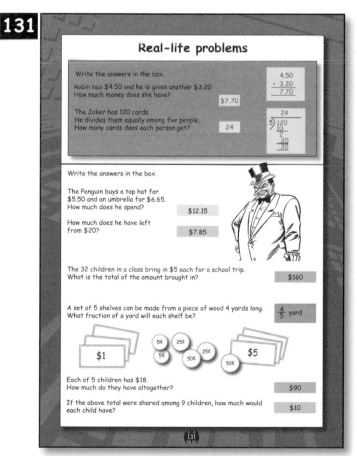

131

Real-life problems

Write the answers in the box.

Robin has $4.50 and he is given another $3.20. How much money does she have? $7.70

```
 4.50
+3.20
 7.70
```

The Joker has 120 cards. He divides them equally among five people. How many cards does each person get?   24

```
   24
5)120
   10
    2
   20
   20
```

Write the answers in the box.

The Penguin buys a top hat for $5.50 and an umbrella for $6.65. How much does he spend? $12.15

How much does he have left from $20? $7.85

The 32 children in a class bring in $5 each for a school trip. What is the total of the amount brought in? $160

A set of 5 shelves can be made from a piece of wood 4 yards long. What fraction of a yard will each shelf be? $\frac{4}{5}$ yard

$1   5¢ 25¢ 5¢ 50¢ 25¢ 50¢ $5

Each of 5 children has $18. How much do they have altogether? $90

If the above total were shared among 9 children, how much would each child have? $10

This page tests children's ability to choose the operations required to solve real-life problems, mostly involving money. Discussing whether the answer will be larger or smaller than the question will help children decide on their choice of operation.

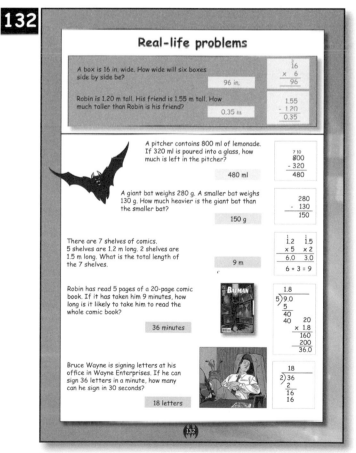

132

Real-life problems

A box is 16 in. wide. How wide will six boxes side by side be?   96 in.

```
   16
 ×  6
   96
```

Robin is 1.20 m tall. His friend is 1.55 m tall. How much taller than Robin is his friend?   0.35 m

```
 1.55
-1.20
 0.35
```

A pitcher contains 800 ml of lemonade. If 320 ml is poured into a glass, how much is left in the pitcher?   480 ml

```
 7 10
 800
-320
 480
```

A giant bat weighs 280 g. A smaller bat weighs 130 g. How much heavier is the giant bat than the smaller bat?   150 g

```
 280
-130
 150
```

There are 7 shelves of comics. 5 shelves are 1.2 m long. 2 shelves are 1.5 m long. What is the total length of the 7 shelves.   9 m

```
 1.2    1.5
×  5   ×  2
 6.0    3.0
  6 + 3 = 9
```

Robin has read 5 pages of a 20-page comic book. If it has taken him 9 minutes, how long is it likely to take him to read the whole comic book?   36 minutes

```
   1.8
5)9.0
   5
   40
   40      20
         × 1.8
          160
          200
          36.0
```

Bruce Wayne is signing letters at his office in Wayne Enterprises. If he can sign 36 letters in a minute, how many can he sign in 30 seconds?   18 letters

```
   18
2)36
   2
   16
   16
```

This page continues with real-life problems but with units other than money. Note that children must perform three operations to solve the third problem.

Problems involving time

Find the answer to this problem.

A train leaves the station at 7:30 A.M. and arrives at the end of the line at 10:45 A.M. How long did the journey take?

7:30 → 10:30 = 3 h
10:30 → 10:45 = 15 min
Total = 3 h 15 min

3 hours 15 minutes

Find the answer to each problem

Alfred's cake takes 2 hours 25 minutes to bake. If he began to bake it at 1:35 P.M. at what time was the cake cooked?

4:00 P.M.

1:35 + 2 h = 3:35
3:35 + 25 min = 4:00

A film starts at 7:00 P.M. and finishes at 8:45 P.M. How long is the film?

1 Hour 45 minutes

7:00 → 8:00 = 1 h
8:00 → 8:45 = 45 min
Total = 1 h 45 min

Commissioner Gordon takes his car in for a repair at 7:00 A.M. It is finished at 1:50 P.M. How long did the repair take?

6 hours 50 minutes

7:00 → 1:00 = 6 h
1:00 → 1:50 = 50 min
Total = 6 h 50 min

Robin needs to clean the Bat-Costume vault in the Batcave and wash the Batmobile. It takes him 1 hour 10 minutes to clean the vault and 45 minutes to wash the Batmobile. If he starts at 10:00 A.M., at what time will he finish?

11:55 A.M.

10:00 + 1 h = 11:00
11:00 + 10 min = 11:10
11:10 + 45 min = 11:55

Bruce Wayne has to be at work by 8:50 A.M. If he takes 1 hour 30 minutes to get ready, and the trip takes 35 minutes, at what time does he need to get up?

6:45 A.M.

8:50 - 1 h = 7:50
7:50 - 30 min = 7:20
7:20 - 35 min = 6:45

Children must remember that hours are based on units of 60 rather than of 10. So, when they regroup, they should add 60 to the minutes instead of the 10 they would add when regrouping numbers.

Elapsed time

Write the answer in the box.

10:40   11:40   12:40   1:20

1 hr   1 hr   40 mins

Catwoman burgles an art gallery. She enters the building at 10:40 P.M. and leaves at 1:20 A.M. How long is she in the gallery?

2 hours 40 minutes

Write the answer in the box.

The ferry leaves Gotham City at 11:00 A.M. and docks across the river at 2:00 P.M. How long is the ride?

3 hours

11:00 → 12:00 = 1 h
12:00 → 2:00 = 2 h

The movie starts at 6:05 P.M. and ends at 9:17 P.M. How long is it?

3 hours 12 minutes

6:05 → 9:05 = 3 h
9:05 → 9:17 = 12 min

Commissioner Gordon works a 9-hour shift at the police department. If he starts work at 9 A.M., at what time is he finished?

6 P.M.

9:00 → 12:00 = 3 h
12:00 + 6 h = 6:00

Alfred wants to videotape a program that starts at 11:30 P.M. It lasts 1 hour and 55 minutes. What time will it end?

1:25 A.M.

11:30 + 1 h → 12:30
12:30 + 55 min → 1:25

HOW MUCH TIME DOES A CRIME CAPER TAKE?

If children have trouble keeping track of the changes in hours or minutes, have them write down each step as in the diagram.

Recognizing multiples

Multiples are found by multiplying a number by another. Circle all the multiples of 10.

14   (20)   25   (30)   47   (60)

TENS ARE THE EASY ONES!

Circle all the multiples of 6.

| 20 | (24) | 56 | (72) | 26 | 35 |
| 1 | 3 | (6) | 16 | 32 | (36) |

Circle all the multiples of 7.

| (14) | 17 | (35) | 27 | 47 | (49) |
| (63) | (42) | 52 | 37 | 64 | 71 |

Circle all the multiples of 8.

| 18 | 54 | (64) | 35 | (72) | (8) |
| 25 | 31 | (48) | 84 | (32) | 28 |

Circle all the multiples of 9.

| 64 | (81) | (36) | 35 | 33 | 98 |
| (45) | 53 | (27) | (18) | 92 | 106 |

Circle all the multiples of 10.

| 44 | 37 | (30) | 29 | (50) | (100) |
| 15 | 35 | (60) | 46 | (90) | 45 |

Circle all the multiples of 11.

| 45 | (33) | 87 | 98 | (99) | 87 |
| 24 | (44) | 65 | 54 | (66) | (121) |

Circle all the multiples of 12.

| 23 | 34 | (48) | 74 | (24) | (60) |
| (72) | 66 | 29 | 109 | (108) | (132) |

Success on this page basically depends on knowledge of multiplication tables. Where children experience difficulties, it may be necessary to reinforce multiplication tables.

Bar graphs

Use this bar graph to answer each question.

CAPS SOLD

What color cap was sold the most?

red

How many more green caps were sold than blue caps?

10

Use the bar graphs to answer the questions.

Tickets sold

How many tickets were sold on May 4

100

How many more tickets were sold on May 3 than on May 2?

10

On which date were 90 tickets sold?

May 1

Distance run by cross country teams

Which team ran 40 miles?

Gotham Greens

Which team ran the same distance as the Grunts?

Gotham Giants

How much farther did the Greats run than the Greens?

5 miles

Children will be required to read information, to look for specific information, and to manipulate the information they read on a bar graph to answer the questions. They may need to be reassured that a horizontal bar graph can be read in much the same way as a vertical bar graph.

Triangles

Look at these different triangles.

Equilateral
(all sides equal;
is also isosceles).

Isosceles
(at least two sides
are of equal length)

Scalene
(all sides
different)

Right angle
(may be isosceles or
scalene, but one angle
must be a right angle)

1	2	3	4
5	6	7	8
9	10	11	12

List the triangles that are:

Equilateral	5, 6, 11
Isoceles	1, 9, 12 (also 5, 6, 11)
Scalene	2, 3, 8 (also 4, 7, 10)
Right Angle	4, 7, 10

LOTS OF TRIANGLES. (I PREFER DIAMONDS, MYSELF)

This page will highlight any gaps in children's ability to recognize and name triangles. Make sure that children can identify the triangles that have been rotated.

EVERYONE SHOULD KNOW THEIR PLACE.

Place value to 10,000,000

| How many hundreds are there in 7,000? | 70 | hundreds (70 x 100 = 7,000) |
| What is the value of the 9 in 694? | 90 | (because the 9 is in the tens column) |

Write how many tens there are in:

200	20	tens	800	80	tens	400	40	tens
500	50	tens	1,400	140	tens	4,600	460	tens
5,300	530	tens	1,240	124	tens	1,320	132	tens
2,700	270	tens	5,930	593	tens	4,530	453	tens

What is the value of the 8 in these numbers?

| 86 | 80 | | 820 | 800 | | 138 | 8 |
| 8,122 | 8,000 | | 84,301 | 80,000 | | 124,382 | 80 |

What is the value of the 3 in these numbers?

| 324,126 | 300,000 | | 3,927,142 | 3,000,000 | | 214,623 | 3 |
| 8,254,320 | 300 | | 3,711,999 | 3,000,000 | | 124,372 | 300 |

How many hundreds are there in:

| 6,500 | 65 | hundreds | | 524,600 | 5,246 | hundreds |
| 18,800 | 188 | hundreds | | 712,400 | 7,124 | hundreds |

What is the value of the 9 in these numbers?

| 9,214,631 | 9,000,000 | | 2,389,147 | 9,000 | | 463,946 | 900 |
| 297,034 | 90,000 | | 9,110,827 | 9,000,000 | | 105,429 | 9 |

Explain to children that finding how many tens there are in a number is the same as dividing by 10. In the number 400, for example, there are 40 tens, because 400 divided by 10 is 40.

Multiplying and dividing by 10

To multiply by 10, add a zero. To divide by 10, move the decimal point one place to the left. Write the answer in the box.

| 42 x 10 = | 420 | | 68 ÷ 10 = | 6.8 |

Write the product in the box.

SOMETIMES, ALL YOU NEED IS A ZERO...

84 x 10 =	840	13 x 10 =	130		
36 x 10 =	360	58 x 10 =	580	54 x 10 =	540
256 x 10 =	2,560	412 x 10 =	4,120	836 x 10 =	8,360
4,700 x 10 =	47,000	687 x 10 =	6,870	2,145 x 10 =	21,450

Write the quotient in the box.

82 ÷ 10 =	8.2	58 ÷ 10 =	5.8	38 ÷ 10 =	3.8
19 ÷ 10 =	1.9	79 ÷ 10 =	7.9	82 ÷ 10 =	8.2
245 ÷ 10 =	24.5	367 ÷ 10 =	36.7	279 ÷ 10 =	27.9
379 ÷ 10 =	37.9	924 ÷ 10 =	92.4	674 ÷ 10 =	67.4

Find the missing factor.

24	x 10 = 240	75	x 10 = 750	99	x 10 = 990
37	x 10 = 370	14	x 10 = 140	35	x 10 = 350
55	x 10 = 550	87	x 10 = 870	76	x 10 = 760

Find the dividend.

47	÷ 10 = 4.7	78	÷ 10 = 7.8	47	÷ 10 = 4.7
257	÷ 10 = 25.7	99	÷ 10 = 9.9	807	÷ 10 = 80.7
409	÷ 10 = 40.9	679	÷ 10 = 67.9	269	÷ 10 = 26.9

Remind children that multiplying by 10 adds a zero to the original figure. Dividing by 10 moves the decimal one place to the left. Whole numbers can be written with a decimal point (e.g. 16 as 16.0). Inverse operations in the later sections give the number that begins the equation.

Appropriate units of measure

Choose the best units to measure the length of each item.

| inches | feet | yards |

| notebook | car | swimming pool |
| inches | feet | yards |

Choose the best units to measure the length of each item.

HOW DO YOU MEASURE UP?

| inches | feet | yards |

| TV set | bicycle | toothbrush | football field |
| inches | feet | inches | yards |

| shoe | backyard | canoe | fence |
| inches | feet or yards | feet | yards |

The height of a door is about 7   feet

The length of a pencil is about 7   inches

The height of a flagpole is about 7   yards

Choose the best units to measure the weight of each item.

| ounces | pounds | tons |

| kitten | train | tomato |
| ounces | tons | ounces |

| hamburger | elephant | refrigerator | sweatshirt |
| ounces | tons | pounds | ounces |

The weight of a tennis ball is about 2   ounces

The weight of a bag of potatoes is about 5   pounds

The weight of a truck is about 4   tons

Children might come up with their own examples of items that measure about 1 inch, 1 foot, and 1 yard, as well as items that weigh about 1 ounce, 1 pound, and 1 ton. They can use these as benchmarks to find the appropriate unit.

141

Identifying patterns

Continue each pattern.

Intervals of 6:	1	7	13	19	25	31
Intervals of 3:	27	24	21	18	15	12

Continue each pattern.

0	10	20	30	40	50	60
5	10	15	20	25	30	35
3	5	7	9	11	13	15
3	10	17	24	31	38	45
4	7	10	13	16	19	22
1	9	17	25	33	41	49

Continue each pattern.

46	42	38	34	30	26	22
33	29	25	21	17	13	9
65	60	55	50	45	40	35
50	43	36	29	22	15	8
28	25	22	19	16	13	10
49	42	35	28	21	14	7

Continue each pattern.

5	7	9	11	13	15	17
56	53	50	47	44	41	38
3	8	13	18	23	28	33
47	40	33	26	19	12	5
1	4	7	10	13	16	19
81	72	63	54	45	36	27

JUST FOLLOW THE PATTERN!

Point out that some of the patterns show an increase and some a decrease. Children should see what operation turns the first number into the second, and check that the same operation turns the second number into the third. They can continue the pattern.

142

Factors of numbers from 31 to 65

Factors are numbers that divide evenly into another number.
The factors of 40 are: 1 2 4 5 8 10 20 40
Circle the factors of 56: ①②3④5 6 ⑦⑧⑭㉘32 ㊏

Find all the factors of each number.

The factors of 31 are	1, 31
The factors of 47 are	1, 47
The factors of 35 are	1, 5, 7, 35
The factors of 50 are	1, 2, 5, 10, 25, 50
The factors of 42 are	1, 2, 3, 6, 7, 14, 21, 42
The factors of 52 are	1, 2, 4, 13, 26, 52
The factors of 48 are	1, 2, 3, 4, 6, 8, 12, 16, 24, 48
The factors of 60 are	1, 2, 3, 4, 5, 6, 10, 12, 15, 20, 30, 60

Circle all the factors of each number.

Which numbers are factors of 39?
① 2 ③ 4 5 6 7 8 10 11 12 ⑬ 14 ㊴

Which numbers are factors of 45?
① ③ 4 ⑤ 8 ⑨ 12 ⑮ 16 21 24 36 40 44 ㊺

Which numbers are factors of 61?
① 3 4 5 6 10 15 16 18 20 24 29 30 ㊳

Which numbers are factors of 65?
① 2 4 ⑤ 6 8 9 10 12 ⑬ 14 15 30 60 ㊄

Some numbers have only factors of 1 and themselves. They are called prime numbers. Write all the prime numbers between 31 and 65 in the box.

31, 37, 41, 43, 47, 53, 59, 61

YOU NEED A SYSTEM!

Children often miss some of the factors of a number, especially when the number is large. Encourage a systematic method of finding factors. Children may forget that 1 and the number itself are factors of the number. If needed, discuss prime numbers.

143

Greatest common factor

Circle the common factors. Find the greatest common factor (GCF).

24: ① ② ③ 4 ⑥ 8, 12, 24
60: ① ② ③ 4, 5, ⑥ 8, 10, 12, 60
42: ① ② ③ ⑥ 7, 14   The GCF is 6

HA! HA! YOU CAN RUN RINGS AROUND THEM!

Circle the common factors.

45:
①③ 5, ⑨ 15, 45

36:
① 2, ③ 4, 6, ⑨ 12, 18, 36

28:
①② 4, 7, 14, 28

54:
①② 3, 6, 9, 18, 27, 54

Circle the common factors. Write the GCF.

35:
①⑤ 7, 35

80:
① 2, 4, ⑤ 8, 10, 16, 20, 40, 80

The GCF is 5

32:
①②④⑧⑯㉜

64:
① ② ④ ⑧ ⑯ ㉜ 64

The GCF is 32

Circle the common factors. Write the GCF.

12:
① 2, ③ 4, 6, 12

48:
① 2, ③ 4, 6, 8, 12, 24, 48

15:
①③ 5, 15

The GCF is 3

18:
①②③⑥⑨⑱

72:
① 2, 3, 4, 6, 8,

54:
①②③⑥⑨⑱

The GCF is 18

⑨ 12, ⑱ 24, 36, 72   27, 54

It is common for children to skip some of the factors of a number. List the factors in pairs and then write them in order, from least to greatest.

144

Writing equivalent fractions

Make these fractions equal by writing in the missing number.

$\frac{20}{200} = \frac{2}{10} = \frac{1}{5}$ $\frac{1}{4} = \frac{2}{8}$

Make these fractions equal by writing in the missing number.

$\frac{10}{100} = \frac{1}{10}$	$\frac{3}{5} = \frac{6}{10}$	$\frac{5}{100} = \frac{1}{20}$
$\frac{2}{20} = \frac{1}{10}$	$\frac{2}{3} = \frac{8}{12}$	$\frac{2}{8} = \frac{1}{4}$
$\frac{11}{12} = \frac{22}{24}$	$\frac{5}{6} = \frac{15}{18}$	$\frac{6}{20} = \frac{3}{10}$
$\frac{2}{12} = \frac{1}{6}$	$\frac{9}{15} = \frac{3}{5}$	$\frac{5}{8} = \frac{10}{16}$
$\frac{7}{8} = \frac{28}{32}$	$\frac{5}{20} = \frac{1}{4}$	$\frac{6}{24} = \frac{1}{4}$
$\frac{5}{25} = \frac{1}{5}$	$\frac{25}{100} = \frac{5}{20}$	$\frac{1}{5} = \frac{2}{10}$
$\frac{5}{30} = \frac{1}{6}$	$\frac{12}{14} = \frac{6}{7}$	$\frac{25}{30} = \frac{5}{6}$
$\frac{9}{18} = \frac{1}{2}$	$\frac{40}{100} = \frac{2}{5}$	$\frac{1}{3} = \frac{5}{15}$
$\frac{3}{8} = \frac{9}{24}$	$\frac{4}{100} = \frac{1}{25}$	

$\frac{1}{8}$ =	$\frac{2}{16}$ =	$\frac{3}{24}$ =	$\frac{4}{32}$ =	$\frac{5}{40}$ =	$\frac{6}{48}$
$\frac{20}{100}$ =	$\frac{5}{25}$ =	$\frac{2}{10}$ =	$\frac{1}{5}$ =	$\frac{10}{50}$ =	$\frac{40}{200}$
$\frac{2}{5}$ =	$\frac{6}{15}$ =	$\frac{8}{20}$ =	$\frac{4}{10}$ =	$\frac{20}{50}$ =	$\frac{40}{100}$
$\frac{1}{6}$ =	$\frac{2}{12}$ =	$\frac{3}{18}$ =	$\frac{4}{24}$ =	$\frac{5}{30}$ =	$\frac{6}{36}$
$\frac{2}{3}$ =	$\frac{16}{24}$ =	$\frac{24}{36}$ =	$\frac{14}{21}$ =	$\frac{6}{9}$ =	$\frac{200}{300}$

Remind children that fractions retain the same value if you multiply both the numerator and denominator by the same number or divide the numerator and denominator by the same number.

Fraction models

Write the missing numbers to show what part is shaded.

$\frac{3 \text{ shaded parts}}{4 \text{ parts}} = \frac{3}{4}$

$\frac{4}{4}$ 1 $\frac{2}{4} = \frac{1}{2}$

So, shaded part = 1 $\frac{1}{2}$

Write the missing numbers to show what part is shaded.

$\frac{5}{9}$ $\frac{2}{3}$ $\frac{5}{8}$ $\frac{5}{12}$

Write the fraction for the part that is shaded.

$\frac{10}{12}$ or $\frac{5}{6}$ 1 $\frac{3}{6}$ or 1 $\frac{1}{2}$ 2 $\frac{2}{6}$ or 2 $\frac{1}{3}$

Write the fraction for the part that is shaded.

1 $\frac{4}{8}$ or 1 $\frac{1}{2}$ 2 $\frac{6}{8}$ or 2 $\frac{3}{4}$ 3 $\frac{1}{8}$

Some children may need further explanation of all the models of mixed numbers. Point out that when all the parts of a model are shaded, the model shows the number 1.

Multiplying by one-digit numbers

Find each product. Remember to regroup.

465	391	278
× 3	× 4	× 5
1,395	1,564	1,390

ARE YOU GETTING FASTER?

Find each product.

573	920	438	813
× 2	× 2	× 3	× 2
1,719	1,840	1,314	1,626

582	832	405	396
× 4	× 3	× 5	× 6
2,328	2,496	2,025	2,376

Find each product.

317	224	543	218
× 3	× 3	× 4	× 3
951	672	2,172	654

128	276	798	365
× 4	× 5	× 6	× 6
512	1,380	4,788	2,190

100	373	882	954
× 5	× 4	× 4	× 3
500	1,492	3,528	2,862

Solve each problem.

Gotham middle school has 255 students. The high school has 6 times as many students. How many students are there at the high school?   1,530 students

255
× 6
1,530

A train can carry 375 passengers. How many can it carry on four trips?   1,500

six trips?   2,250

375   375
× 4   × 6
1,500   2,250

Make sure children understand the convention of multiplication, i.e. multiply the ones first and work left. Problems on this page may result from gaps in knowledge of the 2, 3, 4, 5, and 6 times tables. Errors will also occur if children neglect to regroup.

Multiplying by one-digit numbers

Find each product. Remember to regroup.

465	823	755
× 6	× 8	× 9
2,790	6,584	6,795

BIGGER AND BETTER!

Find each product.

395	734	826	943
× 7	× 8	× 8	× 9
2,765	5,872	6,608	8,487

643	199	823	546
× 7	× 6	× 7	× 8
4,501	1,194	5,761	4,368

Find each product.

502	377	845	222
× 7	× 8	× 8	× 9
3,514	3,016	6,760	1,998

473	224	606	514
× 9	× 8	× 6	× 7
4,257	1,792	3,636	3,598

500	800	900	200
× 9	× 9	× 9	× 9
4,500	7,200	8,100	1,800

Solve each problem.

A crate holds 230 oxygen cylinders. How many cylinders are there in 8 crates?   1,840 cylinders

230
× 8
1,840

Commissioner Gordon drives 457 miles a month on patrol. How many miles does he drive on patrol in 6 months?   2,742 miles

457
× 6
2,742

Problems encounted will be similar to the previous page. Gaps in knowledge of the 6, 7, 8, and 9 times table will result in children's errors.

Real-life problems

Harley Quinn spent $4.68 at the store and had $4.77 left. How much did she start with? $9.45

4.77
+ 4.68
9.45

Azrael receives a weekly allowance of $3.00 a week. How much will he have if he saves all of it for 8 weeks? $24.00

3.00
× 8
24.00

Gotham City theater charges $4 for each matinee ticket. If the theater sells 560 tickets for a matinee performance, how much does it take in? $2,240

$1

560
× 4
2,240

Robin has saved $9.69. His friend has saved £3.24 less. How much does his friend have? $6.45

9.69
- 3.24
6.45

The cost for 9 children to go to see a Batman film is $54. How much does each child pay? If only 6 children go, what will the cost be? $6 per child $36 for 6 children

9) 54

6 × 6 = 36

Harley Quinn has $2.95. The Joker gives her another $5.25, and she goes out and buys a coffee for $3.25. How much does she have left? $4.95

2.95
+ 5.25
8.20

8.20
- 3.25
4.95

Nightwing has $60 in savings. He decides to spend $\frac{1}{4}$ of it. How much will he have left? $45

60 ÷ 4 = 15

60 - 15 = 45

THIS IS THE REAL WORLD!

This page and the next provide children an opportunity to apply the skills they have practiced. They will need to select the appropriate operation. If they are unsure, discuss whether the answer should be larger or smaller. This can help them decide on the operation.

149

Real-life problems

A boy has an hour to do his homework. He plans to spend $\frac{1}{3}$ of his time on math. How many minutes will he spend on math?
20 minutes

$$1 \text{ hr} = 60 \text{ min}$$
$$3\overline{)60} = 20$$

In a gym class, one of the girls makes 2 long jumps of 1.78 m and 2.19 m. How far does she jump altogether?
3.97 m

$$1.78 + 2.19 = 3.97$$

Poison Ivy has a vial of poison containing 40 ml. She uses $\frac{1}{4}$ of it. How much poison is left?
30 ml

$$40 \div 4 = 10$$
$$40 - 10 = 30$$

Batgirl runs 40 m in 8 seconds. At that speed, how far did she run in 1 second?
5 m

$$40 \div 8 = 5$$

A large jar of coffee contains 2.25 kg. If 1.68 kg is left in the jar, how much has been used?
0.57 kg

$$2.25 - 1.68 = 0.57$$

The Penguin has an umbrella factory. The factory can produce 25 umbrellas in 15 minutes. How many are produced in 1 hour?
100

$$1 \text{ hr} = 60 \text{ min}$$
$$60 \div 15 = 4$$
$$25 \times 4 = 100$$

In the Batcave, the computer is 41.63 cm wide and next to it is a printer which is 48.37 cm wide. How much space is left on the shelf for a scanner if the shelf is 1.5 m wide?
60 cm

$$1.5 \text{ m} = 150 \text{ cm}$$
$$41.63 + 48.37 = 90.00$$
$$150 - 90 = 60$$

This page deals with units other than money. Note solving the final problem requires two operations.

150

Problems involving time

Alfred spends 35 minutes cleaning the Batmobile each day. How many minutes does he spend cleaning it from Monday through Friday?
175 minutes

$$35 \times 5 = 175$$

The Joker spends 175 minutes eating breakfast from Monday through Friday. How long does he spend eating breakfast each day?
35 minutes

$$5\overline{)175} = 35$$

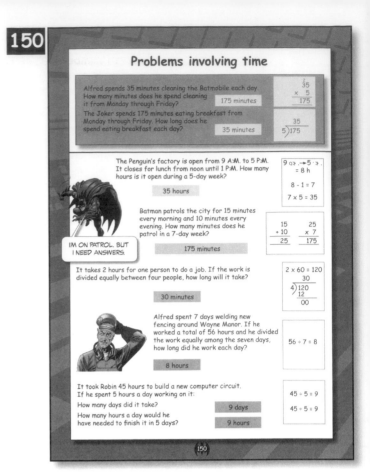

The Penguin's factory is open from 9 A.M. to 5 P.M. It closes for lunch from noon until 1 P.M. How many hours is it open during a 5-day week?
35 hours

$$9 \text{ a.m.} \to 5 \text{ p.m.} = 8 \text{ h}$$
$$8 - 1 = 7$$
$$7 \times 5 = 35$$

I'M ON PATROL, BUT I NEED ANSWERS.

Batman patrols the city for 15 minutes every morning and 10 minutes every evening. How many minutes does he patrol in a 7-day week?
175 minutes

$$15 + 10 = 25$$
$$25 \times 7 = 175$$

It takes 2 hours for one person to do a job. If the work is divided equally between four people, how long will it take?
30 minutes

$$2 \times 60 = 120$$
$$4\overline{)120} = 30$$

Alfred spent 7 days welding new fencing around Wayne Manor. If he worked a total of 56 hours and he divided the work equally among the seven days, how long did he work each day?
8 hours

$$56 \div 7 = 8$$

It took Robin 45 hours to build a new computer circuit. If he spent 5 hours a day working on it:
How many days did it take?
9 days
How many hours a day would he have needed to finish it in 5 days?
9 hours

$$45 \div 5 = 9$$
$$45 \div 5 = 9$$

151

Multiplying and dividing

Write the answer in the box.

$26 \times 100 =$ **2,600** $400 \div 100 =$ **4**

Write the answer in the box.

$34 \times 10 =$ **340**	$41 \times 10 =$ **410**	$56 \times 10 =$ **560**
$95 \times 100 =$ **9,500**	$36 \times 100 =$ **3,600**	$75 \times 100 =$ **7,500**
$413 \times 10 =$ **4,130**	$204 \times 10 =$ **2,040**	$524 \times 10 =$ **5,240**
$787 \times 100 =$ **78,700**	$834 \times 100 =$ **83,400**	$254 \times 100 =$ **25,400**

Write the quotient in the box.

$120 \div 10 =$ **12**	$260 \div 10 =$ **26**	$480 \div 10 =$ **48**
$500 \div 100 =$ **5**	$800 \div 10 =$ **80**	$700 \div 100 =$ **7**
$20 \div 10 =$ **2**	$30 \div 10 =$ **3**	$60 \div 10 =$ **6**
$800 \div 100 =$ **8**	$100 \div 100 =$ **1**	$900 \div 100 =$ **9**

Write the number that has been multiplied by 100.

46 $\times 100 = 4,600$	**723** $\times 100 = 72,300$
325 $\times 100 = 32,500$	**250** $\times 100 = 25,000$
12 $\times 100 = 1,200$	**456** $\times 100 = 45,600$
84 $\times 100 = 8,400$	**623** $\times 100 = 62,300$

THIS IS VERY PRODUCTIVE.

Write the number that has been divided by 100.

300 $\div 100 = 3$	**700** $\div 100 = 7$
1,200 $\div 100 = 12$	**1,800** $\div 100 = 18$
8,700 $\div 100 = 87$	**2,300** $\div 100 = 23$
1,000 $\div 100 = 10$	**6,400** $\div 100 = 64$

Children should realize that multiplying a whole number by 10 or 100 means writing one or two zeros at the end of the number. To divide a multiple of 10 by 10, simply take the final zero off. In the two final sections, solve by using the inverse operations.

152

Identifying patterns

Continue each pattern.

| Steps of 2: | $\frac{1}{2}$ | $2\frac{1}{2}$ | $4\frac{1}{2}$ | $6\frac{1}{2}$ | $8\frac{1}{2}$ | $10\frac{1}{2}$ |
| Steps of 5: | 3.5 | 8.5 | 13.5 | 18.5 | 23.5 | 28.5 |

Continue each pattern.

$5\frac{1}{2}$	$10\frac{1}{2}$	$15\frac{1}{2}$	$20\frac{1}{2}$	$25\frac{1}{2}$	$30\frac{1}{2}$
$2\frac{1}{4}$	$4\frac{1}{4}$	$6\frac{1}{4}$	$8\frac{1}{4}$	$10\frac{1}{4}$	$12\frac{1}{4}$
$8\frac{1}{3}$	$9\frac{1}{3}$	$10\frac{1}{3}$	$11\frac{1}{3}$	$12\frac{1}{3}$	$13\frac{1}{3}$
$65\frac{3}{4}$	$55\frac{3}{4}$	$45\frac{3}{4}$	$35\frac{3}{4}$	$25\frac{3}{4}$	$15\frac{3}{4}$
$44\frac{1}{2}$	$40\frac{1}{2}$	$36\frac{1}{2}$	$32\frac{1}{2}$	$28\frac{1}{2}$	$24\frac{1}{2}$
$4\frac{2}{3}$	$7\frac{2}{3}$	$10\frac{2}{3}$	$13\frac{2}{3}$	$16\frac{2}{3}$	$19\frac{2}{3}$
7.5	6.5	5.5	4.5	3.5	2.5
29.3	26.3	23.3	20.3	17.3	14.3
82.6	73.6	64.6	55.6	46.6	37.6
6.4	10.4	14.4	18.4	22.4	26.4
14.2	16.2	18.2	20.2	22.2	24.2
21.8	28.8	35.8	42.8	49.8	56.8
$13\frac{3}{4}$	$19\frac{3}{4}$	$25\frac{3}{4}$	$31\frac{3}{4}$	$37\frac{3}{4}$	$43\frac{3}{4}$
57.5	48.5	39.5	30.5	21.5	12.5
$11\frac{1}{2}$	$10\frac{1}{2}$	$9\frac{1}{2}$	$8\frac{1}{2}$	$7\frac{1}{2}$	$6\frac{1}{2}$
8.4	11.4	14.4	17.4	20.4	23.4

The patterns on this page are formed by adding or subtracting whole numbers, but the items in each row are mixed numbers or decimals. Children should see which operation turns the first number into the second, the second into the third, and then continue the pattern.

Products with odd and even numbers

Find the product of these numbers.

3 and 4	The product of 3 and 4 is 12
6 and 7	The product of 6 and 7 is 42

AGAINST ALL ODDS, I'LL MAKE THINGS EVEN.

Find the products of these odd and even numbers.

6 and 5	The product of 6 and 5 is 30.	2 and 3	The product of 2 and 3 is 6.
4 and 7	The product of 4 and 7 is 28.	3 and 8	The product of 3 and 8 is 24.
3 and 6	The product of 3 and 6 is 18.	9 and 2	The product of 9 and 2 is 18.
10 and 3	The product of 10 and 3 is 30.	5 and 12	The product of 5 and 12 is 60.
What do you notice about your answers?		The product of odd and even numbers is always an even number.	

Find the products of these odd numbers.

7 and 5	The product of 7 and 5 is 35.	1 and 9	The product of 1 and 9 is 9.
11 and 5	The product of 11 and 5 is 55.	5 and 7	The product of 5 and 7 is 35.
9 and 5	The product of 9 and 5 is 45.	9 and 3	The product of 9 and 3 is 27.
3 and 7	The product of 3 and 7 is 21.	3 and 13	The product of 3 and 13 is 39
What do you notice about your answers?		The product of two odd numbers is always an odd number.	

Find the products of these even numbers.

4 and 2	The product of 4 and 2 is 8.	2 and 8	The product of 2 and 8 is 16.
6 and 8	The product of 6 and 8 is 48.	4 and 6	The product of 4 and 6 is 24.
10 and 2	The product of 10 and 2 is 20.	6 and 10	The product of 6 and 10 is 60.
8 and 4	The product of 8 and 4 is 32.	2 and 4	The product of 2 and 4 is 8.
What do you notice about your answers?		The product of two even numbers is always an even number.	

Can you write a rule for the products with odd and even numbers?
The product of two numbers will always be even unless both numbers are odd.

Children may need help answering the questions on what they notice about the products. Accept any rule about products that children write, as long as it indicates that they have grasped the concept.

Factors of numbers from 66 to 100

The factors of 66 are: 1 2 3 6 11 22 33 66

Circle the factors of 94: (1) (2) 28 32 43 (47) 71 86 (94)

Write the factors of each number in the box.

The factors of 70 are	1, 2, 5, 7, 10, 14, 35, 70
The factors of 83 are	1, 83
The factors of 63 are	1, 3, 7, 9, 21, 63
The factors of 85 are	1, 5, 17, 85
The factors of 75 are	1, 3, 5, 15, 25, 75
The factors of 99 are	1, 3, 9, 11, 33, 99
The factors of 69 are	1, 3, 23, 69
The factors of 72 are	1, 2, 3, 4, 6, 8, 9, 12, 18, 24, 36, 72
The factors of 96 are	1, 2, 3, 4, 6, 8, 12, 16, 24, 32, 48, 96

Circle the factors.
Which numbers are factors of 68?
(1) (2) 3 (4) 5 6 7 8 9 11 12 (17) (34) 35 62 (68)

Which numbers are factors of 95?
(1) 2 3 4 (5) 15 16 17 (19) 24 59 85 90 (95) 96

Which numbers are factors of 88?
(1) (2) 3 (4) 5 6 (8) 10 (11) 15 (22) 33 38 (44) 87 (88)

Which numbers are factors of 73?
(1) 2 3 4 6 8 9 10 12 13 14 15 37 42 (73)

Some numbers have only factors of 1 and themselves. They are called prime numbers. Write all the prime numbers between 66 and 100 in the box.

67, 71, 73, 79, 83, 89, 97

Children often miss some of the factors of a number, especially for large numbers. Encourage a systematic method of finding factors. Children may forget that 1 and the number itself are factors of a number. If necessary discuss prime numbers with children.

Multiplying by two-digit numbers

Write the product for each problem.

```
   56        45
 x 32      x 43
  112       135
1,680     1,800
1,792     1,935
```

NO TIME TO WASTE – START MULTIPLYING!

Write the product for each problem.

```
    84        47        23        56
  x 22      x 25      x 24      x 23
   168       235        92       168
 1,680       940       460     1,120
 1,848     1,175       552     1,288
```

```
    75        64        51        45
  x 24      x 33      x 32      x 34
   300       192       102       180
 1,500     1,920     1,530     1,350
 1,800     2,112     1,632     1,530
```

Write the product for each problem.

```
    65        72        84        85
  x 54      x 68      x 61      x 79
   260       576        84       765
 3,250     4,320     5,040     5,950
 3,510     4,896     5,124     6,715
```

```
    94        58        37        75
  x 63      x 57      x 92      x 26
   282       406        74       450
 5,640     2,900     3,330     1,500
 5,922     3,306     3,404     1,950
```

Children should understand that multiplying a number by 32 is the same as multiplying the number by 2 and then by 30, and adding the two products.

Multiplying by two-digit numbers

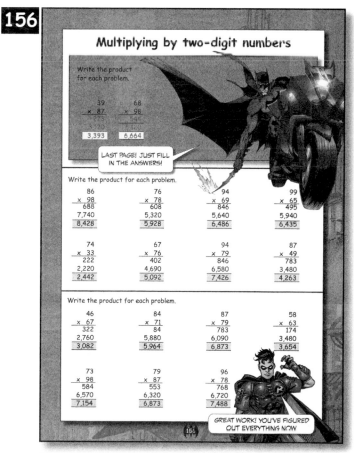

Write the product for each problem.

```
   39        68
 x 87      x 98
  273       544
3,120     6,120
3,393     6,664
```

LAST PAGE! JUST FILL IN THE ANSWERS!

Write the product for each problem.

```
    86        76        94        99
  x 98      x 78      x 69      x 65
   688       608       846       495
 7,740     5,320     5,640     5,940
 8,428     5,928     6,486     6,435
```

```
    74        67        94        87
  x 33      x 76      x 79      x 49
   222       402       846       783
 2,220     4,690     6,580     3,480
 2,442     5,092     7,426     4,263
```

Write the product for each problem.

```
    46        84        87        58
  x 67      x 71      x 79      x 63
   322        84       783       174
 2,760     5,880     6,090     3,480
 3,082     5,964     6,873     3,654
```

```
    73        79        96
  x 98      x 87      x 78
   584       553       768
 6,570     6,320     6,720
 7,154     6,873     7,488
```

GREAT WORK! YOU'VE FIGURED OUT EVERYTHING NOW

This page gives further practice of multiplication as on the previous page. Make sure that children do not neglect to regroup when necessary.

LONDON, NEW YORK, MUNICH, MELBOURNE, AND DELHI

Produced by
The Brown Reference Group plc.
for Dorling Kindersley Limited

DESIGNERS Joan Curtis, Steve Laurie, Lynne Lennon, and Mary Walsh
EDITORS Deborah Evans, Leon Gray, Tim Harris, and Tom Jackson
MANAGING EDITOR Bridget Giles
ART DIRECTORS Jeni Child and Sarah Williams

Batman created by Bob Kane

First published in the United States in 2007 by DK Publishing
375 Hudson Street, New York, New York 10014

07 08 09 10 11 10 9 8 7 6 5 4 3 2 1
LD079 – 06/07

DK books are available at special discounts when purchased in bulk for sales promotions,
premiums, fund-raising, or educational use. For details, contact:
DK Publishing Special Markets, 375 Hudson Street, New York, New York 10014,
or SpecialSales@dk.com

A catalog record for this book is available from the Library of Congress.

ISBN: 978-0-7566-2999-1

Reproduced by Icon Reproduction Ltd., UK
Printed and bound by Donnelley's, US

Discover more at
www.dk.com